PRAISE FOR *The Great Fatsby*

This book is an honest look at what's **glorifying, silly, and important** about the lessons we learn on a bike. Anyone from a pro to a regular Joe will see a little bit of themselves in these pages and walk away with a new perspective. **Fatty's stories will transport you into the moment** and make you want to get out and throw a leg over your bike...only with a bit less fumbling than he does.
—*Rebecca Rusch, MTB Legend*

It might be too late for me, but the worst thing a cyclist can do is forget how ridiculous it is to shave your legs and ride a $5,000 bicycle through traffic. Elden's new collection is **full of wisdom that reminds us not to take pedaling too seriously.**
— *Phil Gaimon, Pro Cyclist*

The lightness of the writing doesn't detract from the importance cycling holds in our lives — instead, **it helps you appreciate and enjoy your passion all the more.**
—*Bill Strickland, Editor-at-Large, Bicycling Magazine*

What's great about Fatty's writing is his ability to entertain and educate — not just for the cycling audience, but for all readers who enjoy taking a peek behind the curtain of niche cultures. Fatty reminds us of the true joys of cycling, and **his self deprecation will keep you laughing cover to cover.**
—*Kathryn Bertine, Pro Cyclist / Author of* As Good As Gold

The Great Fatsby is, of course, very funny and sheds a comedic light on a sport that often takes itself too seriously. **The far more pleasant surprise is its raw, poignant, and introspective truth about why we simply love to ride bicycles.**
—*Levi Leipheimer, Pro Cyclist*

It's a difficult thing to be funny in print. Such is Elden's talent. Perhaps the truest thing I can say of this book is that I envy his gift for finding laughs in the flattest light.
—*Patrick Brady, RedKitePrayer.com*

As a proud recumbent rider and a fiercely Marxist beard-grower I was severely disappointed with this book. However, I am sure all other cyclists will love it.
—*Carlton Reid, Executive Editor, BikeBiz.com*

In the years since his first effort, **Fatty's sarchasti-meter has been finely tuned,** and for that fact, we should all give thanks. However, with the exception of also having a disdain for selfies, and never shaving my eyebrows, **I now know everything I've thought and done up to this point is wrong.**
—*Stevil Kinevil, AllHailTheBlackMarket.com*

This book is better than some movies!
—*Tyson Apostol, Winner of Survivor: Blood vs. Water*

THE
GREAT
FATSBY

ISBN-13: 978-0692338452
ISBN-10: 0692338454

Book design by Kim Dow, dowhouse.com

Manufactured in the United States of America. Rock on.
www.fatcyclist.com

This book is dedicated to everyone who reads and comments at fatcyclist.com. Some people might love to write for the sake of writing, but some of us need an audience. If it weren't for you, there's no way I would have stuck this out for ten years.

More importantly, this book is the funniest stuff I've written, during the hardest and darkest period of my life. You readers got me through this incredibly difficult time. I'll owe you a debt of gratitude forever for the kindness you've shown me.

Contents

ELDEN NELSON

THE GREAT FATSBY

ABSURD CYCLING STORIES
DISGUISED AS EXPERTISE & INSIGHT
{ALONG WITH PLENTY OF HOW-TOS & FAKE NEWS}

AKA

THE BEST OF FATCYCLIST.COM

VOLUME 2: 2007-2010

Preface

ELDEN NELSON

THIS BOOK COMPLETELY IGNORES THE ELEPHANT IN THE ROOM. ON PURPOSE. That elephant, of course, is the fact that this *Best of FatCyclist.com* volume overlaps more or less perfectly with the period during which my first wife, Susan, fought, endured, and eventually died of cancer. None of the posts covering that challenging subject matter are included in this book.

Why? Because Susan's battle deserves a volume of its own, and I wanted to do the easy book — the fun book — first. *Fight Like Susan* will be the next volume in the *Best of FatCyclist.com* series.

So, all that said, this is the best of about four years' worth of FatCyclist.com posts, with a few modifications. First, I shuffled the stories out of their chronological order and into a "story type" categorization. I did this primarily to confuse you.

Next, I added some context: why I wrote each story, what kind of feedback I got, what was going on at the time I wrote it. And then I footnoted every post, with the objective of having no page in the book *not* have at least one footnote. (I failed in this, but I came pretty close.) Essentially, these are new bits that occurred to me as I was editing and revising the stories.

Then, I went through and cherry-picked some of my favorite comments from each post. It was a lot of fun to go back and see how many people have contributed to this blog, as well as how *much* readers have contributed. Honestly, I should list my friends Dug Anderson (a real-life friend as well) and Al Maviva (never met him in real life) as co-authors for this book.

And finally, I added to, deleted from, and otherwise edited each of the stories. The fact is, when I post something to FatCyclist.com, I generally publish it as soon as I get the first draft done, and then barely, if at all, edit it here and there during the day.

If you're new to my writing, I hope you enjoy it. If you've been with me for years, well, this should be a really great walk down memory lane.

xoxo,

Fatty

Foreword

DAN WUORI

WHEN ELDEN NELSON ASKED ME TO WRITE THE FOREWORD TO HIS NEW BOOK, A WHOLE LIST OF QUESTIONS SPRANG TO MIND: WHEN WOULD HE need it? What was the pay? And who the hell is Elden Nelson?

After a little Internet research I put two and two together. Of course I know Elden. It's just that, like you, I know him best by his Christian name: Fatty.

While briefly weighing his invitation, I remembered that writing is awfully hard work and resolved that I would ignore his subsequent efforts to reach me, even going so far as to hide in the one place I knew he would never look: Google Plus. But then you don't blog three times a week for a decade without a little persistence. Let me tell you, Fatty does not take "no" for an answer.

When his overtures continued, I decided I would need to play my trump card. Knowing Elden had already resolved to subtly name this book after his penis (I wish I could tell you that is a joke...but I'll let him explain later on),[1] I agreed to introduce this volume on the condition that I alone could choose its title.

What author in his right mind, much less one with a surprisingly good dick joke in hand, would let a relative stranger demand naming

---

1   See "Lament of the Purple Snipe," p.62.

rights to a portion of his life's work? Just to ensure my safety I insisted on the single dumbest title I could muster: *The Great Fatsby*.

And so, here we are.

I probably still could have refused. I'm not a man of great principle. But in the end I consented, not because I have any great loyalty to Fatty, but because I care for you, the reader.

The thing is, what you hold in your hands is a book about cycling. I'm not sure if you've been paying much attention, but cycling books are a challenged genre of late — which is a polite way of saying that they're mostly full of crap. I hate to spoil the ending for anyone who DVR'd the Oprah interview, but let's just say that sometimes people tell stories that aren't entirely true. And often they wear spandex. (I will give credit to Floyd Landis here for marketing an almost entirely fictional account of his 2006 doping positive — as non-fiction — under the brilliantly apt title *Positively False*. Can't say he didn't warn you.)

Yes, cycling books are best read with a cynic's eye. Which brings me back to the original question: Just who *is* Elden Nelson? And is it possible that he too is being less than truthful? If you bought this book with the expectation that his Fat Cyclist blogger persona is anything more than a sophisticated ruse you might want to sit down before you consider the following:

Elden Nelson is not fat. At least not in any real sense.

And while he puts himself forth as just some affable schlub who likes bikes, the truth is that he has finished the Leadville Trail 100, arguably America's most physically grueling day of bike racing, *seventeen times*. With the last three on a singlespeed.

The truth is out there, people.

As you follow me down this rabbit hole over the next few hundred pages, I encourage you to ask yourself hard questions over whether Elden Nelson, if that is in fact his real name, is who he says he is. Oh sure, he'd have you believe that he's raised more than $2.6 million for charities including World Bike Relief and Livestrong, but is it possible that maybe, just maybe, this is actually some form of court-ordered restitution?

I don't pretend to know. But I've read too many cycling books to take anything a thin guy named "Fatty" is selling at face value.

1.

Things You Already Know
(But Your Friends Don't)

LET'S KICK OFF THIS BOOK YOU JUST BOUGHT — OR, IF YOU HAVE REALLY GOOD FRIENDS, YOU JUST RECEIVED AS A GIFT — WITH A SECTION YOU can skip. If you're a cyclist, this whole section is full of stuff you already know. You don't need to read it *at all*.

Instead, tear out this page and throw it away. Then tear out the rest of this section and give it to your non-cycling friends.

This will serve two incredibly valuable functions:

1. *For them:* They will know the answers to all the rudimentary cycling-related questions they would otherwise be asking you.
2. *For you:* Most people don't realize it, but it feels incredibly empowering to tear pages out of a book. Most of us never get the chance, though, because we're all terrified a librarian or angry anti-censoring activist will jump out and accuse us of ruining a book. Well, now you can hold this page out to them (or you could have, if you hadn't thrown it away) and triumphantly say, *"The author told me to. So THERE."*

Oh, and for those of you who are reading this as an e-book, never mind. You can't do any of this tearing out, discarding, and giving-away stuff. So maybe you should have sprung for the extra couple of bucks and bought the paper version of this book, huh?

I'm sorry. I've gotten completely off-track. I promise it won't happen again. Just kidding. That's really pretty much all that I can guarantee *will* happen in this book.

Anyway, if you decide not to give this first part of the book away, but instead choose to read it for some reason, you'll find it full of information that both new and experienced cyclists might consider valuable. Things like, what cycling gear you should buy, why knee warmers are stupid and you shouldn't get any. And why cycling hurts. And whether it's a good idea to fix your bike yourself. And what can happen if you drink too much.

And more. Much more.

Maybe too much more.

ASK A CYCLIST

This post originally had an ulterior motive. Specifically, I wrote it because the "Bloggies," an annual popularity contest among bloggers, had just kicked off, and I had managed to get a nomination. That meant a different audience would be coming by for a few weeks and I thought this would be a good way to introduce them to my blog so they would hopefully choose to vote for me.

Unfortunately for me, I was nominated in the "Best-Kept Secret" category, which is a nicer category name than "Blog Nobody Reads."

Even more unfortunately for me, I was up against a blog called "The Pioneer Woman," which would eventually become so big that it would spin off a couple of TV shows, children's books, and, eventually, have a state named after it.

Which is to say, I did not win.

But still, it did result in a pretty good story.

As a non-cyclist,[1] I am certain that you have many questions about the strange subculture that has grown up around riding bicycles. Likely, you have been so put off by the pungent smell and crazy eyes of cyclists that you have not dared ask those questions.

I don't blame you. I, too, avoid cyclists whenever possible.

I have, however, been immersed in the world of cycling long enough that I think I can both anticipate your questions and answer them to your satisfaction.

Why do cyclists shave their legs?

There are in fact two answers. First, there's the answer cyclists would have you believe: "We shave our legs in order to make it easy to clean gravel out of our legs when we fall and to make it easier for the masseuse to give us a good post-race massage."

Unfortunately, this answer is a lie.

---

1   Or possibly, as a beginning cyclist. Or maybe even as a very experienced cyclist who nevertheless would like my very valuable advice, because you accidentally mistook me as someone who knows something.

The honest reason cyclists shave their legs is very simple: *vanity*. We've worked so hard to get the legs we've got; we want to show them off.[2]

Why do you wear those clothes?
Cyclists wear tight lycra shorts with a sewn-in "chamois," which is French for "diaper-like item that is supposed to keep your butt from being rubbed raw, but doesn't." The lycra's job is to keep the chamois in place. The lycra's secondary job is to make your package[3] fall asleep from being compressed into one place for hours on end.

Cyclists also wear a polyester zip-up "jersey," a shirt designed to quickly evaporate all the sweat from your upper body, while expertly retaining the stink the sweat creates. Modern jerseys are so well-made that they will smell terrible after even one use and will retain that smell forever.

Fun fact: The proper way to dispose of an old jersey is to call your friendly local HazMat squad, which will properly discard, incinerate, bury, or dissolve in acid said jersey at the nearest nuclear waste facility.

What's going on with your shoes?
Really dedicated cyclists *never* want to be separated from their bicycles, no matter what. So we've invented special shoes that actually snap on to our pedals, much like ski boot bindings and skis, except that comparison kind of breaks down when you consider that nobody has to try to ski in rush hour traffic.

The idea behind these special shoe/pedal combinations is to let cyclists transfer as much power as possible from our legs to our bikes, pulling up on the cranks as well as pushing down on them.

The practical effect of these pedals is that when cyclists come to a stoplight, there is a 70% chance we will not be able to detach our shoes from their pedals, causing us to fall over sideways, as if we were somehow filming an episode of *The Benny Hill Show*.

If you ever witness this,[4] be certain to take pictures or hopefully a

---

2   And by "showing them off," I very definitely include showing them off to ourselves. I can't even estimate the hours I've spent staring at my legs in the mirror. Or I could, but I don't want to. I'm comfortable with knowing that you know I'm vain, but I don't want you to realize, quite yet, exactly how vain.

3   "Package" is a euphemism for "junk."

4   By "this," I mean a cyclist tipping over, not *The Benny Hill Show*.

video. There's nothing quite as memorable as a cyclist wrestling his[5] bike as if it were a rabid badger. You and your family will treasure these images for generations to come.

Sometimes when I'm in my car and pass a cyclist, I get an urge to either shout at the cyclist, honk, or throw a beer bottle. Is that OK?
You bet it is. All we ask is that when you yell at us, you shout *slowly* and *clearly*. Even as often as it happens, I have not yet once understood the actual words automotive passengers yell at me as they go by.

And I feel poorer, somehow, for not knowing what you're shouting at me as you very nearly commit vehicular homicide.

What's the point of cycling? I mean, you're just turning your feet around in a circle. How can you call that a sport? How can you even call that fun?
Most cyclists wrestle with this question their entire lives, without ever coming close to the answer. The best I can offer is something a wise man once told me:

"*Life is pain. And cycling hurts. A lot.*"

Why do you ride in groups? And why do you wear matching outfits?
We ride in groups because we like to imagine that our silly outfits don't look as silly in a group as they do individually. We wear matching outfits to avoid the likelihood that we'll otherwise look sillier than one another.

It's a vicious cycle and must be broken.

I have met three recumbent cyclists in my lifetime. All three were angry and had beards. Why is this?
A recumbent bicycle is a bicycle that lets the rider sit in a reclining position, rather than in an upright position. "Bent" cyclists, as they like to call themselves, are angry because they are convinced their way of doing things is absolutely correct, but nobody cares or wants to join them.

Nobody wants to join recumbent cyclists, ironically, because recumbent cyclists are so angry.

Recumbent cyclists all have beards, by the way, because they are all also Marxists.[6]

---

5 I say "his" because this doesn't happen to women.
6 And Marxists all have beards. Don't even bother trying to contradict me.

I've noticed that road bikes have "drop bars" that curve down so you can grip them much lower than you otherwise would. What's the reason for that low position?

Cyclists almost always put their hands on the part of handlebars above the brake levers.[7] The sole exception is when they are pretending they are Lance Armstrong.[8] If you see a cyclist riding with his hands "in the drops," so to speak, you may be assured that he (or she) is conducting a narrative about how he (i.e., Lance Armstrong[9]) is dropping the competition, putting them in a spot of bother, and otherwise forcing them to unpack their suitcase of courage.

I apologize for the weird metaphors.[10] Your cycling friends got them, I promise.

I often hear about doping running rampant in cycling. Are there any clean cyclists out there?

Anything's possible.

Is cycling all you think about?

No. I also think about eating. And I dedicate a fair amount of time to thinking about eating while cycling. And to what I will eat after I finish cycling. And to how long I have to wait after eating before I can ride.

One of my neighbors is seriously into bike riding and has asked me to join him for an easy ride. Should I go?

Under no circumstances. When cyclists invite non-cyclists on an "easy ride," we intend to take you on a four-hour tour across three mountain passes. We will ride just a little bit faster than you *the entire time,* using

---

7   We call them "hoods."

8   When I originally wrote this, it was true: we all were imagining we were Lance Armstrong. Now, however, we're imagining we're someone who looks and rides like Lance Armstrong, but has a different name. And no, we haven't decided whose name that is yet.

9   Or the unnamed Lance Armstrong-like figure.

10   They're things famous cycling commentator Paul Sherwen said once, and then we all started saying them when we wanted to sound like Paul Sherwen. And now he says them because we expect him too. Cycling is a cyclical sport in more ways than one.

body language to urge you to keep up. Within two hours, your lungs will be burning, your heart will explode, and you will wish for death.

Worst of all, we will not realize the misery we have put you through and will tell our riding buddies that we think we've got you "hooked."

I hear that bike saddles make you impotent. Is that true?
I don't know. This numb sensation I've got down below won't go away, so it's difficult for me to find out.

I'm interested in getting into shape and think a bicycle might be a good way to do it. How much money do I need?
You're in luck. Bikes are relatively inexpensive. You just need a few things to get started: a bicycle, a helmet, bike shorts, bike jerseys, bike socks, bike shoes, floor bike pump, extra tubes, seat bag, tire levers, CO_2 cans, CO_2 adapter, lube, water bottles, bike rack for the car, bike gloves, bike glasses, energy bars, energy drinks, recovery drinks, a bike computer, a coach, plus a few other accessories.

The great news is all of this together shouldn't cost much more than a typical Lexus.

COMMENT FROM AL MAVIVA
Doping isn't rampant in cycling. Cycling, however, is rampant among dopers.

COMMENT BY MILES ARCHER
Recumbent cyclists also all run Unix on their home servers.

COMMENT BY YUKIRIN BOY
I recently opened my briefcase of courage and shaved my legs. No one mentioned how weird it felt wearing regular suit pants afterwards.

SO YOU WANT TO BE A CYCLIST?

You have purchased this book, or have been given this torn-out book section, because you are very curious about cyclists and the world of cycling, and would like me to tell you everything you need to know about what you need to do to join the ranks of this fast-growing sport.

Well, you've done the right thing.

As a well-known and much-beloved ambassador of cycling culture, it will be my honor to give you a whirlwind tour of the different kinds of cycling, the equipment you will need to purchase, and what you will need to do to get maximum enjoyment from your new hobby.

Let's begin, shall we?

One of the really great things about cycling is how inexpensive it is. However, there are a few things you'll find absolutely essential to enjoying the sport.

Obviously, you'll need a bike. And you can get a reasonably good bicycle for around $500. This is, in fact, an excellent amount of money to plan on spending on your bicycle...if you want to draw the scorn and derision of every other cyclist you ever meet.

That would be just *awful*.

And the fact is, if you spend just $500 on that bike, you're going to find that you want to trade it in on a much nicer bike within a few months anyway.

So, you'd better plan on budgeting around $2500 for that bike.[11]

Also, I was kind of misleading you a little bit when I talked about your "bike" in the singular sense. You can't have just one bike; that would severely limit the grand experience that cycling has to offer. You've got to have your main road bike (I know I said $2500 earlier, but $3500 will get you one you *really* like), your rain bike ($750), your fixie ($1666), your cross-country mountain bike ($2750), your freeride/downhill bike ($3800 each if you're going to do it right), your cyclocross bike ($1500), your singlespeed ($1200), and your recumbent ($1900, plus $75 for a good-quality beard trimmer).

That's about $18,966, because I was just kidding about the recumbent.

---

11   Or, as you'll soon discover, that's actually just what your *first* bike will cost.

A HELMET

The bike's just the beginning of the story, though. You'll also need a helmet, because — even though as a cyclist you are otherwise completely unprotected — safety has got to be your first concern.

Now, some people will tell you that a helmet is a good place to save money, since even the cheapest helmets must pass the same tests before they go on the market. But those people haven't told you about the "do you look like a brain surgery patient on the way back to the hockey rink" test.

No, if you want to be a *real* cyclist, you need to get yourself a nice-looking helmet.[12] There's an easy pair of criteria to help you discern whether a helmet looks nice:

1. The helmet has at least 20 vents. More is better. Ideally, in fact, there should be enough vents that you have a difficult time believing that the helmet will actually protect you in a crash.
2. The helmet costs at least $150.

SHOES

If you are a man, you likely have never spent more than $150 on shoes before. Those days are over, my friend. To be a real cyclist, you need cycling-specific shoes. This may seem odd, since — unlike in most sports, where your shoes actually touch the ground — your shoes do nothing but get between your feet and the pedal.

You'll be pleased to know, that cycling shoes are in fact the most special-purpose footwear you will ever own, not to mention the most expensive. Plan on spending anywhere from $250 to $600. These shoes, combined with special pedals, actually *lock you to your bike*, making it so you theoretically can pull up on the pedals as well as push down on them.

In reality, of course, their main purpose is to entertain your fellow cyclists when you fall down at a stoplight, hopelessly tangled with and pinned down by your bicycle.

Anyway.

---

12   Ideally, one for each kind of riding. Even more ideally, a black and a white one for each kind of riding, to match the cycling gear you're wearing and bike you're riding.

Cycling shoes have stiff, inflexible soles, giving you extra power when you pedal, as well as, when combined with the hardware that locks you to your pedals, making you look ridiculous when you walk.

Important safety tip: Do not walk on concrete, asphalt, or tile when wearing cycling shoes, because you are likely to slip and fall. Do not walk on grass or dirt, because you are likely to jam up the inner workings of your cleats. Do not walk on hardwood floors, because you are likely to be killed by your significant other.[13]

Oh, and you're going to want — no, make that *need* — different sets for your road and mountain bikes.

CLOTHES

You might assume that you should be able to wear any clothes when riding a bike...and you would be right! However, you would also notice that your normal natural fiber clothes start to chafe a bit after you've ridden for an hour or so.

And they start to get soaked with sweat.

And they billow in the wind something *awful*.

Which is why you need to buy extremely bright, form-fitting polyester and lycra clothing,[14] including:

- **Bike jerseys**: Bike jerseys are designed to fit you very comfortably, as long as you are a professional cyclist with arms in an advanced stage of attrition. Otherwise, you might find them a bit...um...*snug*. And, after wearing these jerseys a couple times, you might find them a bit stinky. Don't try to get that stink out. It's your street cred. Also, try to get a jersey that advertises your favorite consumer product. And finally, since bike jersey pockets, which are in the back of your jersey, are practically impossible to get to you may want to have your elbows replaced with ball joints.
- **Bike shorts**: Bike shorts have the distinction of being both the world's most- (and yet, somehow, also world's least-)

---

13   It's probably best, in fact, if you never walk with these shoes at all. Instead, remove them as soon as you get off the bike and hold them high above your head, protecting them from any incidental dirt and grime that may be in the area.

14   You won't feel self-conscious wearing that super-bright, super-tight pair of shorts and matching shirt as you clack-clack across the floor in the coffee shop, will you? No, of course you won't.

comfortable clothing, depending on what you are doing at the moment. If you are on a bike, the big diaper-y thing between your nether regions and the saddle clearly falls into the "boon" category. The lycra wicks sweat away as it stretches to accommodate the motion of your legs and your — let's face it — unnatural sitting position. Once you're *off* the bike, however, the diaper becomes dank and cold and starts breeding bacteria so fast you can actually hear the cells divide. Plus, thanks to muscle memory from when you were a toddler, you will be unable to prevent yourself from walking with a distinct waddle. The shoes will augment this motion.

- **Layers upon layers:** You never know when the weather might change. It could become wetter. Or drier. Or colder, or warmer, or windier. Non-cyclists might simply live with these kinds of changes up to a point and then, if the weather got bad enough, go home. Cyclists, however, are prepared for any shift in the weather. Hence, you are going to need to not only own, but carry with you at all times, each of the following:
  - Arm warmers
  - Knee warmers[15]
  - Extra gloves
  - Vest
  - Wind jacket
  - Rainproof jacket
  - Shoe covers

And how much should these clothes cost? That's easy: simply take the cost of an ordinary, comparable article of clothing, then imagine that article of clothing encrusted in diamonds. But still washer-safe.[16]

EMERGENCY REPAIR GEAR

Good news: once you've got your bike and clothing, you're almost ready to ride! But not quite. Because while cyclists celebrate the simplicity and efficiency of their machines, the reality is that bicycles are required by law to break down every nine miles.

---

15   I hate these. I will explain why shortly.
16   Unless you're acting all retro and wearing wool, in which case all bets are off.

So as to avoid being stranded, you need to make sure you always have the following with you when riding your bike:

- Patch kit
- Tire levers
- Extra tube of glue for the patch kit because the first tube of glue has certainly dried out
- Extra tube for when the patch still doesn't hold (true fact: in the history of cycling, only four field-applied patches have ever held)
- Spare tire
- CO_2 tire inflator system
- Mini-pump for when the CO_2 system doesn't work
- Frame pump for when the mini-pump doesn't work
- Cell phone for when the frame pump doesn't work
- Set of allen wrenches (metric and the other kind...non-metric?)
- Spoke wrench
- Duct tape (3 rolls)
- Extra rear derailleur (better safe than sorry)
- Road flare
- First aid kit
- Change of clothing
- Pillow
- Road atlas of the world
- Pistol and ammo, just in case you find that you need to live off the land for a while
- 5-gallon jug of water
- Acetylene torch and welder's goggles
- $500 in cash in case you need to buy a cheap used car to get yourself home
- Something to read
- Russian phrasebook in case you get very, very lost
- Extra Powerbar[17]

These are, of course, merely the bare essentials. If you're going to be out for more than a couple of hours, bring everything else you can imagine possibly needing on the road.

---

17   You can tell I wrote this a long time ago, because as far as I know, Powerbars have not actually been made since 2008. Which means the Powerbars you still see stocked at REI have been there a while.

Depending on the size of your jersey pockets, you may want to invest in a pannier[18] setup.

With these simple and inexpensive purchases made, you're ready to ride.

No, I was just kidding. You're not even remotely ready to start riding your bike. Before you dare embark on the simple, carefree cyclist lifestyle, you must first understand cycling culture, etiquette, training techniques, nutrition, and a few other simple, intuitive cycling fundamentals.

In other words, you must make cycling your entire life. Here's how.

STEP 1: DECIDE WHY YOU RIDE.

As someone new to cycling, perhaps you think that the reason you might want to ride a bike is to get outdoors, see the world, have some fun, and get some exercise, all at once. And this would be a fine reason to ride a bike, if it weren't completely, adorably wrongheaded.

To be a cyclist, you don't ride your bike because it's fun. That kind of riding is what we call "junk miles" and is frowned upon by real cyclists.[19]

Let me be perfectly clear: *riding a bike to enjoy yourself is not an acceptable reason to get on your bike.*

You need to *train*. And that means having a goal. For your convenience, I have several acceptable cycling goals listed below. Feel free to adopt two or more as your own:

- **Race Across America (RAAM)**: An exercise in pain and sleep deprivation
- **24 Hours of Moab,**[20] Solo: This means you ride your mountain bike in a 12-mile sandy loop as many times as you can in 24 hours. That sounds like fun, doesn't it?
- **The Iditarod**: A 350-mile (or more, if that seems too easy) race across the Alaska tundra in the middle of winter. The person who survived this race says it's awesome.
- **The Tour de France**: Don't just slum it, like most of the riders. Make a point of winning a stage.

---

18   "Pannier" is a French word that means "a giant purse affixed to one side of the back of your bike." Panniers always come in pairs, because you want that ungainly, awkward canvas monstrosity to be symmetrical.

19   I'm frowning at you right now. Do you feel my frown?

20   RIP.

STEP 2: RIDE WITH PURPOSE

Once you've made your decision to make a race the center of your life, you're all set to start training. Of course, many of you are new to this sport, so I'll define this unfamiliar term:

Train (verb): To exercise according to a set schedule, with the dual objectives of becoming more proficient at that sport, and learning to hate the sport at which you are working so hard to become proficient.

Oh, and there's a side benefit too. If you're training, you're guaranteed to be scheduled to do a set of road hill intervals the day all your friends want to go on a group ride. Or you'll be having an enforced rest day when all your friends want to ride an epic stretch of singletrack.

But all this training will pay off and one day you will be the fastest and strongest rider of all the people who used to be your riding buddies, back when you had friends. You know, back before you started training.

Of course, all this training is going to hurt. A lot. As a cyclist, you need to pretend to enjoy this kind of pain. You need to talk about "putting your head down and suffering up a mountain" in reverential tones. You need to act like being in self-inflicted, entirely recreational pain has taught you wisdom and has given you a certain self-sufficiency and quiet confidence.

And not that it, in fact, makes you seem kind of creepy to everyone else.

STEP 3: EAT LIKE A CYCLIST

It's not a well-known fact, but cyclists do not eat food. Instead, they consume synthetically-manufactured, food-like substances, engineered to deliver fuel to blood cells as efficiently as possible, without the inconvenience of being enjoyable to eat.

All cycling food substitutes are required by law to be, or at least taste like, one or more of the following:

- An insoluble powder that tastes somewhat, but not quite, like Kool Aid with too much sugar mixed in. A handful of Cream o' Wheat[21] is usually mixed in as well, with the intent of settling to the bottom of the bottle, which is in turn required to taste like a pool filtration system (i.e., delicious!).
- Glucose from an IV bag. But thicker. Much, much thicker. With raspberry flavoring.
- Carob-coated rawhide.

---

21   Or chalk dust, because chalk dust has more protein.

STEP 4: LOOK LIKE A CYCLIST

Like many tight-knit communities, cyclists want to identify with each other by looking exactly alike. This entails, first and foremost, shaving your legs.

Never lift anything, or your arms won't atrophy properly.

Get a goofy tan. The tops of your legs and forearms should be dark as can be. The tan, however, should not extend to the back of your legs, nor beyond the jersey line.

And above all, you should have the reverse raccoon look, where all of your face except your eyes — where the glasses go — is deeply tanned.

STEP 5: PRIORITIZE LIKE A CYCLIST

Here's an interesting fact about cycling: once you get your legs into decent shape, you can go for hours and hours and hours without your legs really tiring out. That's not true of most other sports.

So guess what? In order to get a challenging workout, you're going to need about four hours per day. Except weekends, when you're going to need to go for about *six* hours.

This, of course, is something you'll need to inform your significant other of, at some point.[22]

Luckily for your family, they'll think it's lots of fun to spend family vacation time traveling to a bike race and then sitting on the side of the road for 2.7 hours until you whiz by, focusing on the road and nothing else.[23]

STEP 6: THINK AND TALK LIKE A CYCLIST

It's all well and good to have chosen to be a cyclist, but it's not enough. You have to talk the talk. Use the following guidelines when conversing with other cyclists:

- **Cars**: You're against them, especially when they do something that nearly (or actually) gets you injured. Never ever ever consider the possibility that you might sometimes be at fault.
- **Cars, Part II**: You're not against cars when you're driving one to the trailhead. Furthermore, your bike rack is something you should have thought about as obsessively as the bike itself.

---

22   Maybe while she or he is sleeping, watching television, or is otherwise preoccupied.

23   Later, after the race, you should pretend you did see them. You know, to be nice.

- **Other cycling disciplines:** If you're a road cyclist, regard mountain bikes as clumsy, inelegant toys. If you're a mountain biker, shake your head in wonder at the fact that anyone would choose to mix it up with cars all the time. If you're a trackie, try to puzzle out why nobody else you know wants to join you for a couple of hours of riding around and around and around on a banked oval. If you're a recumbent rider, be sure to keep your beard well-trimmed and please try to not be so angry all the time.
- **Other sports:** Be unaware of them.
- **Doping:** Despise it, unless you actually do it. In which case, *act* like you despise it.

There is, of course, more. And I'd gladly reveal it to you, but the fact is my coach told me to keep my typing rate down to 35 words per minute today and to not spend more than 85 minutes on the keyboard.

COMMENT BY JASON

Thanks for providing the breakdown of the requisite items to be a cyclist. This may in fact save my marriage as I can now demonstrate to my wife that my cycling obsession is normal and the amount of money I spend to support my addiction is, in fact, healthy.

COMMENT BY TIM E

Fatty, you exaggerate. It took 8 full months before I bought the second bike to replace my starter bike.

COMMENT BY JENNI LAURITA

What about the $600 computer with GPS/power meter/et al? And how could you leave out the butt balm?!

COMMENT BY AARON

Funny thing is, all the non-cyclists reading this think you're probably exaggerating. You also forgot the 5 different-sized backpacks for mountain biking. You know, depending on how long the ride is, the type of trail, and whether or not you need to carry armor.

COMMENT BY LUCKYLAB

You really didn't touch on the next level where you have absolutely no clue how much the bike cost. You know, the one where you've upgraded the dang thing part by part and have left the prices somewhere deep in your memory, in a dark corner with the recurring nightmare you had as a child, so you can go ride the thing without sobbing uncontrollably every time you hit a rock.

TOP TECHNIQUES FOR GETTING TIME TO RIDE

As I sit down to write about cycling each day, I sometimes find myself uncomfortable. Often, this is because my pants are too tight.

But not always.

Sometimes, I'm uncomfortable about what I'm writing because I'm telling too much truth, revealing not just my own secrets, but the secrets of every cyclist who lives the incredibly imbalanced lifestyle we have chosen. Namely, riding at the expense of pretty much everything else.

When I write these kinds of things, I become acutely aware of the lopsidedness of my life. And that very few people I know understand or appreciate my compulsion. And that it's in fact, possibly, time for me to start making some changes in my life.

More than any of this though, I'm afraid that any of the millions of other cyclists who are just like me are going to want to beat me up for laying plain our secrets.

Then I reassure myself: this is not a real concern, since none of us have any upper-body strength.

It is common knowledge that if you want to be a rider of any consequence, cycling must be the only thing you think about, ever.[24]

Sadly, there are those who, bizarrely, think that there are other things in the world that approach the importance of cycling. These people are often called "family members," and for reasons that have never been made clear, they believe they have some sort of claim on your time.

Pfff.

And since, for the time being anyway, you live in the same house as your family, there's probably going to be a little awkwardness if you simply ignore these people and go about the very important business of riding of and caring for your bicycles.[25]

How, then, can you get in all the quality bike-riding time you deserve? By using the time-tested time management (also called "manipulation" or "being a weasel") techniques described below.

---

24   For example, I'm thinking about riding right now.
25   I'm still thinking about cycling, by the way. I never stopped. I'm excellent at multi-tasking.

DETERMINE HOW MUCH YOU SHOULD BE PREPARED TO GIVE UP
When you negotiate for time to ride, you must be prepared to give something up in return.[26] The trick is in understanding how to give up as little as possible. Use the following as a guideline:

- **Ride during business hours, when you wouldn't be home anyway:** Do not give up anything for this. In fact, why even reveal that it happened at all?
- **Short ride (which could possibly turn into a longish ride) after work:** Make a phone call on the way home from the ride volunteering to pick up dinner, so your partner doesn't have to cook and so you can eat immediately upon returning home, because you're starving.
- **Long ride (4+ hours) during the weekend:** Volunteer ahead of the ride that you're planning to spend most of the day working around the house, but would like to start the day by getting in a "good-length ride." This is, of course, code for "long ride," but it's crucial you don't actually call it that.[27]
- **Long weekend away with the riding buddies:** Flowers and chocolate.
- **4+ day cycling road trip:** Flowers, chocolate, and jewelry.
- **Month-long trip to go pre-ride the Tour de France:** Anything asked of you, since the only negotiation tactic open to you in this case is pure, outright begging.

GOOD DEEDS: TIMING IS CRUCIAL
I don't even need to tell you the value of pre-emptive good deed-doing (sometimes referred to as "banking brownie points") as a finding-time-for-cycling technique.

But if your sense of timing is off, you run the very real risk of sabotaging yourself and your act of "kindness" will be for naught. Oh, you could say that the act of kindness is its own reward, but neither of us really buys that.

The simple, important rule of "good deeds as a form of currency to be spent on permission to go on a ride" is:

---

26   I think this may be a law of physics or something. Or it might just be a law in Utah. Could go either way.

27   And for sure don't call it an "all-day ride." Especially when it's an all-day ride.

Do not, no matter what, mention the ride you want to go on while you are performing the good deed.

Did you notice how I put that in bold and italics, in its own paragraph? It was that important.

Why? Because if you do mention the ride, your significant other will draw a line connecting the dots so fast, you're likely to be sliced in half by it.

Instead, wait a minimum of six hours — nine is smarter — before mentioning that you'd like to go on this ride. And when you mention this ride, *do not bring up the good deed you did.* Sure, both of you know a transaction is happening, but neither of you should acknowledge it. Kind of like when you give a cop a $50 bill to get out of a ticket.[28]

Abandon the charade at your peril. I say this with the wisdom of experience.

THE "CLEARING THE DECK" STRATEGY

An excellent way to get some riding time to yourself is to sneakily arrange for everyone in the house to be doing something at the same time. Send the kids off to a movie with their friends. Send your partner off to a craft store, hardware store, the horse races, or whatever other thing there is that you both know he or she likes, but you do not.

Suddenly, you've got time for yourself. Gee, what to do?

I expect you'll think of something.

5 TOP TECHNIQUES

You have many, many additional ways to avoid your family in order to spend more quality time with your bike.[29] Try these five top techniques on for size.

1. **"Just this once."** They say nobody likes a whiner, but that doesn't mean that whining doesn't work. Make your case that you work hard, that you don't spend a lot of money on cars (don't say this if you spent a lot of money on your car, or if your bike cost more than a car), that you don't try to stop your partner from doing the things he or she loves. You just like to ride your bike, and, *just this once,* you'd like to get out

---

28   I have never tried this. I honestly can't even imagine trying this.
29   And really, that's what life is about.

on a ride without having to start at 3:00am and be back before anyone wakes up in the morning, as if it were something to be ashamed of and hidden from the neighbors.[30]

The great thing about saying "just this once" is that nobody really believes that you don't ever plan to use this gambit again. Your partner knows you're going to make the same argument again next week.

2. "I have a dream." This one takes planning and foresight. On New Year's Eve, while everyone's talking about the things they wish they had the discipline to stick with but won't, you bring up something you really plan to do. Look your partner in the eyes and say, with all the conviction you can find in that hollow husk where your soul should be, "Honey, I want to get in great shape this year. I want to lose weight and get fit. I would really like to win at local races."

Then, each day after you ride, express gratitude for the "support"[31] you're being given as you strive to reach your goals.

If you can, from time to time, get a little misty as you say this, it makes the lie more palatable.

3. "I'm doing this for you." This technique works best if you have a grotesquely obese neighbor you both know by name. "Would you rather I look like *Dan*?" you could ask. "If you want me to gain fifty pounds,[32] just give the word and I'll stop biking."

Conclude with, "I should probably update my life insurance, since once I stop exercising I'll be at greater risk for heart disease."

Note: If you have picked up a vibe that your partner wouldn't mind seeing you dead (happens more often than you might think), you should probably avoid the above technique.

4. "This is nothing." Again, you'll want to have an unknowing neighbor to bolster the credibility of this argument. This neighbor must be gone or unavailable almost all the time, whether for work or for waxing the

---

30 Try to start crying, just a little, if you can manage it.
31 In this case, "support" means that your partner has not yet murdered you.
32 Or, in my case, *another* fifty pounds.

bmw.[33] Simply say, "You think *I'm* gone a lot? Have you happened to check out *Brad* lately? Would you prefer I be more like him, maybe?"

The flip side of this argument actually works pretty well, too, if you happen to have a local hermit. "ok, how about if I just sit around and never leave the house except to go get the mail, like Bob. You'll see me all you want. Won't that be great?"

5. Mope. To get something, sometimes you've got to give something up. Sometime, don't go on a ride. Don't even ask. And then mope around the house all day. Sigh heavily. Look outside the window.

Eventually, you'll be asked what your problem is. Don't answer right away. Hem and haw. Insist everything's fine.

Finally, admit that there was a group ride you were interested in today, but you decided against it. You'd rather hang out with the family.

I promise, next time you ask, you'll be given a free pass.

---

33   No euphemism intended.

SO YOU WANT TO BE A MOUNTAIN BIKER?

*This is going to freak you out, but there is **actually more than one kind of biking**. Further, it may freak you out even more to know that some cyclists commit to one kind of riding, and one kind only.*

Like, some people ride just on the road. Some ride just on the mountain. Some ride around in circles.

I do not understand these people at all. Road biking and mountain biking are equally awesome, in vastly different ways. I can't imagine why, having invested the time to get strong enough to do one, any cyclist wouldn't want to do both.

This story is to help road cyclists overcome that hurdle and embrace the awesomeness that is mountain biking.

And yes, I did write a corresponding "So You Want to Be a Road Cyclist" piece. It just didn't make the cut for this book.[34]

As a road cyclist, you have no doubt asked yourself, from time to time, the following question:

"What would happen if I rode my bike off-road?"

Well, the answer is quite simple. If you took *your* bike off-road, your brainpan would be shaken loose and your tires would explode, right before your rims crumpled in a heap.

But that may not have been the question you meant to ask. Maybe you meant to ask, "What would it be like to ride a mountain bike on these trails I sometimes see intersecting the tarmac?[35] Would it really be that much different?"

Yes, it would be different.[36] Here are some of the key tips and tricks to help you prepare for your grand off-road cycling transformation.

1. YOU MUST GET A TATTOO.[37]

Before you even begin thinking about shopping for a mountain bike, let alone taking your first mountain bike ride, you must get a rad tattoo.

---

34   This, I suspect, should serve as an answer to the people who are asking themselves, "If this is the *Best of FatCyclist*, what *didn't* make the cut?

35   Yeah, cyclists call pavement "tarmac." We're hoity-toity like that.

36   Wonderfully, gloriously different.

37   Interesting fact about me: For years and years, I told anyone I could that if, someday, I were to finish the Leadville 100, a famous mountain bike race, in fewer

It's the law. There are actual mountain bike police out monitoring the trails, and they are liable to ask you if you have a tattoo. If you don't, they are authorized to give you one of their choosing on the spot.

Now, I'm certain that you are thinking, right this moment, "I'm pretty sure I saw a mountain biker without a tattoo, once." I assure you: that mountain biker had a tattoo. It was just more discretely placed than most, probably because that biker still lives at home and is afraid his mom will find out.

So the question is, what should your tattoo be? Well, mountain biking bylaws stipulate that a chainring must be one of the graphical elements, a mystical Asian glyph must be included, and there must be a whimsical third symbol: wings, a skull-and-crossbones, or a cloud are all good examples. I recommend a yin-yang symbol inside a chainring, peeking out from behind a cloud, as if the yin-yang chainring were the sun.

Feel free to make up your own story as to what this means.

2. NONE OF YOUR EXISTING EQUIPMENT TRANSFERS.

You might think that since you already have an outrageous quantity of cycling gear that you would have significant equipment overlap, making it easier for you to get your foot in the mountain biking door.

That is, naturally, ridiculous.

You will need to buy all new clothes: baggy shorts, jerseys promoting different products, a helmet with a visor. You will need different shoes, and a high volume/low pressure floor pump. You will need different lube and different tools.

And none of the spare bike parts you have accumulated over the years will be of any use. The wily bike part manufacturers have made certain of that.

3. YOUR BIKE WILL BE TOO COMPLEX FOR YOU TO UNDERSTAND.

Here's an interesting exercise: sketch out your road bike from memory. Be thorough: draw where the cables go and the where the brakes are.

That was easy, wasn't it?

Now, ask a mountain biker to sketch out his full-suspension bike from memory. He won't be able to. The frame is just too complex—the

---

than nine hours, I would get a tattoo with my finishing time. A few years ago, I finally finished in under nine hours. I have not gotten the tattoo.

fork moves up and down, the whole back section of the bike flexes around, and disc brakes are black magic that require either a degree in physics or theology[38] to properly repair.

4. YOU MUST CHOOSE A TRIBE.

When you ride your road bike, the bike type describes precisely what you're doing: you're riding on the road. Sure, there are a few outlier bike types (TT bikes, fixies), but even those are minor degrees of difference.

When you decide to go mountain biking, on the other hand, you haven't yet decided anything. You must still narrow down by these oh-so-important factors:

- **Wheel size:** 26", 27.5" or 29"? If you go with 26" wheels, you're a Luddite who can't accept the winds of change. If you go with 29" wheels, you're a sap who believes everything he reads. If you go with one of each, you're just confused.[39]
- **Your riding style: Cross country, Downhill, or Freeride?**[40] "Cross country" means you aren't very good at riding downhill, so tell people you like to be able to climb. "Downhill" means that you wish you could afford a motorcycle, and are making do for now. "Freeride" means you bought into the marketing hype that said if a downhill bike were a pound lighter you could also climb with it.
- **Suspension: Front, Full, or None?** Modern mountain bikes have sophisticated shock absorbers that can very nearly negate the bumps on the trail you claim to have come out to enjoy on the first place. Here's a thought: if you want a smooth, non-bumpy ride, why don't you try a remarkable new invention called "tarmac?"[41] On the other hand, if you ride a mountain bike with no suspension, you'll be called a retro-grouch and you'll be rattled into a state of amnesia.
- **Gears or singlespeed?** When you're on your road bike, of course you want gears. Gears make you go faster. On mountain bikes,

---

38   Or, better yet, both.

39   If you go with 27.5" wheels, you're neither fish nor fowl, and look for consensus where there is none.

40   I'm not sure, but I think freeride is now called "all-mountain." Or maybe it's called "Enduro." *I am so confused.*

41   i.e., pavement.

on the other hand, it's becoming increasingly popular to have no gears, because it's simpler or more pure or something. The prevailing wisdom on this theory is that the only people who subscribe to it are those whose brains have been excessively rattled, due to lack of proper suspension on their bikes.

5. YOU MUST LEARN NEW TACTICS.

When you first start mountain biking, you'll be tempted to draft, riding as efficiently as you always have. You will quickly discover, however, that this tactic doesn't have much benefit at two miles per hour.

And don't point out obstacles. Unlike roadies, who want to help each other stay upright, one of the primary reasons mountain bikers hit the trail is because there's always a good chance someone's going to have a good wipeout, and they don't want to miss it.

Finally, and most importantly, start drinking more beer.

6. BE READY TO WORK HARDER FOR YOUR MILES.

If you go on a three-hour road ride, you've probably covered 50 miles or so. If, on the other hand, you've gone on a three-hour mountain bike ride, you may not get out of sight of the trailhead.

7. BE PREPARED TO BE INJURED IN NEW AND INTERESTING WAYS.

As a road cyclist, you no doubt live in constant terror of road rash. The good news is, as a mountain biker you'll never have to worry about road rash again.

The bad news is, there are numerous new ways you can be injured while mountain biking:

- **Branches at eye level**: On your road bike, glasses are a good idea. On your mountain bike, they're a really really good idea. Really.
- **Branches at other levels**: Have you ever wondered what it would feel like to have a branch catch in the crook of your arm as you blow by at 22 mph? Or to have a branch insert itself between your spokes and fork? Good news: You'll find out soon!
- **Dirt is softer than pavement,**[42] **but not much**: You've probably already figured out that turfing it on the dirt is going to hurt less

---

42   I got tired of writing "tarmac."

than hitting the road. However, when you consider how much more often you're going to fall, that may be small comfort.

- **You're going to get stupid.** By and large, people don't do intentionally stupid things on road bikes. You just ride. This is not the case on mountain bikes. At all. People will look at a nine-foot dropoff and say, "I think I can make it." I'm pretty sure this has to do with all the brainpan rattling.
- **Nasty creatures:** Got room in your jersey pocket for a snakebite kit? Maybe you should make room.[43]

You'll be glad to know, however, that your big, burly mountain bike is built to take the kind of beating you're sure to give it, and it will only rarely have mechanical difficulties.

No, I'm just kidding. Your mountain bike will break as often as, or more than, your road bike.

So please, allow me to conclude by welcoming you, my roadie friends, to the world of mountain biking.

I'm sure you're anxious to dive right in.

---

43   I have come across rattlesnakes four times while mountain biking. One of these times, I didn't even realize it until I heard the rattling. At which point I suddenly found myself capable of riding much, much faster.

THE PROBLEM WITH BEING WELL-HYDRATED

Long before I started writing for FatCyclist.com — in fact, long before I started obsessively riding bikes — I wrote for an off-campus college weekly called Student Review. *As you probably guessed, I wrote a humor column. Mostly innocuous, because, even though this was a college paper and was even off-campus, it did serve the extremely conservative, almost exclusively Mormon, Brigham Young University.*

I was single. I was dating. I wrote about my life, including, once, the awkwardness that can accompany desperately needing to use the restroom while your date is obliviously engaged in a long monologue.[44]

The furor around that story: the outrage, the calls for me to be fired (hilarious because like everyone else there, I worked for free) was...instructive. "I've learned my lesson!" I said to myself. "From this point forward, I'll leave my writing outside the restroom!"

From the way the previous two sentences end in exclamation points, you can tell I was serious about this.

I am happy to report that, twenty years later, in this story, I am completely ignoring that life lesson. Which is my way of saying that if it bothers you to read about peeing, you may want to skip ahead.

Years ago, I edited a computer programmer's magazine (*Visual C++ Developers Journal*,[45] to which I'm sure you subscribed). The publisher was based in California, but I worked remotely, subletting an office from a real estate agent.

Since I worked remotely, I was on the phone almost constantly. Talking to authors. Talking to editors. Talking to layout. Talking to the publisher.

Talking, talking, talking.

DRINK UP

At the time, I was training very seriously, and was trying to get down to racing weight (i.e., the weight at which my knees no longer squoosh into my belly on the upstroke of my pedaling rotation).

---

44   As far as I know, this story is now lost to the world. A true tragedy.

45   I've got lots of copies of back issues of this magazine, oddly enough. Just in case you'd like me to autograph one for you.

Now, any time I want to get serious about losing weight, drinking water becomes a huge part of my day. Even at work, I'll keep a couple water bottles at my desk, drinking one bottle per hour or so.

I'm not absolutely certain why constantly drinking water is so effective at bringing your weight down (also, I'm not interested, so please don't email me with links to informative articles), but I know that it works.

As I would drink, I would, naturally, need to pee. And I'm not talking about needing to pee once every couple hours, nor am I talking about needing to pee once per hour. I'm talking about needing to pee pretty much all the time.

I remember, for example, finishing once, washing up, and returning to my seat...and getting the first glimpse of that special "it's go time" twinge *as I sat down.*

In fact, I have, more than once, contemplated whether it might be possible, if one were to drink just a smidgen more, to both drink and pee at a constant, non-stop rate.

Someone, please try this and get back to me on how it turns out.

THE IMPORTANCE OF GOOD PLANNING

I don't need to tell you that if you're a perpetual water drinker and you're going to be in a ninety-minute meeting, you've got to take steps. Specifically:

1. Taper off on the drinking at least an hour before the meeting.
2. Go use the restroom just before the meeting, even if you don't really feel like you need to.[46]

Sometimes, though, I forgot. And when that happened, meetings seemed to go longer.

And time seemed to slow. Then stop.

Then reverse itself and go backwards.

Of course, there's nothing wrong with excusing yourself from a meeting for a moment for a "bio break," as we euphemized it.

On the other hand, it feels distinctly awkward when you have to excuse yourself to pee for the third time that hour.

---

46 At the time, my friend Dug and I worked in the same office. He worked for the same publishing company as I did and he was also working hard to be a well-hydrated cyclist. As a result, you could always tell when we both were on the same conference call: we'd both be in the bathroom three minutes before the meeting started.

DESPERATE MEASURES

And now we come to the point of this story:[47] the fateful day when I got a phone call from the president of the company.[48]

It was unexpected and it was urgent. I put my headset on and settled in.

But, without thinking, I just kept on drinking.

Ten minutes into the call, I realized I had nervously drunk a whole bottle of water since picking up the phone.

Fifteen minutes into the call, I needed to pee. But this wasn't the kind of call from which you take a break. Nosirree.

Twenty-five minutes into the call, I needed to pee, *bad.*

And thirty-five minutes into the call, I determined it was time to make a new, novel use of one of my water bottles.

I drew the blinds closed, waited until I could tell I wouldn't need to talk for at least a minute, then put my phone on mute. I unscrewed the top of my least-favorite bottle and made additional preparations, which I shall, mercifully, not describe here.

I immediately felt three sensations:

1. **Exquisite relief.** I don't believe I need to explain this sensation nor why I felt it.

2. **Strangeness.** The knowledge that I was peeing while my boss yelled at me about my inability to ask relevant follow-up questions in interviews was peculiar, to put it mildly.

3. **Warmth.** The water bottle was quite warm after I was finished. I shouldn't have been surprised by this, I suppose, but the temperature of fresh urine just wasn't something I had ever previously considered.[49]

PANIC

I was then able to return to the business at hand: being raked over the coals by my employer. But it didn't seem so bad, anymore. I felt calm. At peace. And above all, relieved.

---

47   I know, you had forgotten that I might have one.

48   Calls like this were terrifying, which generally added to whatever pressure you were currently feeling.

49   From a clinical perspective, there's nothing about this sentence that's disgusting, right? And yet, I feel like I owe you an apology for having sprung it on you. I'm sorry.

However, my employer had more to say. Which he did, at some length.

Twenty minutes later, I had rendered both the bottles on my desk unfit for any use. An "X" drawn with a Sharpie on each of those bottles made it clear what those bottles were exclusively for, from now on.

Worse, as I finished filling the second bottle, I had a new problem. I was not finished.

At which point I learned something I had always wondered about, but had not, until that moment, tested. Specifically: it is, in fact, possible to stop peeing before you're done. And the relief, while partial, is still measurable.

I'll take my Nobel prize money in cash, thanks.[50]

> COMMENT BY VINCENZO
>
> I had that same experience but was on watch inside a nuclear submarine.

> COMMENT BY ULTRAROB
>
> I've long said I would never make it in management because I can't last long enough in meetings without a bio break.

> COMMENT BY JAT
>
> I have also contemplated the constant flow experiment: drinking until you are peeing and drinking continuously, but the problem I think is that your electrolytes would get irrecoverably out of whack and then you'd die. You'd fill a lot of bottles before keeling over, though. It would be quite a sight for whoever found you.

> COMMENT BY 29ER
>
> Guys are such cheaters. We women can never do that!

---

50 To this day, I wonder what I would have done if my boss had not finished his call five minutes later.

COMMENT BY DI

Dude. I have to say, just when this post got to where I didn't think it would shock/surprise/whatever me, you kept going... um, yeah, you kept going.

LESSON LEARNED, AGAIN. FOR NOW.

Here's a true fact, as opposed to most everything else in this book, which are false facts: I am the worst bike mechanic in the world. I have spent more money having my repairs repaired than I have spent on new bicycles. I'm not sure how that's possible, but I promise it's true.

When I attempt any bike maintenance beyond putting air in a tire or lube on a chain, I start sweating and second-guessing. And then I start over-tightening bolts and breaking spokes.

If they could, bikes would flee in terror when I approach.

In short, whenever I profess bike repair expertise, you may not want to take it very seriously.

Recently, I bought something bike-related, and then I didn't tell anyone about it. As an over-sharer of epic proportions,[51] this is unusual behavior for me. But I have a very good reason: I have no business owning this thing. I should probably give it up—to charity, to a good home, to anyone but me.

What is it?

It's a bike stand. Specifically, a Bontrager ProWrench Repair Stand. Which I suspect is a terrific bike stand, though I must now admit that I will probably never really know. Because, if things go well and I keep my head, I will use this bike stand primarily as a combination clothesline/scarecrow.[52]

Let me explain.

MECHANICUS INEPTICUS MAXIMUS, DEFINED

I suffer from *Mechanicus Inepticus Maximus* (MIM), a disease that prevents me from successfully executing even the simplest bike repairs and maintenance. When I work on my bike, my hands get clammy.

---

51 See previous story.

52 Also, I'll have it available to loan to people. "Oh, you need to borrow a bike stand? Feel free to use mine. No, don't worry about bringing it back tomorrow. Keep it as long as you like."

I sweat profusely, I forget the meaning of "righty-tighty-lefty-loosey" (except in Australia).[53]

I strip bolts. I drop and lose small parts. I scratch paint, dent metal, and splinter carbon.

I start talking to myself, and not in a very nice way. I will say things like, "You, sir, are a buffoon. An addle-brained, senile, and uneducated buffoon. You are fit to handle neither wrench nor screwdriver. Hex keys scatter in your presence."

As I work, my failures cascade. After trying to replace brake pads, somehow my wheels have come out of true. After I flail around for a bit with the spoke wrench, somehow my left crank has become loose. When I tackle that, my bike's chain shortens by two links.

HERE, LET ME SHOW YOU WHAT I MEAN

Let me use last weekend as an example. I have lately become very comfortable with disassembling bike chains. I have completely disassembled four of them in the past month. So I thought to myself, "It's high time I remove the chain from my Waltworks,[54] give it a thorough cleaning, and put it back on.

Naturally, I went a turn too far with the chainbreaker tool and popped the pin out altogether.

So I thought, "Well, I have a new chain just sitting in the garage. I'll put it on the bike."

Except I made it one link too short. So I added a link back in...except I must have added two, because then the chain was flopping around like it was a foot too long.

So I adjusted the limit screws on either side of the dropout. Evidently, though, not the same amount, because now the wheel wobbles when it spins. Not that it spins very much, of course, because of course it rubs against the brakes.

At this point I abandoned the project before it got worse. And believe me, it would have gotten worse.

MIM: Is it a disease or a curse? I cannot tell. Maybe it's some of both. Like syphilis, but more embarrassing.

---

53   And Japan and England, probably. But you'd be better off asking someone else.
54   The brand of a singlespeed bike I own.

WHAT TRIGGERS MIM?

MIM can remain dormant for as long as the one affected doesn't try anything stupid, like say, working on a bike. In my case, however, I'll occasionally get the urge to improve my bike wrenching skills, thinking that I could save myself a lot of time if I knew how to take care of the basics.

So I'll go and buy the tools for my project. Last week, for example, I got a torque wrench and some hex bits, thinking that I wanted to have everything I need on hand to adjust the settings on my new Superfly singlespeed. Maybe swap out the handlebars, maybe practice changing the tire with those Chris King Fun Bolts installed.

You know. Try to become more self-sufficient.

I've already mentioned how well the bike chain project went. I have not mentioned, however, that I first stripped the adjustment bolt on my new bike's seatpost.

I'm sure this information surprises you. A lot.

I believe I will donate all my tools to a worthy bike shop before I once again get the impression that I have any business doing anything with a bike but riding it.

SECRET SHAME

I do my best to hide the fact that I suffer from MIM. It's not easy, though. When neighbors, who have seen I have a ridiculous number of bikes in my garage, ask me to help them repair their kids' bikes, I have to come up with a different excuse each time. When my bike's broken down at the side of the road and another cyclist stops and asks what the problem is, I have to make something up, rather than simply admit that I have no idea.

When I ride by people suffering from a mechanical on the trail, I have to pretend I am deaf and also have not seen them.

But I am not the only one who suffers from MIM. I know this for a fact, because a few months ago, I stopped by Dug's house, and found him in the garage, muttering over a chain (a purple one, which indicates an entirely different disease).

I offered help. It shows you just how desperate he was that he accepted that help. From *me*.

Eventually, we did in fact get that chain on the bike, but we twisted one end of it 180 degrees before connecting, creating a bike-chain Möbius strip.

And also Dug lost a finger.[55]

THE FIRST STEP

I am convinced that before a MIM sufferer can hope to be cured, he must first acknowledge his sickness, and then publicly vow to never harm a bicycle again. Toward that end, I hereby declare and swear myself to the following:

I, (Your Name Here), have no ability with tools. I have never had any ability with tools and do now freely confess that I will never have any ability with tools. Nothing but harm and sadness will ever come of me trying to convince myself otherwise.

As a cyclist without mechanical skill, I now promise that I will no longer try to do anything with my bike beyond inflating a tire and lubing the chain. I will not change brake pads. I will not true a wheel. I will not try to fix that creaky noise coming from either the bottom bracket or stem, I'm not sure which.

I will not even pretend to think about setting up disc brakes.

I promise to sell — or if necessary, give —all my tools to someone who can use them without causing irreparable harm. When my bike is broken, I shall confess as much and bring it straight to the bike shop before I make things worse. And I shall tip the mechanic generously, for she or he has a skill that I have not.

From this day forward, I will ride my bikes with renewed understanding as I embrace my limitations. Specifically, if my bike ever breaks even a little bit and I'm by myself without a good cell phone signal, I've got a long walk ahead of me. For while the tools in my seatbag may help me survive in the wilderness or perhaps whittle a flute out of a willow branch, in my hands these tools will do the bike no good whatsoever.

At all.

No matter how long I tinker, nor how many knuckles I bloody.

Hi, my name's Fatty, and I have MIM.

---

55 No, not really.

COMMENT BY LORIE

I once got a flat tire. Thinking I could fix it, I got the patch kit out of the seatbag, put the patch on the tire, got the CO2 cartridge, inflated the tire and wondered why it didn't hold the air. Only when I took the bike to the shop and the mechanic nearly died laughing, did I realize that I should have patched the inner tube, not the TIRE. My reply — "Well, there was a hole in the tire too" — only caused more laughter.

Mechanically, for some of us, there is no hope.

COMMENT BY DOM

MIM extends beyond bikes. I put together a swingset once. The directions called for 2 adults. When the muttering turned to curse-riddled rants I understood why they specifically said adults.

COMMENT BY SHARON

I feel so relieved that someone has finally recognized this and named the disease. I somehow feel I am no longer alone in this.

COMMENT BY MIKED

If it jams, force it. If it breaks, it needed replacing anyway.

A SCIENTIFIC EXPLANATION OF WHY CYCLING HURTS

This is one of those stories I waited to tell until I couldn't wait any longer. From the very beginning of my cycling career — about ten years before I started writing about riding — I began thinking about how and why cycling hurts.

I evolved a theory. It made perfect sense, but I still kept it quiet. The world wasn't ready for it.

Finally, after blogging for a few years, I felt I was ready to present my theory, and then to collect the praise, accolades, and, hopefully, large cash prizes that would naturally come my way.

Hm. Evidently, the world was still not ready for this theory.

I'm sure, however, that this time everyone will get it.

Right?

As a very popular, handsome, respected, and award-winning[56] author, I am frequently asked questions regarding bicycles. Here are some I've received recently:

- What kind of bike should I buy?
- What are the best things to eat and drink before, during, and after a ride?
- Is it important that I stretch before riding?
- How should I select the right saddle for my anatomy?

At first glance, these questions do not seem to have anything in common. However, if you will dig a little deeper, you will realize they do in fact share a characteristic: they are all stupid questions.[57]

Let us dismiss them from our thoughts.

Recently, however, I encountered a question that caught my attention, primarily because I am the one who conceived it:

---

56   Three-time "Best Sports Blog" Bloggie winner, "Lifetime Achievement" Bloggie winner, Utah Social Media Awards "Best Blog" winner. And probably a lot of other awards too. Like, sometimes I'll just give myself a trophy, because I feel extremely accomplished at the moment.

57   See, there *is* such a thing as a stupid question.

WHY DOES CYCLING HURT?

The answer is not obvious. Consider other activities, for example. Driving an automobile does not hurt. Watching television does not hurt. Eating nachos does not hurt.

But cycling, in particular, certain aspects of cycling, *does* hurt.

Why?

I am pleased, after considerable research which I suspect will garner me still more awards and accolades, to provide the answer.

INTRODUCING...THE PAIN PELLET

As most of you know, there are four commonly-known elements, from which all substances on Earth are made. These elements are Earth, Wind, Fire, and Cheddar. The more cheddar the better, but that is the subject for another paper.

What most of you do *not* know is that there is a fifth element, and it is not the one starring Bruce Willis.

No indeed.

The fifth element is *Pain.*

Unlike other elements, which can be combined to form other substances (*nachos*, for example, are a combination of Earth, Fire, and Cheddar), Pain keeps to itself, clumping into small balloon-like spheres called *Pain Pellets.*

While difficult to see, Pain Pellets are easy to detect, for when touched by a human, a Pain Pellet will burst, splattering you with a certain amount of pain. The larger the pellet, the larger the pain blast radius.

And if one encounters several Pain Pellets while traveling in a certain direction, one will experience *sustained* pain.

PAIN PELLETS: PROPERTIES AND PROCLIVITIES

The reason, then, that cycling hurts is because cyclists[58] tend to frequent places where Pain Pellets generally congregate. Specifically:

- **Pain Pellets adhere to slopes.** As everyone knows, an upward slope is in tension with the magnetic forces that some call "gravity" (I will discuss the folly of the theory of gravity another time, but for our purposes today, we can pretend that such a force does exist). A byproduct of this tension is

---

58   Due to some cosmic accident, no doubt.

friction, which in turn creates static electricity. Pain Pellets, being very much like balloons in both size and texture, are drawn to this static electricity on upward slopes, and cling to it. The steeper the slope, the greater the density and size of Pain Pellets collected.[59]

- **Pain Pellets settle at the bottoms of treacherous places.** Pain Pellets are subject, to a degree, to the normal forces of "gravity," and will settle where you might expect them to: just below slippery roots, at the base of a three-foot ledge, and just beyond a surprise hairpin are three good examples. Mountain cyclists are particularly adept at uncovering and disrupting these Pain Pellets.
- **Pain Pellets are attracted to heavier people.** A surprising fact is that if two people — let's call them "Brad" and "Fatty" for no particular reason — ride up a given hill, the heavier one ("Fatty") will encounter more Pain Pellets than the lighter one ("Brad"). Indeed, the Pain Pellets will actually move out of Brad's way and wind their way toward Fatty. It is almost as if the Pain Pellets are sentient and find heavy people especially attractive.
- **Pain Pellets grow back quickly.** Cyclists often attribute the "drafting" effect of riding to the thoroughly debunked notion that the cyclist in front of them creates a slipstream. In reality, the rider in front is hitting a disproportionate number of Pain Pellets, allowing the rider behind to ride the route relatively unscathed. Unfortunately, Pain Pellets reform in their original location in a mere matter of moments.

HOW TO AVOID PAIN

Of course, some cyclists find the near-incessant encounters with Pain Pellets sub-optimal, even to the point that the Pain Pellets may impede the cyclist's progress. "How," the cyclist may reasonably wonder, "might I avoid the Pain Pellets?"

There are multiple strategies.[60]

---

59   You see? This is totally scientific.

60   None of which work as well as simply staying indoors, on a couch. Pain Pellets avoid television, except for reality television shows, which many people have correctly observed as being "painful."

1. **Slow down.** When riding up a hill, one notices a surprising amount of pain. Further, the faster one rides up that hill, the more it seems to hurt. It is therefore worth noting, then, that one generally will encounter the same number of Pain Pellets, regardless of whether one is going up the hill very fast or very slow. However, since when going slow one encounters the Pain Pellets at a slower rate, the perceived pain may be decreased.

2. **Weave.** When climbing a hill, one may reduce the frequency of Pain Pellet encounters by "paperboying" up the hill. Some theorize that Pain Pellets grow in long uphill strands and that by weaving one's way up the hill, one may avoid at least some of these strands of Pain Pellets. In reality, though, one is actually encountering perhaps more Pain Pellets over the course of the climb, but since one is hitting them at a slower rate the perceived pain is again reduced.

3. **Don't fall.** One universal truth about Pain Pellets is that they remain on the ground. When one remains upright on one's bicycle, one is merely splattered by the exploding Pain Pellets as one's bicycle wheels burst aforementioned Pellets. However, when one crashes off one's bicycle, one is almost certain to land directly on several Pain Pellets, soaking the cyclist in pain.[61]

In summary, Pain Pellets and the cyclist seem to have a strange mutual attraction. Cyclists are drawn to inclines and treacherous locations, which are the natural habitat of Pain Pellets.

And in short, the question "Why does cycling hurt" has a sensible answer based on pure physics. Cycling hurts because cyclists are drawn to pain.[62]

> COMMENT BY KALGRM
>
> I guess they are afraid of fibre: I know if I don't have enough fibre in my diet, I get pain pellets.

---

61   It should be further noted that Pain Pellets do very little to cushion the cyclist's fall.
62   Pain Pellets, that is.

COMMENT BY ATOMIC

Ha! I knew it couldn't be because I'm out of shape! I'm just bigger and the pain is attracted to me! You're a genius!

COMMENT BY RANTWICK

Wow! I loved that post. I am drawn to pain pellets, and my heaviness brings them to me as well. It finally all makes sense. Someone mentioned Nobel. I agree, and I will look into nominating the Unified Theory of Pain Pellets.

You know, if you only spelled your name Elbon (come on, it's only two letters), it would be jumble of Nobel! How freaky is that? I need to lie down...

COMMENT BY BIG MIKE IN OZ

As a trackie I'd like to add to this whole pain pellet theory. It is a well known (and well-covered already today) fact that pain pellets adhere to slopes, the steeper the slope, the higher the concentration of pellets. Now think carefully about the steepest slope you've ever seen cyclists continually attack and conquer. Think again. Think clean. Think smooth. Think indoors maybe. That's right, the velodrome with its 30, 35, even 40 degree banking is a haven for pain pellets. And more than that is the fact that the velodrome is an enclosure means that the pain pellets just keep accumulating. Until some poor soul touches a wheel. Then they land right in the middle of the greatest concentration of pain pellets known to man.

COMMENT BY WHEELDANCER

I've noticed that the more I ride the less effect the pain pellets have on me so I suspect that their is some sort of immunity that can be built up. I can confirm, unfortunately, that hitting the ground negates any immunity that has been built up.

I HAVE A PREPARED STATEMENT
I WOULD LIKE TO MAKE

I did not intend to be born a male. I was just born that way. And I am, by and large, just fine with it.

Also, I'm white. And middle-aged. And straight. So I probably don't need a lot of sympathy from very many people.

And yet, as a member of the least-interesting group of people there is, I still struggle. I still find myself fighting (and yes, sometimes failing) to express my point of view. To convey the urgency of my plight.

This is the tale of one such battle.

The ride plan was simple, really.[63]

We[64] wanted to find out what the upcoming Ironman bike course felt like in its entirety. So we'd park at the nearby reservoir, do the 22-mile ride to the beginning of the two-lap part of the ride, do the two laps, and then, even though this was not part of the course, we'd ride back to the reservoir.

A 140-mile road ride, give or take. Ambitious, but not ridiculous.

There was just one snag: the weather forecast for St. George, Utah, that day was odd: "Windy," it said. Honestly, I don't recall ever seeing a weather forecast saying that before. "Sunny," sure. "Overcast," "rainy," "snowy," absolutely. But never "windy."

The weather forecast, as it turns out, was inaccurate only to the extent that it should have read, "windy *as hell.*"

I imagine hell as a very windy place. Don't you?[65]

As soon as the ride began, The Hammer and I, as a survival technique, started taking turns drafting, in a decidedly un-time-trial-like fashion.

By the time we had ridden the first half of the first lap of the course, I noticed we were averaging 12.5 miles per hour. I did some math for

---

63   This is probably a good place to cue the ominous music.
64   The Hammer — my wife Lisa — and I.
65   I'm thinking that if you're answering, "what's so hellish about wind?" that you are simply not a cyclist.

what that meant, finishing-time-wise, and didn't like the answer.[66]

I checked my math. I was not wrong.[67] If the wind held (or got stronger, which seemed likely) and we stuck to the original plan, it'd be close to dark before we finished the ride.

I said as much to The Hammer, who replied, "I'm determined to finish this ride." Which was good enough for me.

Until it wasn't.

THE RIGHT THING TO SAY

At Veyo, about 20 miles from finishing the first loop, we stopped at a convenience store.[68] At that point we hadn't gone far enough that either of us should be cooked, but I was cooked. And The Hammer looked tired, too.

But I did not say anything. No, I had already asked for an "out," and had been denied. I, being a macho, macho man, would tough out the ride, no matter what. I would not complain. I would not whine.

Not out loud, at least.

And then we began the ride toward Saint George and the beginning of the second lap. This section is primarily downhill, and should have been an excellent place to recover.

But the wind was coming at us, hard, from eleven-o'clock. Meaning it had all the power of a nice hard headwind *plus* the exciting challenge of a brutal crosswind.

I did more math. And the math looked bad. I arrived at a conclusion: *I really really really*[69] *did not want to do the second lap.*

But how to tell The Hammer this? I used the ample time I had, courtesy of the murderous headwind/crosswind, to think of a convincing argument.

Here is what I came up with:

I am so tired. I don't think I can handle a second lap. What do you say we just cut it short and head back to the truck?

I didn't like that, though. Saying "I am so tired" is an admission of

---

66   140 miles/12.5mph = more than eleven hours. And since there'd be some definite slowing as we fatigued, it would probably be more like twelve hours. Or thirteen.

67   As if I'm *ever* wrong.

68   The selfsame convenience store referred to in the "Convenience" story in the "Strong Opinions, Trivial Matters" section of this book.

69   If I use three "reallys," you can rest assured I mean and have considered each and every one of them.

weakness, and as a man, I am contractually obligated to never ever admit weakness.

So I formulated another speech, this time in the form of a story problem:

You know, we're going eleven miles per hour right now. It will be dark in four hours, and if we do a second lap, we will have seventy more miles to ride. I'm not sure it's a good idea to finish this ride in the wind and the dark and the rain.

No good. She already knew all of that. She didn't need me shepherding her.

I crafted a casual dismissal of the second lap:

Really, I think we've got a good idea of what this course has in store for us. I don't think it's going to be necessary for us to ride it again.

I liked this approach at first, but as I practiced saying it in my head, I realized she'd see right through it.

I considered the pathetic approach:

I'm in my small ring, going downhill. *I don't think I want to do this again in the dark and rain. And I'm cold, I'm tired, I hate the wind, my nose is running, and this just isn't fun anymore and I want to go home.*[70]

In addition to this approach being pathetic, it was in fact also the most honest approach, and I was just about to go with it.

Then The Hammer said, "There's no way we're doing a second lap today."

And my speeches, my wonderfully crafted and extremely persuasive statements, suddenly became unnecessary.

My relief, well...there was only one word for it: exquisite.

COMMENT BY ERIC P
Nothing is more manly than a direct declarative statement.

COMMENT BY MARKG
Fatty, you are my hero. If only I would learn to shut up until my wife makes the right decision, my life would be sweet bliss.

---

70 And then start crying, to drive the point home.

COMMENT BY DREW

Traffic? Feh, no problem. And I'll ride in the rain until I grow gills, I'll ride in the heat until I burst into flames, I'll ride in humidity until I have a Cajun accent, and I'll ride up mountains until my legs explode. All of that can happen and I'll still say it was a fun ride.

Five minutes in the wind and I weep uncontrollably.

COMMENT BY HEIDI

Guess we know who wears the bike shorts in your family!

THE GRAND ILLUSION

I wrote this piece back in the early months of 2010: five years ago, more or less. The main thought behind it, that cycling fools you into thinking you're not subject to aging, is still something with which I wrestle.

In my head, I realize that I'm pushing fifty (48.5 at the moment). But whenever I get on a bicycle, I am faster, fitter, and more daring than I was when I was thirty.

Seriously, I would love to meet my thirty-year-old self and kick his butt. Because I could.

This point of view is not, however, without its problems.

I don't mean to boast (yes I do), but I've made it through the winter without gaining much weight at all. Maybe five or seven pounds. Maybe nine or ten at the most.[71]

Okay, I've gained eleven pounds[72] during winter. But compared to my usual annual weight gain/loss pattern, that's practically like *losing* fifteen pounds. Practically.[73]

And so it was with no small amount of pride a few days ago that I, at the beginning of the South Suncrest climb, marked another rider so far ahead of me that I couldn't even tell what color his (or her) clothes were. A veritable dot of a cyclist, on the mountain equivalent of the horizon.

Then I closed, caught, briefly chatted with, and dropped him, for it was indeed a him.

"Clearly," I thought to myself, "I am a force to be reckoned with."

I continued my ride, feeling strong. Feeling fit. Feeling like I am — as I have possibly recently mentioned — a force to be reckoned with. My legs turning smooth circles, my arms applying exactly the correct amount of counterbalance to my downstroke, so that I ride a smooth, clean line.

I was powerful. I was efficient. A cyclist in the prime of my life.

Then, once home, I swung my right leg over the saddle (I always dismount on the left, though I've never considered why) clicked out of my left pedal, and was on the ground once more.

---

71 And for sure no more than fifteen or twenty.
72 Well, eleven if you round down to eleven from twenty-five.
73 This is the new math, kids.

And then I limped through my front door and up the stairs to my bedroom, leaning heavily on the rail, because I could barely walk.[74]

I stripped and turned on the shower, then attempted my "while the water heats up" ritual: doing sets of pull-ups. For today's ritual, my sets were remarkably consistent: 0, none, and zero. This is because I have, once again, recently injured my shoulder, and it hurts too much to haul my weight up to the chin-up bar.

As I stood[75] in the shower, I contemplated the ride and the events that followed. Which was when I had the following great epiphany:

Cycling is popular with middle-aged people because it gives us the illusion of being in great shape, even as our bodies completely fall apart.

WHAT THE ILLUSION FEELS LIKE

Cycling, by being no-impact on road and only moderate-impact on cross-country trails, gives you the sensation that you are whole and healthy. And why not? You're climbing up mountains and flying down them, all under your own power.

And the bonus is, if you've been doing it for a few years, your legs magically transform and you can — in spite of being middle-aged — show those young'uns a thing or two.

And if you keep it up, you continue to improve, getting stronger and faster while everyone you know complains about getting slower and older.

It's like the Fountain of Youth.

THE REALITY

The problem, against which I just recently banged my head, is that cycling makes you fit, but only within a tiny little narrow set of parameters.

Specifically, cycling has made me very fit to turn my legs in small, smooth circles, under heavy load, almost indefinitely. And it's made my forearms very fit at counterpulling against the downstroke of my pedals. Again, almost indefinitely.

This kind of fitness translates, once I'm off the bike, to...um... nothing. As I mentioned before, walking *hurts* right now. Running is out of the question.

---

74   I'd exaggerate here if I could think of a way to. But no, this is just how it really is.
75   Or, possibly, sat, due to exhaustion.

And while my arms look toned, having done near-infinite low-effort reps, I am *not* the guy you want to help move your piano.

And I'm far from the only example of this kind of pseudo-fitness. Take my good friend Kenny, for example. He looks strong, and on the bike he is nigh indestructible.

Off the bike, however, he walks gingerly, hobbling as if pride is the only thing keeping him from using a walker to get around.

If you punch him in the arm, it will break.

And the thing is, this illusion perpetuates itself. Off the bike, I'm human.[76]

On the bike, I'm strong like bull.

So, given an opportunity, where do you think I'm going to be?

> COMMENT BY ERIC THE SWEDE
> I can ride all day. I played pick-up hoop for an hour Sunday afternoon and I still can't walk proper.

> COMMENT BY RANTWICK
> Leave my middle-aged illusions alone, you dork. They're all I have.

> COMMENT BY DUG
> We're all Mr. Glass off the bike.

> COMMENT BY BIKEMIKE
> Just wait. When you turn 50 all of these issues will pale in comparison to the whole other set of issues waiting for you. Oh yeah, it gets better...and by "better" I mean "horribly worse."

> COMMENT BY KANYONKRIS
> Better narrowly specialized fitness than no fitness (which is where I'd be without cycling). But you're right, it is an illusion of all-around fitness. Even doing a wimpy sprint triathlon showed me this.

---

76 OK, fine: subhuman.

THE FAT CYCLIST EXPLAINS: CARBON FIBER

From time to time, I like to explain difficult cycling techniques and technologies in clear, simple English. Except for when it makes better sense for me to explain in French, in which case I will of course explain in English anyway, because I don't know French.

If you have a cycling-related question you would like explained, simply email me; my address is fatty@fatcyclist.com. Due to the volume of email I receive, however, I cannot respond to all questions individually. In fact, I respond to hardly any email at all.

OK, the truth is I haven't checked that email address in months. But I will soon. I promise.

And now, on with the explainification!

I recently received an email which I had slightly less-recently sent to myself. This email went as follows:

> Hi Fatty,
>
> First, let me begin by saying that I'm a big fan of your blog. I don't know how you come up with your insightful, witty, and down-to-earth cycling commentary on a near-daily basis. The only person I'm aware of who writes more about cycling than you is Lennard Zinn. Oh, and Bike Snob NYC writes more than you, too. So that's two people who write more cycling-related stuff than you. And they're both better than you, too. No offense.
>
> Anyway, the reason I thought I'd email you is to ask a question that's been bugging me lately. It seems that more and more biking stuff is made from carbon fiber. Frames, cranks, handlebars, seat posts, brake levers, stems, bottle cages. Practically everything.
>
> I understand why they're doing this: carbon fiber is light, it's strong, and it can be made into practically any shape. Fine, I get that.
>
> But what the heck is carbon fiber? I mean, I know what the two words are, kind of. "Carbon" is what pretty much everything in the universe is made of, and "fiber" is a thread of some sort or

another, and if you eat enough of it, you poop on a regular basis.
Excellent.

But when you put those two words together — "carbon
fiber" — somehow you've suddenly got this outrageously strong
stuff that's really light that you can make into any shape?

It sounds like dark magick to me, Fatty.

Please help me understand what this stuff is and how it works,
so I can explain it to other people without giving you credit.
Best Regards,
Duane
PS: *Please also explain how CDs work.*

Duane, you've asked an interesting question, and a timely one at that, since I am currently in the process of revising the Wikipedia entry on carbon fiber for accuracy and completeness. And also, quite frankly, for interestingness, because the current entry is so dull I simply have not been able to bring myself to read it.

Here, in plain and understandable English, is my explanation of what carbon fiber is, how it can be shaped into practically anything, and why it is so light and strong.

WHAT IS CARBON FIBER?

Carbon is the most plentiful element on Earth. Except hydrogen, I think. And oxygen too, maybe. And probably nitrogen, or was it helium? But after that, carbon for sure.

My point is that there's a lot of carbon.

But what does carbon look like? Well, coal is pretty much pure carbon. So there you go. Carbon is black and flaky, and it's pretty heavy. And if you drop it, it shatters into a bunch of pieces.

"But Fatty," I hear you say, "Heavy and rock-shaped and flaky and brittle aren't the kind of properties I generally associate with carbon fiber bikes at all! Or at least not for the past couple years!"[77]

And that's because carbon is only like that (heavy, brittle, and coal-colored) before you turn it into fibers. Now a "fiber," as you know, is really

---

77 Which is too bad, really. Back in the day, you could plan on getting a new frame pretty much every year, thanks to generous crash replacement programs at major bike manufacturers.

nothing more than a thread. And threads are flexible (not brittle) and light (not heavy) and don't shatter when you drop them on the sidewalk.

So you definitely want to make your carbon fiber-y if you're going to make a bike out of it.

To do this, you extrude coal through something that's kind of like a pasta maker, except the pasta is really, really thin. And it's not extruding a semolina-based dough, it's using carbon.

And then, once you've put the coal through the pasta machine, you boil it for eight minutes. Any longer than that and you've got soggy, limp carbon fiber and no amount of pasta sauce and cheese will ever fix it. Believe me, I've tried.

[Note: Since coal is 99% pure carbon, and coal burns, and most threads burn, be aware that your carbon fiber bike is very, very flammable! And it will give off a thick black smoke when it burns, and the EPA will come and have a very stern conversation with you. Still, the knowledge that your bike burns can be useful in survival situations. But if someone dares you to jump your carbon fiber bike over a bonfire, do NOT take the dare.]

WHY IS CARBON FIBER LIGHT?

Now that you understand what carbon fiber is, your next question is, undoubtedly, "Why is it (i.e., carbon fiber, not your question) light?" The answer to this (i.e., your question, not carbon fiber) is really quite simple. Carbon fiber is light because a fiber is nothing more than a thread, and threads are light.

Here's a way to prove this to yourself and friends.

First, pick up a thread, maybe a foot or so long. See how light it is? Put the thread on your bathroom scale. On most scales, it doesn't even register. Pretty amazing, if you ask me.

Now, just for fun, put another thread of about the same length on the scale. See? Still doesn't register, does it? You know why? Because fibers *have no weight* whatsoever. Mysterious, I know, but demonstrably true.

The real question is: since fibers are weightless, *how come carbon fiber bikes weigh anything at all?* My personal theory is that bike manufacturing companies put ball bearings in the downtubes to add weight, putting in slightly fewer ball bearings each model year. This allows them to claim less and less weight (and hence a reason to upgrade) every year.

It's a lousy trick.

Bicycle manufacturers of the world, I'm putting you on notice. Stop putting ball bearings in the down tubes and give us our weight-less bikes *now*!

WHY IS CARBON FIBER STRONG?

As you know, carbon is the primary element in diamonds, and diamonds are unbelievably strong. Here, try this. Look around you and pick up a handy diamond — the biggest one you can find. Now, try to bend it.

You can't, can you?

Now, place it between your palms and try to crush it, like you would an orange.

Not easy, is it?

See how strong diamonds are? That's why carbon fiber bikes are strong.[78]

But there's even more to why carbon fiber bikes are strong. In fact, the strength of your carbon fiber comes from a number of different factors:

1. **The weave of the carbon fibers.** Three-strand braids are extremely strong, but are rarely used. The reason why is quite interesting. Long ago braids were almost exclusively used in factories, but since most guys cannot braid to save their lives, most of the carbon fiber braids were executed by women. A discrimination lawsuit was brought to bear by a man who felt put upon, and that was that. Now the basket pattern is used most often, although some people are working on a new "interlocking pretzel" pattern, which sounds both promising and delicious.[79]

2. **The thickness of the carbon fibers.** Thicker is of course stronger, and the best carbon fiber bike would be where each tube is one *really thick* fiber. But science doesn't know how to do that yet, and I haven't told them because they haven't offered me enough money.

3. **The kind of glue they use to hold the fibers in place.** Most manufacturers go with a kind of epoxy, which is fine. Be aware, however, that some of the cheaper manufacturers

---

78   I could totally be Bill Nye the Science Guy. Speaking of whom, I once had a phone conversation with Bill and he loves cycling.

79   Disclaimer: I have no idea at all here what I am talking about.

use straight-up Elmer's school glue. The best way to tell if your carbon fiber bike is mixed with Elmer's is to smell it. If it smells like Elmer's, it probably is. The *best* kind of glue to use, of course, is Super Glue, because that stuff is *strong*. But hardly anyone ever uses this anymore — even though it's incredibly strong — due to the fact that factory workers kept gluing their fingers together.

HOW IS CARBON FIBER SHAPED?

The final aspect I'll cover is how carbon fiber can be formed into practically any shape. Well, first the manufacturing plant mixes some glue up and then they slather it over a layer of the carbon fiber weave, and then they do that same thing again and again — sort of a glue-and-carbon-fiber lasagna — and somehow make it into the shape they want it to be.

Or something like that.

Honestly, I have no idea how. Maybe they pinch it into the shape they want just before the glue hardens. Or maybe it's magic. It's a total mystery to me.

Anyway, that's how carbon fiber works. I'm glad I could explain it to you.

PS: CDs work by using lasers!

COMMENT BY BIKEMIKE
If I were to go to the local grocery and buy bags of charcoal, how much and how long would it take to build a nice carbon frame? I really like the new Specialized S-Works Roubaix but I can't afford retail prices.

COMMENT BY MIKE ROADIE
So....if my bike floats, then it's a duck?

COMMENT BY THE OTHER MATTC
You realize you just destroyed some lazy junior high schooler's research for his or her science project.

KNEE WARMERS ARE STUPID

It's pretty uncommon for me to write something I actually mean. But when I wrote this story, I was dead serious. I really did hate knee warmers, for the reasons I explain below.

And so convinced was I in my rightness that I was completely stunned by the reaction I received. People disagreed with me? How could that be possible?

Well as it turns out, it was possible because I had, up to that point, never had anything but terrible, badly-made knee warmers. Knee warmers that gripped either too tightly, or not at all.

About a week after I wrote this, I bought some good knee warmers.[80] *And now I realize they're actually kind of useful.*

But I still think they're stupid.

I am a nice person. An accepting person. A tolerant person. While "live and let live" is not my motto, I think I can safely say that this is more due to the fact that I have never seen the value of having a motto than it is a repudiation of the sentiment. In short, I tolerate practically everything and am not quick to judge.

That said, I hereby assert that knee warmers are idiotic and must, without exception, be immediately destroyed.

I shall now prove my thesis, through the medium of making several irrefutable observations, and also with some highly persuasive photographic illustrations.[81]

---

80   Specialized brand. They actually are sewn together in such a way that they are leg-shaped and expect that you might bend your legs at the knee sometimes, as opposed to thinking your leg is just a cylinder that tapers a little bit.

81   You know what's an easy way to tell when someone's setting up a straw-man argument? When they start writing as if they were constructing a legal brief. This goes for lawyers, too.

THE INTENDED FUNCTION OF THE KNEE WARMER IS RIDICULOUS

Here is a photograph of a cyclist's legs:

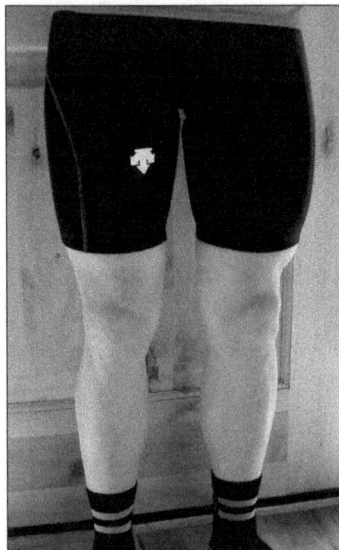

Apart from the non-relevant observations that these are my legs, that my legs have not been shaved in nearly a week,[82] and that I am flexing so hard that my knees are likely to explode any second, we can tell from this photograph that my knees are uncovered.

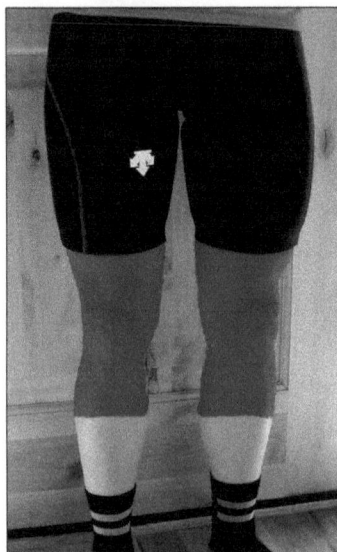

Now, let's take a look at how my legs would look if I were wearing knee warmers.[83]

An impartial observer of a cyclist wearing knee warmers would be right to ask the following questions:

What is the temperature range for such clothing? At what temperature is it warm enough for you to expose your shins and calves to the cold, but cold enough for you to cover your knees? (Answer: *never*)

How comfortable is it to have an elastic grip constricting around your quads? Knee warmers, while ostensibly keeping your knees warm (because we

---

82   And yet, they are somehow nevertheless incredibly attractive and well-defined.
83   Yes, they're Photoshopped in. And not very well. Can you *please* just try to accept that this is for illustrative purposes only and just move on?

do *not* want chilly knees!) are in reality applying a gentle tourniquet to the quads, the muscles you use most when cycling. As a rider, you must ask yourself: *which will help me stay warmer: a thin layer of lycra, or not having my limbs turn blue and falling off?*

What are you supposed to do with these things when/if you manage to remove them? Of course, the (supposed) benefit of knee warmers is that you can take them off partway through the ride. Which means, if you're with a group, you get to make everyone stand around and start hating you as you try to wrestle your knee warmers over your shoes, sticking and ripping as they go over your bike shoe cleats. Awesome.

And then, once you manage to get the blasted things off (by which time a couple of the people in your group have grown bored and left), you need to find a place to put those knee warmers, which is going to be your jersey pockets. Unfortunately, the bulk of the wadded-up knee warmers is going to be so great that you will now have two unsightly humps just above your butt.

It doesn't sound attractive, and it doesn't look attractive, either. It does, however, make your jersey stretch and pull against your stomach, making you look like you bought a jersey two sizes too small.[84] Super awesome.

KNEE WARMERS DO NOT KEEP YOUR KNEES WARM

Everything we've mentioned so far presumes that even with their inherent logistical disadvantages, knee warmers at least do their job.

Except they don't.

Suppose, like most human beings, you have legs that taper from wide to narrow (see helpful illustration at right). Furthermore, suppose that gravity pulls things down. Now, just for the sake of crazy argument, suppose you start flexing your leg about ninety times per minute. Under these bizarre circumstances, do

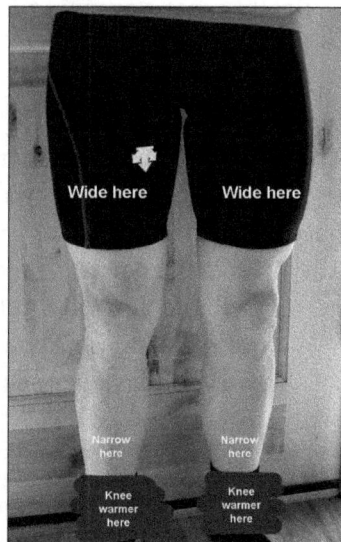

---

84   Instead of just one size too small, which is perfectly normal for cyclists.

you think it's safe to assume that anything that can settle, will settle? (The correct answer is "yes.")

Translation: Since your legs are wedge-shaped and you're constantly pumping them up and down, it's not going to be long 'til your knee warmers become ankle warmers. Unless, of course, you hike them up every three minutes or so.

But I'm sure you've never experienced that effect, have you?

KNEE WARMERS SLOW YOU DOWN

While it's true that knee warmers serve precious little practical purpose, and it's also true that knee warmers fail to serve the dubious purpose for which they were created, we can all at least take comfort in the fact that they do make you a slower cyclist.[85]

You think it doesn't take extra effort to stretch that extra lycra twice (once for each leg) per crank revolution? And you think that at 90 crank revolutions per minute, that extra effort doesn't add up?

Let's conduct a little thought experiment. Say a knee warmer increases pedaling resistance by 1%. Fine. Now say you turn the cranks ninety times per minute — that's 2 (because you have 2 legs) x 1% x 90 turns per minute. Yes, the math proves it: **your knee warmers increase pedaling difficulty by 180% per minute.**[86]

Really, what's amazing is that when wearing the stupid things you can move *at all*.

REPURPOSING OPTIONS

The only question is the manner of disposal. Are knee warmers entirely useless, or can they be repurposed into something with actual value? I have a few ideas:

- **Mask:** Poke a few holes in a knee warmer, pull it over your head, and you're all set to rob a convenience store. And since your mask does not have a top, you're less likely to overheat or have your dark glasses fog.

---

85   I swear that this is true. I *always* feel slower when I wear knee warmers. And I in no way think that this could be due to the possibility that when weather gets cooler, I tend to start exercising less and gaining weight. That is a simple coincidence.

86   Hey, did I tell you that for my day job I'm an analyst at a well-known, well-respected research organization? I sure hope they never read this.

- **Headbands**: Cut your knee warmers into strips. One knee warmer should be able to make up to 14 headbands.
- **Handbag**: Sew one end of a knee warmer shut, then use a spiral cut to transform the other knee warmer into a shoulder strap. This is neither stylish nor practical, but it's at least better than their original purpose.

I am willing to entertain other possible uses of knee warmers. I am not an unreasonable man. For the love of all that's good in the world, though, just, please, keep them off your knees.

COMMENT BY SANS AUTO

I had a cycling coach that said, "cover your knees til it's 70 degrees" (cute, huh?). I just got the official word from a doctoral student in Athletic training behind me, "bologna."

COMMENT BY DUG

Knee warmers and arm warmers, when worn with no other clothing, makes for a spectacularly stylish look. Also, stop asserting that you are a nice person. Show some evidence. Second, your calves and shins don't really have joints. That is, no moving parts.

COMMENT BY RICK S.

You know what knee warmers are good for? Dropping a hint to your wife that you would really like to get a ride in that day. If I walk around the house with just my knee warmers on, she gets the hint and usually gives me the hall pass for a ride.

COMMENT BY BIKEMIKE

If you wear them backwards, they will fall up.

COMMENT BY MARK

I can't believe a guy who used to rollerblade to work is doling out advice on what to wear.[87]

---

87   It's true. I used to rollerblade.

COMMENT BY ONE OF SEVEN

"Man, I hope my husband reads this knee warmer report — I think he looks like a dork with them on.

2.

Things That (Mostly) Really Happened

MORE OFTEN THAN NOT, THIS PARTICULAR BOOK IS ABOUT BIKE-RELATED TOPICS. YOU KNOW, BIKE PHILOSOPHY AND ETIQUETTE AND CULTURE AND opinion and analysis.

This section, on the other hand, is about actual rides. And about riding. About getting outside (or in one case, staying inside) and... riding my bicycle.

Yes, a section in a book about bikes that talks about riding bikes. Crazy.

Also, I should perhaps mention that this is my favorite chapter in the book. So if you've been thumbing around, wondering where the good stuff is, well...it's here.[1]

---

1   Also, hopefully you agree that it's everywhere else in this book, too. Because if not, well, I could have made this book a lot shorter.

LAMENT OF THE PURPLE SNIPE

I very nearly made "Lament of the Purple Snipe" the title of this entire book. I really wanted to. I loved how hoity-toity it sounded. And I loved the insider joke behind it.

Luckily for you, my wife was violently opposed to this idea. As was everyone else I met. Which means you do not have to carry this book in a plain paper bag so as to avoid having to explain to other people what "Lament of the Purple Snipe" means.[2]

You're welcome.

That said, this story may be unsafe for reading during work or on airplanes, assuming your co-workers/co-passengers tend to read over your shoulder, and are very offended by the very thought of certain anatomical realities.

Furthermore, I can safely say that if this story had photos, it definitely would be not safe for work/air travel/any kind of travel. So, a promise from the outset: this story does not have photos.

Once again, you're welcome.

I need to do some disclaiming. In order for me to tell this story without a lot of ridiculous, circuitous language, we need to directly and frankly acknowledge men have a part that women don't.

In short,[3] in this story I will in fact mention the portion of the male anatomy that is often called a "penis." Although, to make you more comfortable with this post — I understand some people find the word "penis" offensive and prefer to not ever hear or see the word "penis" at all — I will not use the word "penis" throughout this post. Instead, I will use a code word for "penis." The word I will substitute for "penis" throughout this post is "snipe."

I have chosen the word "snipe" because it is an anagram of the word "penis."

---

2   Briefly, "snipe" is used here as an anagram for "penis." Hence, a "purple snipe" is what I got after having an especially painful accident, where my...snipe...smacked good and hard against the stem of my bike as I flipped over the bars. Which is, I think you'll agree, lamentable. However, it's probably not something you want to explain to strangers on the subway.

3   Too late for that, really.

By the way, "pines" is also an anagram of "penis," but I chose not to use it, because it is a plural word, which would be confusing.[4] Also, it could be considered unnecessarily metaphorical, not to mention boastful.

So, "snipe" it is. And I'm going to stop putting quotes around the word snipe, because hitting the quote key twice per use of this word is just too much work.

Also, one final disclaimer: I am not just talking about any snipe. I am talking about *my* snipe. So, if you find you are capable of reading a story about a generic snipe but not about an actual snipe belonging to a beloved, multiple-award-winning cycling celebrity author, you have two obvious options:

1.   Stop reading.
2.   Pretend I'm actually talking about someone else. A favorite movie star.[5] A fictional someone, even.

You also have an easy third option, which is to read this story and then send me an angry email,[6] saying you simply cannot fathom how I would dare to write about my snipe. Note, however, that at press time I am about 1900 email messages in arrears. Hence, your message may not receive the attention it deserves.[7]

And now, at long last, on to the story.

MY THIRD-MOST PAINFULLY MEMORABLE CRASH

Among the strange-but-true axioms of mountain biking is this: slow crashes can be every bit as painful as fast ones. If you're not moving in the horizontal plane quickly — or at all — your body can take the vertical brunt of your fall in one place.

Thus, while my most painful crash of all — rocketing off the road and down a boulder-strewn embankment[8] — was definitely fast, my second-most painful crash happened at approximately zero miles per hour: I stalled out and fell over sideways while attempting a technical move on Porcupine Rim, and separated my shoulder on impact.

---

4   Not to mention distracting.
5   Stanley Tucci? No, better go with someone else.
6   My email address is fatty@fatcyclist.com. I recommend you use "I Am Insulted by Your Vulgarity" as the subject line.
7   For some reason, however, when people offer me cool free stuff, I manage to find time to read and respond to their email.
8   Leadville 100, 2009.

And my third-most painful crash — which is the subject of this story and to which I swear I will eventually get around to talking about[9] — was low-speed, as well.

The reason for the crash was quite ordinary, as was the crash itself: it was just an uphill endo.

Specifically, I was climbing Tibble Fork.[10] About a mile and a half up the trail, there is an eight-inch ledge where an exposed root crosses the trail. On its own merits, there's nothing especially difficult about this ledge. But, since you've just ridden an incredibly difficult 1.5 miles of climbing in order to get to that ledge, the level of difficulty for cleaning it rises significantly.[11]

Anyway, as I approached the ledge, I wheelied to put the front tire over the root and onto the trail beyond.

But not...quite...high...enough.

My front wheel hit the root solidly, bringing the front of the bike to a halt. The front wheel then magically became a fulcrum, levering me up and, *partially*, over the bike.

Gravity took over then, and I crashed down heavily, landing with my center of gravity — my snipe — on my bike's stem.

Eventually, I hit the ground.

My screams could be heard in the next county. And the one after that.

I writhed. The pain was so overwhelming that I really, honestly, thought I had severed my snipe's ancillary componentry.[12] I had waves of nausea. I groaned. I expressed interest in dying, right there, just to be done with it.

Looking back, perhaps I should upgrade this crash to second-most painful. I'm pretty sure that, at the moment of impact at least, it hurt worse than separating a shoulder.

After some time — minutes? hours? days? — I found that I no longer wished for death, and found furthermore that I could stand without feeling like I would heave.

---

9   You can tell I'm stalling, can't you?

10   My favorite mountain bike trail in the whole world.

11   I'd say "exponentially," but I'm sure that someone will eventually challenge my reasoning, and then I'd have to admit that I'm no good at math and just like the sound of the word "exponentially."

12   Also known as "testicles."

And in fact, after verifying that my snipe and all associated hard-ware[13] were present and, to my great relief, intact, I finished the ride.

THE NEXT DAY

Aside from some expected soreness, my snipe gave me no special reason to pay attention to it for the rest of the day.

Overnight, however, a change occurred.

The change was as startling as it was obvious, but was located in a place I could not exactly show off to strangers in the street.

At least, not without legal consequences.

However, there was one person who I knew would appreciate what had happened: my friend and co-worker, Dug. Furtively, I called him into my office, closed the door, and said, "You have to see this."

Then, I made appropriate disclaimers about how what I was about to do should not be construed as anything untoward, nor should any undue significance be attributed to said action.

After which, I showed Dug my snipe.

Which was completely, entirely, and utterly the deepest, darkest purple you could imagine.

I had planned to ask Dug whether he thought maybe I should go see a doctor, but I then thought better of it, because Dug was collapsed on the floor, laughing so hard he could not breathe.

Moral: be wary of uphill endos. Also, don't show your snipe to Dug.

> COMMENT BY MICHAEL RHODUS
> You and Dug must be very good friends for you to show him your purple snipe. Everyone should have such a friend. I think.

> COMMENT BY JIM
> Wow. I hate whacking my snipe on the stem. It really hurts.
> But not as much as when I jumped onto my bike, catching my scum rot on the back of my saddle during a recent 'cross race.

> COMMENT BY KIMBERLEY
> Makes me glad I am snipeless!

---

13 Software?

COMMENT BY LARRY
I crashed once where I flew off my bike and landed on a downed tree. A branch from said tree impaled my snipe. When we regrouped, I had to show my snipe to the doctor in our group (he is a veterinarian).
He had the same reaction as Dug.

COMMENT BY ERIC
I too have had snipe-to-stem impact. I would rank it as my most painful mountain biking experience, and I did not have any color change. I cannot imagine how bad your impact was.

COMMENT BY BUCKYTHEDONKEY
You know you have great mates when you share your most painful secrets with them, and they laugh. :-D

THE DAY I HATED BRAD

Brad Keyes is one of my best friends, a member of the core team of guys with whom I ride. He's one most tenacious, innovative, interesting people you could ever meet. When he has an idea, he makes it real. For example, several years ago he disliked the current state of sports drinks, both the way they tasted and the what's in them.

So he invented his own: CarboRocket. It's awesome, I use it in every endurance race. Check it out at carborocket.com.

You owe me $200 for that, Brad.

Brad is also one of the most positive people I know. He always seems happy, he sees the humor and fun in every situation. This is fantastic, usually. Just about any time you go riding, Brad is the guy you want to have along.

But not always. No, definitely not always. There are times when what you need is a voice of reason on a ride, someone who says, "This is beginning to feel more like a three hour tour[14] than a bike ride."

Ten-or-so years ago, Brad, Rocky, Alan (a friend of Rocky's) and I planned to ride the Kokopelli Trail as a two day ride. We planned to ride from Moab to Dewey Bridge the first day,[15] camp there, and then continue to Colorado the second day.

Unfortunately, it rained the night before.

A lot.

Waking up and looking at the ankle-deep water in the parking lot of our hotel, I recommended we forget the epic ride we had planned, go back to sleep, and in a few hours go for a ride on Slickrock, which would be dried out by then.

Rocky and Alan were right with me. In fact, I think they admired my courage. I had been the brave one, saying what everyone else was thinking: that riding out into the wilderness after a big rainstorm was not a good idea.[16]

---

14   This is a *Gilligan's Island* reference. Ask your parents about it; they'll explain.
15   About a seventy-mile ride.
16   Understatement of the year.

Brad was astounded. We had planned this ride for weeks! We were prepared! The trail was probably fine![17]

And then, finally, he said, "Let's just try. If it's no good, we can always turn around."

Rocky, Alan, and I caved. In the face of such enthusiasm, how could we not?

Had I known what the day held in store for us, of course, I would have simply murdered Brad on the spot, hidden his body, gone back to bed, then gone for the aforementioned ride on the Slickrock Trail later that afternoon.

When I consider the day that followed, I would have been justified in doing so.

THE BEGINNING OF THE CLIMB

The Kokopelli Trail begins at the Slickrock trailhead. With three of us (i.e., everyone but Brad) casting a wistful look back at the ride we'd prefer to be doing, we began the ride up Sand Flats Road.

Here's the thing about Sand Flats Road: there's a lot of it that isn't sand at all. Oh sure, there's *plenty* of sand, but it's not *all* sand.

There's also a considerable amount of clay.

Usually, of course, you don't even notice the clay. It's all hard and baked and easy to ride on during the 362 days of the year when it doesn't rain in the hot Moab desert. Nearly every day, clay is an awesome riding surface.

On the other three days of the year, however, it's a bad riding surface.

I need to be clear, here. By "bad riding surface," I don't mean that it's suboptimal. By "bad riding surface," I mean that it was actually wicked and spiteful.

And in short, we each had to frequently stop, scraping mud from our bagel-esque tires, scraping mud from our derailleurs, scraping mud from our pedals, scraping mud from our brakes.

You get the picture.

After an hour or so of this, during which we had traveled perhaps a dozen yards,[18] I said that this seemed like enough. We could turn

---

17   I don't put these exclamation points in here lightly. Brad's voice was loud and high-pitched. He was *exclaiming*.

18   I'm exaggerating by roughly fifty percent, which means that during this hour we had actually gone eighteen yards.

around now and still get in a good ride on the Slickrock trail, then go get dinner at the Moab Brewery.[19] The day was not too late to salvage.

Brad — who, I'd like to point out, had never done this ride before and had no idea of what was ahead of us[20] — insisted things would shortly get better, and we should go on.

Brad must be a Jedi[21] or something, because his mind trick worked. We went on.

WHEREIN I BECOME MENTALLY SCARRED FOR LIFE

About ninety minutes later than we had originally planned (meaning we were about fifty percent behind schedule already), we got to the point where you turn off Sand Flats Road and onto singletrack.

Ordinarily, this is one of my favorite parts of the ride. While almost all of the rest of the Kokopelli Trail is on wide dirt roads, this section feels a little more like mountain biking.

Ordinarily.

But not this day.

After the night's rain, this trail — no, let's call it what it really is: this "ravine" — was a soupy mess in some places. In other places it was a running stream. In still other places, it was the exactly perfect material for making adobe bricks, complete with straw already mixed in, so as to make the binding compound stronger. As if that were somehow necessary.

Within yards, our bikes were completely immobilized. The only way to continue was to shoulder our bikes and trudge on, hiking for four miles uphill in alternately slippery and sticky mud in our bike shoes.

"This," I told Brad, "sucks."

"Are you kidding?" asked Brad, brightly. "This is a total adventure! I'm loving this!"

We eventually got to the pavement part of the ride, which I have never been so glad to reach. On previous Kokopelli rides, we're usually just getting warmed up by this point; we've been out a couple hours and are typically just getting into our endurance groove, looking forward to the sun coming out soon and warming us up.

This time, we had been out six hours. Yes, it had taken us *three times*

---

19 A good place, but don't get the fish tacos. Just sayin'.
20 I, on the other hand, had done this ride half a dozen times. But what do I know?
21 One of the evil Jedi. There are evil Jedi, right?

as long as usual to reach this point.

"The math is impossible," I told the group. "We won't make it to camp before dark. We need to turn around."

Rocky and Alan nodded their heads, a chorus of consent. Brad, however, said, "We don't even know if it's been raining on other parts of the trail. It could be totally dry. Besides, this is fun!"

Seriously. He said it was fun.[22]

BRAD STRIKES OUT ON HIS OWN

So, in a demonstration of how weak-willed the rest of us were, we pressed on. Things weren't so bad as we rode on the pavement for several miles, climbing up to Beaver Mesa. The only difference, being, of course, that we were much more exhausted and demoralized than we had ever been before.

Except Brad. He chattered on happily about what an awesome time we were having.

I believe Brad may have been on drugs.[23]

When we reached the top of Beaver Mesa, the paved road ended, yielding to a good gravel road. This good gravel road lasted for nine inches, approximately.

It, in turn, yielded to brownie batter.

Our bikes were instantly jammed up. Wheels wouldn't turn. Drivetrains were completely obscured. And since we were about to begin another climb, followed by a descent that would leave us committed to a night huddled in mud — because, as I mentioned, there was *no way* we were going to make it to camp — I decided to try convincing Brad, one more time.

"Brad," I said. "We've got another climb here, in horrible *mud*. This will be followed by a treacherous descent, with cliffside exposure, through *mud*. Then we've got to ride through Fisher Valley, which will be more *mud*, and climb and descend Seven Mile Pass. In the *mud*."

"Brad," I pleaded, "This spot, right here, is the last place we can turn around and make it home and still have a chance of not sleeping in the mud tonight."

"I'll tell you what," said Brad, cheerily. "I'll ride on ahead for a couple

---

22 I'm genuinely ashamed at how easily Brad bent us to his will.
23 And he didn't even offer to share.

miles and see if the trail improves."[24]

"Whatever," I replied, exhausted.

So Rocky, Alan, and I waited, dejectedly trying to get our bikes into rideable condition. Then we waited some more.

And then, just to mix things up a bit, we continued waiting.

Finally, I, as the person responsible for bringing Brad out on this misadventure, rode on, hoping that I could catch up with him.

As I rode, I bellowed, every few seconds, *"Brad! Get back here!"*

THE SENSIBLE THING

And what do you know? It worked. Brad came back. "Is it still muddy?" I asked.

"Yep!" he replied, brightly. "But I didn't finish the climb, so I don't know if it's muddy on the downhill."

What Brad didn't understand, of course, is that the climb continued *for another six miles.*

"We're going back to Moab," I said.

"But," he replied.

"Not. Another. Word." Finally, I was taking a stand. "We've got *maybe* three hours of light left and the most technical part of the whole ride is in front of us. And it's muddy. We're going back."

Dejected for the first time that day, Brad agreed.

We took the pavement back to Moab. Rocky, Alan and I, relieved at the certainty we would not be huddling together for warmth in a cave built of mud and sticks that night, were much happier.

Brad was glum. He had been having a great day, until this sad reversal of events.

AFTERWARD

It took Rocky and me years to forgive Brad for cheerfully dragging us through eighty miles of mud. I don't know if Alan ever forgave him. Alan's not the forgiving type.

Of course now, Brad and I are about as good of friends as friends can be. In fact, ten years later, Brad and I still both tell this story.

Brad, of course, tells it a little bit differently than I.[25]

---

24 I swear, my blood pressure rises factorially just recalling this conversation.
25 He has never written it down, though, because that would be an admission of guilt.

COMMENT BY ROCKY

I am a second witness to Brad's psychosis on that day. My 23 lb. Ibis Mojo easily ranged from 30 lbs. to 400 lbs., depending on the consistency of the mud. Once we started to descend back into town (the mud on Beaver Mesa was, no exaggeration, a foot deep), it took ten miles of fast pavement descending to remove all of the mud from our tires.

In Brad's defense, he is one of those guys that is easy to hate but impossible not to love. Enthusiasm is contagious. But then so is the plague.

I echo the clamor for Brad's version as I would like a glimpse at the inner workings of a scarred psyche.

COMMENT BY TASHA

Brad is the eternal optimist... "things will get better just around the corner." Don't feel bad about succumbing to his enthusiasm. I have been pulled in time and time again for the last eighteen years! He has a way.

COMMENT BY ALAN

Fatty, Why did you go and have to bring this event up again? I've spent the last ten years trying to forget. Now I've got to poke my minds eye out with a stick again. You failed to mention that we were subjected to rain, sleet, snow and 20 yards of black ice on the road while doing 40 mph. And wasn't there a near miss with a deer crossing the road as we descended? Good times!

As for Brad, that is the only time I had ever met him. One has to respect his optimism and skill. He probably is a great guy, but I will never know. Because I still hate him.

HOW I RUINED TWO SUITS IN ONE SECOND

As an award-winning storyteller, I know the rules of storytelling. And the first two of them are:

1. *Don't talk about politics or religion.*
2. *Seriously, just don't.*

In general, I am more than happy to heed these rules. But there's no avoiding talking about religion in this story. Well, maybe that's not true, because I'm still not going to talk about religion here, but I will mention it, because there's no getting around it.

Because, you see, this is a story about me riding my bicycle, in Finland, as a Mormon missionary.

For those of you wondering how I wound up in Finland, no, I did not choose it. Mormon missionaries have no say at all in where they go. However, back in the eighties prospective missionaries were given a language aptitude test. Those who did well often wound up going to China, or to Navajo reservations. Or to Finland.

The problem with this test, of course, was that it was actually a lot better at discerning whether someone has an aptitude for taking tests than for learning and speaking languages.

Wow, I'm off-track already. I can tell this is going to be a hard story to keep reined in.

About a year or so into my time in Finland, I found myself in a little town called Kemi. Kemi's main claim to fame was its delightful-smelling paper mill.[26]

My missionary partner — "companion" in Mormon jargon — and I lived a few miles outside of town in a farmhouse's upstairs apartment. It was a rustic place, with only cold-running water (we heated water on a big pot to wash dishes and took showers at the local public gym). Not super fancy, but we did have access to the sauna in the basement and the rent was cheap, so we figured we had it pretty good.

After I had been in Kemi a few months, I was assigned a new

---

26   It was also known for its proximity to Russia. Fun fact: I lived in Kemi when the Chernobyl reactor melted down. "Don't go out in the rain" was pretty much all the guidance we were given.

companion: Derek White. Derek was a great guy to be around; he made the long days riding around on bikes from apartment complex to apartment complex downright fun.

A natural ham, Derek knew several tricks on bikes. He could sit facing backward on the handlebars and backpedal, riding down the street that way. He could ride a wheelie.

It goes without saying that he could ride no-handed for any distance, and in any situation. At first, I was wary when riding with him; I'd keep my distance as we rode, expecting him to veer wildly. I was certain that with all these hijinks, eventually Derek would crash.

But he did not.

So we began to ride side-by-side, so I could listen to him tell stories, gesturing as he talked and rode, with no trace of self-consciousness. Confident. No-handed.

Eventually, this would lead to a serious problem.

The thing about anything done well is that it doesn't look difficult. It looks easy. Natural. These days I understand this visual contradiction as I watch my friends fluidly clean mountain bike moves that I know I should never attempt.

But back then, I just thought, "Well, *I* could do that."

And so, as I was telling a story of my own, I did. I pushed off the handlebars, moving into an upright position. And there, for one glorious moment, we were. Two teenage Americans,[27] each wearing cheap business suits,[28] riding no-handed down a bike path in Kemi, Finland. Really, what could be more natural?

And then, of course, I veered toward Derek. And before I could get my hands down to correct myself, the "veered toward" became a "plowed into."

The next few moments are confusing, and quite possibly subject to interpretation. But I'm pretty sure he reacted to my plowing into him by leaning into me (his theory). Or maybe our handlebars just locked (my theory). Regardless, we didn't just crash. We crashed *into* each other.

---

27   I believe that we were both actually nineteen years old.

28   Fun fact: most Mormon missionaries buy their suits at a store that has grown up around selling suits to these young men. It's called "Mr. Mac," and the suits are as durable as they are ugly. Also, they generally come with two pairs of pants, because missionaries tend to wear them out as they ride their bikes along.

I am quite certain I was the first to hit the ground, because I distinctly remember how the ground-up layering went: my bike, then me, then Derek's bike, and then Derek.

Sort of a Mormon-missionary-and-bike club sandwich, if you will, with a generous side order of blood.

I learned at that moment that, at least up to a certain point, embarrassment is a stronger and more acute sensation than pain.

It probably really only took forty-five seconds for us to disentangle ourselves from our bikes, but during that time, a pair of old women trudged by, one using her wheeled sled as a walker/grocery cart.

"Mormons," she said, rolling her eyes and shaking her head both wisely and disapprovingly. Then she pushed her sled around us and kept going, not giving us another look.

At which point Derek observed that my front wheel was taco-ed (though neither of us knew the term at the time) and the tire was blown.

Then he started laughing.[29] Derek has that infectious kind of laughter and before long, we were both sitting down on the ground, considering ourselves:

Two Yankee kids, far from home, in cheap, torn, bloody shirts/slacks/ties, sitting on the pavement and laughing like fools beside their mangled bikes in Kemi, Finland.

Really, what could be more natural?

PS: I do not remember for certain, but I believe we did not win many converts that day.

COMMENT BY SAM MACCUTCHAN

I have crashed many times in cycling as well as snowboarding. If you can laugh about it, it was a good crash!

COMMENT BY JOHNEBOY

Great story. I too was involved in a crash with my companion in Denmark. He looked worse than he was and a kind motorist stopped and called an ambulance explaining that two Americans had crashed their bikes and one needed help. My companion, still woozy from the cracked helmet, was able to summon the strength to speak up and say. . . . "I am from Canada."

29 What else could he do?

COMMENT BY DEREK WHITE
I was there and it hurt.

THIS VIDEO WILL BE SO AWESOME

I live in Utah and hope to never leave. There's great road biking. There's great mountain biking. The variety of terrain is incredible, and people generally get along with each other. While mountain biking here, I've been offered more beer by guys on horseback than from anyone else, anywhere else.

In particular, I live in Alpine, Utah. It's a tiny little town. We have one gas station. We don't have a grocery store.

But we do have out-the-door access to world-class riding, both mountain biking and road biking.

So of course, I want to show it off, to put a camera on my head and capture it for the all the citizens of YouTubia to admire.[30]

Which is what I had in mind when I began the ride I'm describing in this story.

American Fork Canyon is, quite simply, the main reason I wanted to move to Alpine, Utah. Which is to say, American Fork Canyon is home to Tibble Fork,[31] the Ridge Trail,[32] Timpooneke, South Fork Deer Creek (aka Joy),[33] and Pole Line Pass. That's right: American Fork Canyon is home to the royal flush of mountain biking.

But those are all mountain bike trails, and American Fork Canyon is home to an exceptional road ride, too: the Alpine Loop. Thinking it was high time I show off the great road ride I've got here, I put on the helmetcam, set it to record — with more than five hours of recording time on a card, it's easier to just record the whole ride than to capture clips — and rode out to meet the rest of the group.

We made our way to American Fork Canyon, getting ready for the carnage the climb would no doubt create. This would be the first group ride of the season, up a serious climb.

There was no *way* it would not turn into a battle.

---

30   And then, of course, to comment on those videos that it was both "fake" and "so gay."

31   My very favorite mountain biking trail in the world.

32   About fifty or so miles of perfect, hardly-used-by-anyone singletrack.

33   Allow me to recommend you watch my video called "Six Minutes of Joy," which I have — naturally — given an "Ode to Joy" soundtrack. I think you'll get a feel for why I love this place. http://bit.ly/fatsby06

I'M 120% THE MAN I USED TO BE

Here's the thing: two of the guys there, Eric and Jason, were working hard to get a fast time at Leadville this year. They took off of the front. Dug, briefly torn between obeying his shepherding instincts[34] and wanting to see if he could contest the lead, rode with me for a few minutes and then bridged the gap.

This gave me an excellent opportunity me to contemplate what thirty pounds equates to. For example, a very lightweight freeride bike. Or a three-year-old child. Or three gallons of water (imperial gallons, not u.s. gallons).[35]

Or my big ol' layer of fat.

I may not be the walrus, but I look the part.

"Oh well," I thought. "Maybe I'll be able to hang with the group on the descent." I thought of the video and how it would show Dug bridging the gap and how much he would like that part of the video and decided I would edit it out.

I CAN SUFFER WHEN NEEDED

Between the Timpanogos Cave parking lot and the Tibble Fork turnoff, the road levels off for a couple of miles. And, luckily for me, Jason, Dug, and Eric were not trying to devastate me even further by forming a paceline and increasing their gap on this section.

In short, I managed to catch up.

"This will be an excellent section on the video," I thought, as I pulled even with the group. "Perhaps I will play it in slow motion with dramatic sound effects."

We passed the Tibble Fork turnoff, veered right, and were at the base of the main climb.

Jason and Eric immediately shot off the front. Dug kept me company for a few moments until he realized that I had nothing interesting to say[36] and then he went on ahead.

But I couldn't just sit back there, letting everyone go miles ahead of

---

34   Dug is the guy who likes to make sure everyone's okay. That nobody's left behind. That likes to keep the group together, if at all possible. Hence his nickname: The Shepherd.

35   I actually have no idea if there's a difference. And also, I don't care enough to Google it.

36   More to the point, I was breathing too hard to be able to say anything at all.

me. Not without at least a token fight. So I pushed. Hard. Like there was something at stake.

Which of course there was.

There *always* is.

TAKING TURNS

Giving it everything I had, I reeled Dug in. And then together, we reeled Eric in. Jason was up ahead in the distance; sometimes you could see him, sometimes he was around a corner. So I pretended he didn't exist.

Thinking that perhaps I had just a little more in me, I pushed harder, and dropped Dug and Eric for good.

Except I hadn't.

The thing about giving a climb everything you've got is, the sound of blood in your ears pretty much blocks out every other sound. So I was surprised when Dug and Eric caught up with me about one minute later. "At least," I thought, "They are having to work for it."

It was, I should say, my fervent *hope* that they were working for it.

For the rest of the climb, Dug, Eric, and I took turns setting the pace for our group of three. Each time one of the others passed me, I thought to myself, "That's it. I'm done. I'm about to slide backwards."

But each time I managed to hold on. *Barely.*

Once, I even considered saying to Dug as he passed me and I fought to grab his wheel, "If you want to crack me now, all you've got to do is stand up and attack for two seconds."[37]

Even through the haze of pain, though, I thought to myself, several times, "All this passing and re-passing is going to make terrific video."

And, just to put an exclamation point on it, I stood up and sprinted to what I decided was the turnaround point, where snow still blocks the road.[38]

It's easy to declare yourself the winner when you choose the finish line in secret.

---

37 I of course did *not* say this. I'm not stupid.

38 One of the very best things about riding up American Fork Canyon in early spring is that until late spring, a gate blocks the road, preventing all motorized traffic from using it until Memorial Day, when the road is snowplowed and opened for general use. Until then, road cyclists can ride this section of the road with no fear of cars. It's the very definition of awesome.

NEAR DEATH EXPERIENCE

In early spring, the first mile or so of the Alpine Loop descent is two parts awesome to one part freaky. One awesome part is due to the road itself: it's a twisty, fast-descending smooth mountain road. The next awesome part is that the top part of the road has not been opened to motor traffic for the year, so you can use both sides of the road as you descend.

The freaky part is that there are boulders, tree trunks, and scree[39] galore lying scattered on the road from winter rockslides. Those are bad to hit at thirty miles per hour.

I made a point of looking down so I'd catch some of that craziness on video.

Once you're past Pine Hollow, the descent opens up and you can go as fast as you dare — and I mean that very literally. I have never quite spun out on that part of the descent because I always chicken out.

Eric, however, did not chicken out, and attacked hard. He blew past us on the left side of the road, fully committed. And, I suspect, really really really hoping there was no oncoming traffic around the bend.

I leaped — my legs are strong, and my big gut isn't so much of a disadvantage on the descents — and caught Eric as we passed the Tibble Fork turnoff. He and I started working together in a furious bid to keep Dug, Jason, and Mark from bridging.

You see, there's always a sprint finish at the bottom of American Fork Canyon: the toll booth. Big bragging rights for the winner.

I didn't have a GPS on my bike, but would guess we were working north of 40mph on this fantastic downhill. Pedal with all your might for the fifteen seconds of your pull, then drift left and coast, feathering your brakes in the other guy's slipstream for fifteen seconds.

Rinse and repeat.

I knew this, along with the sprint at the end, would be the centerpiece of the video.

Or at least, that's what I thought until we came around a bend and suddenly faced the broadside of a bright yellow jeep, in the middle of executing an 18-point U-turn in the middle of a blind mountain bidirectional road.

---

39   "Scree," according to Wikipedia, is "collection of broken rock fragments at the base of crags, mountain cliffs, volcanoes or valley shoulders that has accumulated through periodic rockfall from adjacent cliff faces." Isn't this book educational?

I was pulling the group at that moment and locked up my rear brake, keeping the front brake open enough so I could still steer. Later I would be grateful that the fifteen years of riding I've done had given me this useful conditioned reflex.

Simultaneously I yelled "SLOW!" at the top of my lungs, hoping, but not really believing, that Eric would be able to get to his brakes and swerve before he touched my rear wheel.

But he did. He veered to my left, braking hard.

And there, somehow, was Dug, having just about managed to finish bridging to Eric and me, also braking hard and managing to avoid Eric, me, and the jeep.

Disaster averted and back under control, we went around the jeep. I made eye contact and shook my head disappointedly.

Two minutes later, of course, it occurred to me that this would make *great* video.

BIG SPRINT FINISH

Dug, Eric, and I worked together as we finished the big working descent to the toll booth. Strangely, Dug was taking waaaaay too long of pulls, tiring himself out before the big sprint.

I, however, am not one to complain.

So, from my comfortably-rested second position in the group of three, I opened up and sprinted as hard as I could when I saw the toll booth. In truth, I attacked too early, but Dug had given me such a long rest that I felt I had it in me.

And I did.

Eric threw his bike (almost too far) at the end, but I think we have consensus that I had won my first ever toll booth sprint.

A glorious moment. And I knew I had caught it on video, to boot.

LESSONS LEARNED

I had grand intentions of riding up to Suncrest with the group...until we actually got to the climb and I discovered the headwind was two or three shades beyond brutal. "Hmmm," I asked myself, "Which should I do? Turn around and coast home, or fight a hard headwind for a four mile climb?"

Four minutes later, I was home.

I pulled into my garage, and took off my helmet, wanting to dash up to my computer and upload the video so I could start editing it down to the good parts.

I knew I had a winner.

Which, of course, is when I discovered that I had left the lens cap on.

COMMENT BY MIKE ROADIE

That's still better than, "And then I woke up!!!"

COMMENT BY JASON

That's funny, when we hit that wind going up Suncrest, I also thought about turning around and going to your house.

COMMENT BY FREDDY FRESHLEGS

"It's like, how much more black could this be? And the answer is none. None more black." — Nigel Tufnel

COMMENT BY MIKE

Did Dug, Mark, Eric and Jason all know the cap was still on? "Hey guys, let's let him win this one (wink-wink, nudge-nudge, point at the lens cap)."

COMMENT BY SYSTEM6

Q: What's the difference between a great victory and a simple daydream?
A: Lens cap.

COMMENT BY ERIC

I've yet to unpucker from the yellow Jeep encounter.

MANO A MANO: THE RACE REPORT

There is a universally-understood cycling axiom that states:
Any time two or more cyclists ride together, that ride is actually a race.
And here are the universally-understood corollaries to that axiom:

- *At no point shall any party to that race state that a race is about to begin.*
- *At no point shall any party to that race acknowledge that a race is in progress.*
- *After the race, the loser shall decide whether to acknowledge the winner's superiority, or to instead make a lame excuse.*
- *If the loser makes a lame excuse, the winner shall treat the aforementioned excuse as implicit acknowledgment of the loser's loss, and may in fact treat said excuse as more valid than an explicit admission of the winner's superiority.*

The original axiom is immutable. The corollaries...well, the corollaries have exceptions.

A few years ago, Dug and I were both signed up for a local race. Due to rain, however, neither of us decided to do that race. And in fact, I admitted something: the only reason I was interested in the race at all was because I wanted to see who is faster: him or me.

Dug admitted he was curious about the same thing. So after work, we duked it out. Two laps, on the same course we would have been racing on the previous weekend.

The objective? To find out which of us, right at that moment, was the less pathetic of us two.

If Dug were a car racing video game, he would be one of those where you have to *earn* your turbo boost — but once you've got it, you get to keep it.

If I, on the other hand, were a car racing video game, I would be the kind where you have nitrous and turbo boost right from the first moment of the game, but you only get a finite amount of each.[40] I would also be the kind where somehow the console senses you're about to press Start and immediately turns on the nitrous, turbo boost, and mashes the gas button clear into the controller without asking whether

---

40   I am thinking, of course, of the Crash Bandikoot Team Racing video game from about 1999, back when I had eye-hand coordination.

you really want to go that fast right from the gun.

And, in short, in spite of the fact that Dug clearly explained before we started the race that he was going to hang back and let me cook myself to a crisp, I went right to my redline and kept it there. By the time I got to the bridge that signals the base of the big climb on the first lap, I could no longer see Dug.

Which, in my mind, proved that I was, at that moment, the greatest cyclist who has ever lived.

Never mind that this is a full-gas, no strategy, boneheaded approach to racing. It worked. While Dug suffered badly for the big climb, I put enough of a gap between us that even though I knew I had a good chance of completely discombobulating on the second lap, he would be psychologically destroyed and hence unable to catch up.

THEORY OF SUBJECTIVE SPEED

As we raced, I craned my neck around ten thousand times to see if Dug was closing in.[41] Especially during the second lap up Clark's, I felt eminently catchable.

This brings me to a couple of things I noticed during this race.

First, in the absence of any kind of real measuring device (a bike computer, GPS, or even a watch), my sense of speed was incredibly subjective. During the first ascent up Clark's, my iPod[42] played about three songs. On the second climb up Clark's, I felt like I was barely moving, like I might tip over at any moment. And yet, I started the climb about halfway through one song, and finished about three complete songs later.

In other words, I did the climb in three songs when I was fresh, and 3.5 when I felt completely broken.

Now of course, songs can be of variable length and I might have been more than halfway through a song at the beginning of one of the climbs and blah blah blah, but still: while I felt like on the second climb I was twice as slow, in reality I was likely a minute or three slower.

By the way, I have just now decided that from now on I shall measure all climbs in Song Units. Please do likewise.

---

41   More often during the second lap than during the first.
42   This was back before we used phones for everything.

MORE SUBJECTIVE SPEED THEORY

As I say, actual amount of time notwithstanding, I felt like I was crawling during the second climb up Clark's. Several times, I considered getting off my bike, resting while I waited for Dug to catch up, then proposing that races are stupid and that we're both closer to our mid-forties than early forties and what business do we have racing one another?

But I kept going. For you.

During this (subjective) crawl, I noticed that the distance between trees was greater than I had previously thought. I noticed that the distance between a couple of landmarks on the climb is about twice as far as I used to think.

Above all else, I noticed a *lot* more false summits than usual.

ADRENALINE IS NOT MY FRIEND

Of course, since the course is a loop, it can't be all uphill.[43] The big down-hill is called Ghost Falls, a switchback-y, wide, clean stretch of singletrack with several bridge crossings and a few whoop-de-doos up top.

The first time down Ghost, I was terrible, for two reasons. The first and most important reason is that I was too amped up. I wasn't *riding* the trail, I was attacking it. And on a twisty course, that just doesn't work. I kept overbaking the switchbacks, surging in any little straight-away, and in general being a herky-jerky mess.

By riding so aggressively, I'm almost certain that I was slower than when I just ride this trail normally, flowing with it and enjoying myself.

THE WORST DOWNHILLING SONG EVER

The second reason I did so badly on the first descent was that my iPod chose to shuffle Johnny Cash's cover of "Hurt" into play.

Now, let it be known that I love this song. Cash brought soul and an ache to it that makes his version vastly superior to the original (and I like the original too).[44]

That said, I cannot imagine a worse song to downhill to.

However, just for fun, I just took a look at my "One Good Gig" playlist

---

43   Because that would suck.
44   By all means, feel free to send me your dissenting opinion. Just realize that your opinion happens to be wrong.

(a carefully-chosen set of songs to fit on a 1Gb iPod),[45] and decided that if my iPod really hated me, it should play the following songs from that list the next time I'm on a nice, long downhill:

- "Hurt (Nine Inch Nails cover)," Johnny Cash
- "Loser," Beck
- "Under the Milky Way," the Church
- "Round Here," Counting Crows
- "Baby Got Back (Sir Mix a Lot cover)," Jonathan Coulton
- "Superstar (Carpenters cover)," Sonic Youth
- "Pennyroyal Tea (Live)," Nirvana

As long as I'm at it, though, here are the seven songs on my "One Good Gig" playlist I would *most* like to get shuffled into play during a downhill:

- "Renegades of Funk," Rage against the Machine
- "Don't Take Me for Granted," Social Distortion. (As an aside here, I'd like to proclaim that this is my favorite song from my favorite album from my favorite band. This song is the archetype for straight-ahead rock and roll.)
- "Under My Thumb (Rolling Stones Cover)," Social Distortion
- "Uncontrollable Urge (Live Version)," Devo
- "Nice Guys Finish Last," Green Day
- "Whisper to a Scream," Icicle Works
- "Bad Reputation," Joan Jett

DEFIANCE OF PHYSICS

After climbing Clark's and descending Ghost Falls, the race course had us doing a short little loop of singletrack I call "Last Dance" because it's generally the last thing we ride before finishing the ride.

Last Dance starts with a climb, and then drops down to the main Corner Canyon artery trail. It's that climb that boggles me. For some reason, it's the easiest climb in the world. Even though my legs are cooked from a hard climb and working descent, I seem to just float up that climb. It only lasts a minute or two, but, even on the second lap of a race, where I was fully out of gas, I zipped right up it.

It's a climb that rides like a downhill. Weird. And wonderful.[46]

---

45 One gigabyte? Oh, technology used to be *adorable*.

46 I'm not aware of any other uphills in the world that ride like downhills, but I know of dozens of downhills that require as much work as a climb. This seems manifestly unfair.

AFTERWARD

I am not, generally, an intense person. But when I race, I am not myself. I take each and every race very seriously. So I finished the race pushing myself as hard (albeit much much slower) as when I started, and kept looking over my shoulder to the very end.

Reaching my truck without Dug in sight, I hurriedly put my bike up on the rack, took off my helmet, got out a drink, folded down the truck bed's gate, and sat down, doing my best to get into an "I've been here forever" position as quickly as possible.

A few moments later, Dug rolled through the parking lot, no-handed and casual. We sat and talked for a while, while Dug picked off the dozens of caterpillars that had accumulated on his jersey.

The next morning, my throat was still raw from two hours of open-mouthed hyperventilating. I had a hard time walking down stairs. And I found myself worried at the prospect of that afternoon's group ride to the summit of the Alpine Loop.

Which of course was ridiculous. I'd be fine. After all, it's not like it was going to turn into a *race*.

COMMENT BY DUG

The song that came on for me just as I crested (and I use the word crested very loosely here) the top of Clarks on the first lap: Wake Up Dead Man, by U2.

Too little, too late.

COMMENT BY JOSH

If we are now judging our ride time with songs, I am leaving one song on my iPod: "In a Gadda Da Vida," by Iron Butterfly.

COMMENT BY WEILAND

Isn't this a best of seven series?

A MEDITATION ON THE PAIN CAVE

Not every story needs to be a joke and this one certainly isn't. This one is just about me, riding hard. This one is about how incredible riding feels. It's about how hurting on a big climb can be something in which you take an extraordinary amount of pride.

Mostly, when I'm off the bike, I'm a goofball. This story is about who I am when I'm on the bike.

This one is about who I am when I'm nothing but legs, lungs, and willpower. You might recognize yourself in this one, too.

I had planned to do a short ride on the flats. A nice little spin, focusing on high cadence and low torque.

But it was so hot outside. And one secret every cyclist who lives near mountains knows is: you can climb out of the heat. It's always ten or fifteen degrees cooler in the canyon, and maybe even cooler as you get toward the summit.

So when I had to decide whether to turn right and head toward the flats in the valley, or turn left and head to the canyon, I turned left.

Which meant I would not be doing an easy spin.

NEW PLAN

By the time I got to the mouth of the canyon, I could tell something: my legs felt good.[47] Unusually good. Like they wanted me to see what was possible.

I stepped it up. Still felt great. Went to a higher gear. Wanted more.

By the time I got to the toll booth, I was in my big ring, about three cogs down the cassette. That is not a common gear selection for this ride. But for whatever reason, that's where I wanted to be.

THIS PAIN IS MINE

I generally climb the Alpine Loop in the second and third gear, shifting up to third and fourth when I'm standing. Today, though, I rode in fifth and sixth. At a cadence that seemed higher than normal.

---

47   "My legs felt good" is such a common, yet odd, expression in cycling. Occasionally, they really *do* feel good. More often, however, I think you just have a day when you're more open to the idea of accepting the pain that comes with a hard cycling effort.

It hurt. It hurt gloriously.

I think other cyclists who love climbing will agree: there is nothing quite so exquisite as pain you have chosen to suffer, and manage to keep right below the threshold that breaks you. You are controlling chaos. You are mastering your body. You have the time trialist's smile: a grin with teeth exposed, mouth wide open. You're not happy, and yet you are.

And you're begging for more air. It's all around you, but you can't get enough.

You are pushing every single thought, except one, out of your head. *Can I push harder and still not snap?* If the answer is "yes," then you push harder.

It's surprising, really, how often the answer is "yes." More often than you would expect.

When the answer is "no," however, the sense of gratification is immense. You're going as hard as you can. Or are you? You evaluate yourself. Not in a calculating, cerebral way at all, in fact you're not even using words. You're just wondering: am I being overcautious? Or am I really about to pop?

On this day, I was certain, once, that I had hit that point. I had popped. I slowed drastically, the sense of disappointment settling in.

But then I stood up, and I went again. And found I had it in me.

When you can do this, it is a huge victory.

BIG DAY

"Today," I thought, "I am turning in the ride of a lifetime."

And you know what? It's entirely possible that I did. I was light: around 156 pounds. I had been riding a lot recently. So maybe, just maybe, on that day I was the fastest and strongest I have ever been.

But I'll never know for sure.

I had no electronics with me. So maybe I turned in a 52-minute Alpine Loop summit.[48] Or maybe I just turned in a 1:02.[49] Either is possible, but I don't care which it was. On this ride, time didn't matter to me.

What mattered is how I felt. And I felt *fast*. Strong. Like I was proving something about, and to, myself.

---

48 That is a very fast time. Close to a personal record.
49 Still a fast time, but nothing special for me.

RETURN

When I reached the summit, I pulled into the parking lot and rode around the perimeter for a couple minutes in slow circles. Happy. Proud. Throat very raw.

I pulled a bottle out of a cage to take a drink and realized: I had been so focused that I had taken only one quick drink during the entire climb. I made up for lost time (and fluid) and began the descent.

Usually, I attack the downhill of the Alpine Loop pretty hard. It's so fun. But this time, I just coasted, conservatively, drained and content. I just didn't have anything left in me. I felt well and truly exhausted. Spent. Empty.

It was a good feeling.

COMMENT BY BIKECOPVT
I have often found that the best rides happen when there is nobody around to witness it and no electronic gadget to "prove" it. You just know...that was a great ride.

COMMENT BY JOEL
It's been far too long since I've done serious climbing, but you nailed everything I love about it.

COMMENT BY BIKEMIKE
To the pain!

COMMENT BY TUBENERD
You made me want to go on a ride after reading this. So I did. Thanks.

CLEANUP IN AISLE KNEE

I was reluctant to write this story. I had already angered the fearsome god of mountain biking, thus causing a wreck. By writing about this crash, I was inviting the cycling jinx: the mysterious force that guarantees when you talk about a specific kind of cycling misfortune, you are bound to bring that misfortune down upon you.

And I don't need to be courting that kind of juju in my life.

But it's a simple and inevitable fact of cycling: every once in a while we fall. And when we crash, it's only very rarely onto a smooth, sterile, debris-free surface.

Which means there's going to be some work to be done. And that work is going to involve soap, water, ointment, bandages, and pain.

Lots and lots of pain.

We were just riding along. Honestly, that's all we were doing.

My friend Mark and I were really, actually, and truly *just riding along*.

But Betty, the goddess of mountain bikes (yes, that's right, Betty) looked down on Mark and was not pleased.[50] So Betty smote Mark. Just knocked him clean off his bike. No warning or anything. Just tugged his front wheel out from under him and pushed him over.

Unfortunately for both of us, I was right on Mark's tail. I no sooner saw the hand of Betty viciously showing Mark who's boss (hint: it's Betty) than I crashed into the wreckage formerly known as Mark and his bike.

So startled was I by this chain of events that my mouth hung slack. This worked out badly for Mark, because my open mouth was bound to collide with something. In this case, my front teeth would collide with his knee, drawing blood.[51]

Meanwhile, my knee crunched and slid on the hard-surfaced, gravelly trail.

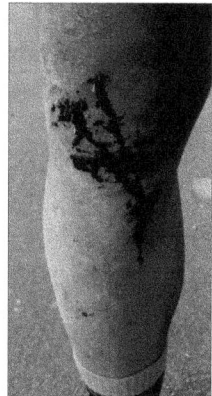

---

50   No, I don't know why. Nobody *ever* knows why Betty isn't pleased. We just know she isn't.

51   For those who are curious about my first impressions of this unintentional foray into cannibalism: tastes like chicken. Disappointing, really.

And, just to round things off, gross most of the rest of you out, and maybe make a few of you uncomfortable with the fact that you're suddenly very interested in Mark, here's him cheerfully showing off his post-crash hip:

"Here," Mark seems to be saying in this photo. "I'd really really like to show you my wound, and perhaps a wee bit more."

Which gets us to the point of this story:[52] after all the fun and games are over, someone's going to have to clean up that mess.

THE SHOWER OF PAIN

A good hard bike wreck, regardless of whether you were riding road or mountain, hurts really bad twice. The first time is when you incur the injury.

The second time is, of course, is when you wash it.

For me, the second time is worse, and for a couple reasons. First, because when you crash, it just happens. But when you're washing an injury out, you're slowly, consciously doing it to yourself.

And second, it's worse because cleaning up after a crash is so much more than soap-lather-rinse. In fact, it's even more than soap-lather-rinse-*repeat*.

It's a ritual. A ritual of pain. It's an assertion that you are willing to suffer for your art, such as it is.[53] And above all, it's an absolute guaranteed way to ruin a white washcloth.

STALLING

I expect there are some people who, when they've got a bike injury to clean up, step into the shower[54] and get straight to it.

I am not one of those people.

Instead, I wash everything else first, slowly and carefully. I wash my face extra-well, because perhaps I'll otherwise break out with my first

---

52   Finally.

53   It's also a way of telling the world, "Hey, I don't really want an infection."

54   Or tub, or whatever. Although I'd think cleaning yourself up in a tub has got to be pretty gross.

acne in twenty years. I wash between my toes. I wash my back, without the aid of a back scrubber.[55]

I wash my hands, which I generally otherwise don't do in the shower, figuring they see plenty of soap and scrubbing action without having to be specifically attended to. Which is unfair, when you think about it.

Perhaps I might even put shampoo on my head, which is a cruel mockery of both my head and the shampoo upon it.

Then maybe I'll squeegee the glass and clean the shower's grout. And then I'll cast about, desperate for something, anything, else to clean besides the wound.

At some point, though, I run out of other things to do and steel myself for the inevitable: the wound must be cleaned.

THIS MAY HURT A LITTLE...BUT IT'S MORE LIKELY GOING TO MAKE YOU WISH YOU HAD OPTED FOR THE GENERAL ANESTHETIC

When it's time[56] to start the process of cleaning the wound up, I tell myself that my wound is just a surface that needs to be cleaned. It is not part of me. Any pain I experience has nothing to do with the actions I am taking, and so I will not stop just because I am in pain.

Saying this doesn't help at all, by the way. I have no idea why I say it to myself.

I then take the two very simple tools I use for cleanup — Dial antibacterial soap and a dark-colored washcloth — and begin to lightly daub at the wound, hoping that perhaps all the blood and dirt and scabs will just fall off, due to the overwhelmingly strong combined forces of gravity and soap.

This is rarely sufficient. Alas.

Then I begin what I call "The Escalation of Scrubbing™." Each stroke just a little bit more forceful than the previous, until the wound has been successfully opened up again and is bleeding freely again and oh no the pain is too much and I think I can see muscle and tissue and cartilage and maybe I need a transfusion because I suddenly am having a difficult time standing and the room is spinning around.[57]

Oh, and I should also mention that I usually make pitiful mewing noises while I do that part.

---

55 It takes more time that way, especially if you're being thorough.
56 Or in my case, well past time.
57 This is how I behave when I have nothing more than a skinned elbow, by the way.

With all the general stuff washed off, the easy part — and by "easy" I mean "just bearably painful" — is over.

Now it's time to get to the stubborn stuff.

The stubborn stuff tends to take the form of very small rocks,[58] twigs, dirt, and miscellaneous crud. Or a riding buddy's front tooth, I suppose. And this stubborn stuff is usually hidden beneath a flap of skin that didn't get torn all the way off. This flap is now acting as a sort of Tupperware lid, keeping the dirt and grime safely sealed away inside you.

That flap of skin is going to have to go. I realize that. And yet, whenever I go to pull one of those flaps off, a very shrill and insistent voice in my head says things like, "YOU ARE NOT SUPPOSED TO TEAR YOUR SKIN OFF, STUPID. BECAUSE WHEN YOU TEAR OFF YOUR SKIN IT CAN NO LONGER PROTECT THE JUICY STUFF UNDERNEATH."

Yep, that voice really says everything in all-caps like that. And don't think I haven't told it how annoying that can be.

So I do my best to ignore the voice and remove the skin that isn't doing me any good anymore, so I can get to the dirt and rocks and dog hair and pieces of asphalt embedded within me.

...

...

Oh, I'm sorry. I seem to have passed out again.

Eventually, the wound is clean. And then comes the rinsing. Which, somehow, seems to hurt just as bad as everything else that has come before.[59] Or maybe worse.

By then my gauge of pain is a little bit fouled up.

AFTERWARD

Once cleaned, I apply an entire tube of Neosporin, because I work under the theory that Neosporin's main job is to prevent any air molecules from getting near my blood.[60]

And then, once the ointment (really, is there an uglier word in the English language?)[61] is applied, I like to discover that the only kind of

---

58   Yes, a *Monty Python and the Holy Grail* reference. Please take the time to enjoy "Witch Village" here: http://bit.ly/fatsby07

59   Almost as if exposed nerve endings are being hit by a forceful stream of water.

60   My science may be just a little shaky here.

61   Candidates include "moist," "moisture," and "nostril." And yes, I'm going to count "moist" and "moisture" separately.

bandages I have left in the house are the tiny little ones that don't quite make it all the way around your pinky finger.

Luckily, each box of Band-Aids comes with around eighty or ninety of this size. With patience, I can make a sort of quilt from these tiny things and apply them to my wound.

Of course, this bandage will not adhere to any place on my skin where there's any Neosporin at all. It will adhere very well to my open wound, and will in fact chemically bond to it within seconds.

I swear, sometimes all this post-crash cleanup takes so much time and effort I wonder why I bother injuring myself at all.

> COMMENT BY STEVE
> Hemorrhoids is the ugliest word.
> Even worse, you put ointment on them.

> COMMENT BY BORN 4 LYCRA
> So were the bikes ok?

> COMMENT BY MIKEONHISBIKE
> Whatever happened to getting your mom to spray some Bactene on it and running back outside to play?

> COMMENT BY JENNEBELLE
> That was really gross.

> COMMENT BY WING-NUT
> Once, just once I got a case of real stupid after a crash and thought that the aerosol skin would help cover the raw nerve endings. After getting up off the floor I realized that I now had to wash that stuff off.

> COMMENT BY JO
> Kris called home once to ask if we had any really big bandaids. Not my favorite question.

SPIN CLASS

When I originally posted this story in my blog, it was...polarizing. Some readers identified closely with it. Others thought I was too harshly critical. Still others thought that I had just happened upon a bad example of a spin class.

All I know is that it was the longest, strangest hour of "cycling" in my life.

We had a nice big snowstorm last night, rendering the streets an icy, snowy, slushy mess. Not great for an outdoor ride.[62]

"There's a spin class at Gold's Gym in an hour. We could do that," my wife said.

I was intrigued. You see, there are three forms of cycling that I had never tried, but had always been curious about, mostly because they seem so bizarre. These include:

- Unicycles[63]
- Recumbents
- Spin class

Well, maybe it was time to tick the "done" box on one of those items. I found an ancient pair of road shoes I knew had SPD cleats, put together a complete, matching cycling kit — I know it's important to look good when going to a Gold's Gym — and headed out the door.

I INSPECT EVERYTHING

We got to the spin room about thirty minutes early. There were about ninety stationary bikes, all adjustable in pretty much every direction. "Oh good, we get a place near the fan," The Runner[64] said, as she picked the bike closest to that fan. I chose the bike next to her. I did not realize at the time how incredibly important that would turn out to be.

I busied myself setting the saddle height. Then the saddle position.

---

62   I know, I know. Some of you go out and ride no matter what, and you are robust, strong-minded people with steely resolve. Also I find you insufferable.

63   As of this writing, I now own a unicycle. Sadly, I have not successfully stayed upright on said unicycle for a period of time that can be measured with a conventional stopwatch.

64   Prior to her earning, via multiple amazing cycling efforts, the more general moniker of "The Hammer," my wife Lisa was lovingly referred to in my blog as "The Runner." You can probably guess why.

Then the bar height. Then the bar position. As others trickled in, I noticed that nobody else adjusted anything but the saddle height. Evidently, I'm a bike fit snob. Or just a goofball.

The Runner and I started warming up: high cadence, low effort. Then I turned the little knob that controls the resistance. One half turn was all it took to go from "virtually no resistance" to "completely locked up." Which meant, basically, that I'd be giving the knob little nudges when asked to increase or decrease my effort, instead of the big manly power-twists I thought would more accurately represent the change in how hard I was working.

Adapting quickly, I began planning other methods I could use to add drama to my spin effort:

- Dramatically squirting water from my bottle into my mouth, onto my head, and down my back
- Dramatically toweling my face off
- Dramatically gritting my teeth during maximum efforts

As we warmed up, I noticed one other guy, in full Pearl Izumi PRO kit, doing the same. I looked at his legs. Hairy. I waited until he made eye contact, then flexed my freshly-shaved quads. He looked down and away, deferentially.

We both knew who was the alpha male in the room.

A BAD OMEN

The instructor came in, and it was her turn to be inspected. The first thing I noticed was...her legs.

No, not for that reason.

I noticed her legs because they were freakishly skinny. Seriously, her quads were no bigger than my calves.[65]

She climbed up on her bike and started warming up.

I observed. I cringed.

It was all I could to not go over there and volunteer to help her get her position set up properly. Her saddle height put her legs at 35 degrees... at maximum extension.[66]

And then there was the cockpit. It was so unbelievably cramped and wrong I was astonished her knees didn't hit the bar with every rotation.

---

65 Which, to be fair, are enormous and muscular.
66 My knees ached in sympathy.

To my credit — and to The Runner's relief — I refrained from going over and setting the bike up for the instructor.

I GIVE 110% (OR POSSIBLY 92%)

The room filled. The spin session began.

The instructor took us on a virtual bike ride, having us adjust the resistance for climbs, sometimes standing up, sometimes sitting down, and sometimes increasing or decreasing our cadence.

All of which is fine, and pretty much what I expected. But there were parts that were hard for me, as a cyclist, to get past.

Allow me to give some examples.

She said we were riding on a mountain road, which definitely indicates a road bike. But then, when she wanted us to just use our legs, not our upper bodies, she'd have us stand up, go to high resistance, and tell us we were riding on a "swinging bridge," which would probably be best handled on a BMX bike.

I don't know about you, but on a swinging bridge I'd definitely stay seated and would go for high cadence, low effort riding so as to keep the side-to-side motion to a minimum.[67]

From time to time, she'd let us know we were on singletrack, which made me start thinking about real singletrack, which made me wish desperately that I were not in a gym at all. In any case, now I'd need to be on a mountain bike, which made me think that this instructor needs to pick a better riding course, because it's hard to pack three different bikes with me.

Sometimes we were asked to "run" on the bike. I was baffled by this instruction until I saw a few people swinging one arm at their sides. I tried this for about one half of one second before my ridiculosity meter went so far off the chart that I had to go back to both hands on the bar.[68]

We were supposed to put our hands behind our backs and ride sometimes. I have a feeling this would be frowned upon in a group ride.

At high effort, when we were supposed to be at a 9 or 10 on a scale of 1 to 10, the instructor would be turning such an incredibly slow cadence

---

67 I was tempted to raise my hand and tell the instructor that I was having a hard time suspending my disbelief, but my wife gave me a look. I remained silent.

68 I looked down, unwilling to meet the gaze of others, hoping nobody I knew had seen me.

that she would have been a swerving mess on a real bike.[69] Curious as to what it would feel like to have that much resistance on a bike, I tried ratcheting the tension until I was going at the same cadence as the instructor.

Unfortunately, my legs are so powerful that the friction caused by the bike's braking motion briefly set the wheel on fire. Fortunately, my sweat quickly doused the flames.

Throughout the session, the instructor called out the effort she wanted us to put out. "Go to a nine," she would call out, which I would interpret as, "You should feel like barfing...but can probably hold it back." And then she'd call out, "Now go to ten!" Which I would interpret as, "This should feel like a sprint finish at the end of a race and should not be sustainable for more than one minute, tops."

And then she said, "Now go higher!"

"But I'm already at ten," I thought. "I'm maxed out." But just to see what would happen, I'd nudge the resistance up a hair.

And I was able to keep going.

So I nudged it again.

Still going.

So, evidently, my perceived maximum effort is really about my 85%. Which means I've been slacking a bit.

Okay, maybe a lot.

CATASTROPHE AVERTED

The thing about spin classes[70] is that riding technique isn't rewarded, or even encouraged. You can thrash around and pedal squares and ride with your hands behind your back, and that's just fine.

Which means that if someone ever wants to go on a ride with you and uses "I've been to spin class a lot" as their riding resume...well, you may want to keep your distance.

And so the irony is super sweet that I — a guy who rides on the road several times per week, and has done so for about two decades — very nearly caused a multiple-bike pile-up in the spin class.

---

69   I wanted to raise my hand and volunteer it would be more efficient to turn a higher cadence at a lower resistance, but had the sense that this kind of feedback was not currently being sought.

70   Or this spin class, anyway.

It was during a standing, 30-second standing sprint, I think at level 7.[71] And then I pulled my left cleat out of the pedal on the upstroke.

My knee *thunked* solidly into to my chin and I leaned heavily and wildly to the right, very nearly crashing into my wife. Had I actually crashed into her, I would have caused her spin bike to fall over into the next person, causing a domino-style crashing cascade of spin bikes and humanity.

Which would have been embarrassing.[72]

I AM STRANGELY COMPETITIVE

My wife and I didn't talk during the spin class. We did, however, have a competition...which she was likely unaware of, but which she was very excited to find out about afterward.[73]

The competition is called, "Who Sweats More?" And the rules were simple. Whoever had the larger diameter sweat puddle at the end of the spin class, wins.

She won. By a landslide. Or by the sweaty equivalent of a landslide, anyway. A tidal wave, maybe?

Before I knew it, the forty-five minutes was over. Which is odd in itself, since forty-five minutes on a bike, even at high effort, kind of feels too short.[74]

My overall impression? Spin classes might in fact be an interesting and fun way to change up your workout, and they probably burn a lot of calories in a short period of time.

And also, they really really suck.

COMMENT BY ALLAN
Spin classes are all about taking what is fun out of cycling.

---

71 I was putting in about a 7.28 effort, though, because that's the kind of guy I am.

72 But also, if caught on video, a YouTube sensation.

73 And even more excited to find out about it by means of reading it along with the rest of the world.

74 And yet, it simultaneously feels like it will never end.

COMMENT BY RABBIE

Spinning is fine, but you need to have decent equipment (e.g. more progressive resistance than just half a turn from zero to max) and an instructor that just concentrates on the basics.

After my spin class today I felt like Tom Boonen. Less to do with my all out final sprint effort, more to do with the instructor choosing 'Cocaine' as the cool down track.

HOW I GOT THE DAISY

One of the things I like best about cycling is the tradition of it. There are certain rides I do every single year: The Leadville 100, Levi's GranFondo, the Rockwell Relay, and the Ride Around White Rim in One Day (RAWROD).

The thing is, after you've done these "tradition" rides a few times, they start to blend together. And I see that entirely as a good thing: you build a cumulative memory of the event, made up of the best parts of individual rides on that course.

Kind of like how when most people think about "Christmas," they don't think about a single, specific Christmas day: they think of their Christmas mashup — their fond memories from numerous Christmas days.

That said, every once in a while, there's a particular event on one of these traditional rides that stands out. A day that you remember completely separately from all those other rides.

"How I Got the Daisy" is definitely the prime example of this fact.

I have a story to tell about riding the White Rim. It is quite a story, featuring a mylar balloon, a brutal serial killer, explosive diarrhea, and a whimsical plush novelty daisy toy affixed to my bike's handlebar.

It's a good story. And to be clear, all of the above elements feature fairly prominently into that story. And make no mistake: this story is true; it is not one of my little tricks.

To entice you into reading the story,[75] I offer the accompanying photograph of the aforementioned daisy.

However, you probably noticed that "explosive diarrhea" is one of the elements in this story, and I assure you it is not a trivial element.

Nosirree.

So, consider this fair warning. If you do not want to read a story featuring — in frank and somewhat repulsive detail — explosive diarrhea, you should skip today's post and perhaps instead watch a video I made last year while riding the White Rim Trail.[76] It's a good video, and

---

75   And to give incontrovertible proof of the veracity of my story.
76   You will find it here: http://bit.ly/fatsby08

does not mention explosive diarrhea.[77]

But it also does not contain a whimsical, smiling, plush novelty toy.

So you'll have to weigh the pros and cons yourself, then make up your own mind. I'm not going to do your thinking for you.[78]

And now: on with the story.

THE SETUP

Kenny's RAWROD ride has grown to be something larger than a group ride. It's an important annual event and a lot of people show up. Enough, in fact, that it's difficult to tell, when regrouping, when the entire group has gotten back together.

To solve this problem, Kenny had an ingenious idea: a totem of sorts, indicating who is the last person on the ride. Whoever was the last person in the group would have to wear a specially-constructed necklace, featuring a snail shell. If (and when) that person passed another person, s/he would hand the necklace off to the new slowest person.

Thus, when the person with the snail shell arrived at a regroup spot, we'd all know that the entire group was back together.

It's a clever idea, as long as you remember to bring the special snail necklace along with you to Moab.

Which brings us to Friday afternoon, the day before the big ride. I got a phone call from Kenny, as he was driving toward Moab. "I forgot to bring the snail shell necklace," Kenny said. "Can you put something together?"

"Sure," I said, though I was not sure at all. "As long as nobody minds that the 'last rider' totem will no longer be a snail shell necklace, but will instead be something I purchase at a grocery store on the way out of town."

Kenny agreed to this.

So, as my wife and I bought groceries for the next day's ride, we bought a mylar balloon, filled with helium. We figured that this, fastened to a seatpost, would be an excellent way to indicate last placemanship.

And it probably would have, too. If not for the serial murderer.

---

77 Nor any other biological emergencies.
78 Please read this story.

A CRY FOR HELP

My wife and I arrived at the campground, ate lots of bratwurst, sat around the campfire, and generally enjoyed the RAWROD Eve atmosphere. As the night darkened and people started heading off toward their tents — what with a 6:30am start and all — the two of us headed to the truck. We were going back into town to stay in a hotel.

Why a hotel instead of camping? For the following excellent reasons:

1. I don't like camping.

We started driving down the dark, quiet dirt road back toward Moab. The cloudy sky obscured the half moon, making it so we could see little or nothing except what was lit by the headlights.

It was eerily dark outside.[79]

Then, suddenly, The Runner screamed in terror, jumping and grabbing my arm.

I looked ahead, then to the sides for her source of fright.

Nothing.

Then I checked the rear view mirror...and there was a head, rising slowly and ominously from the back seat, in exactly the way Jason Voorhees would, if Jason decided to move to Moab and start mountain biking between killing sprees.

I jumped, emitting a (very manly) yelp.

Turns out it was the balloon.

It would be a while before our heart rates returned to normal.

A FAREWELL TO A SERIAL KILLER BALLOON

We continued our drive toward Moab. As would not be unexpected from a couple of people who had just eaten their respective weight in bratwurst and spicy brown mustard, we had the occasional need to fart.

Excuse me, that came out wrong. I meant to say that **I**, and I alone, had the occasional need to fart.[80]

As a courteous and loving husband, I would roll down the windows whenever this important biological function made itself known to me.[81]

At one such time, as I rolled down the windows, the balloon started

---

79 Also, sinister.

80 My wife does not fart, and if she did, her farts would no doubt smell of nothing but peppermint and cinnamon.

81 And me alone.

getting sucked outside. The Runner made a truly heroic grab and actually snagged the ribbon tied to the balloon.

The balloon, however, would not be denied. Snapping the ribbon, it shot outside.

Presumably, it is still at large, sneaking up and terrifying innocent people.[82]

I won't lie: I was grateful to see it go.

Meanwhile, we now needed to get a new "Last Rider in the Group" talisman at 10:30 on a Friday night. Luckily, the daisy you see in the photo at the beginning of this story happened to be the first thing The Runner saw as we entered the City Market in Moab.

Perfect.

A BRUSH WITH FAME

The conditions for RAWROD were really about as perfect as they could be. By 8:00am, it was pleasantly warm, but not hot, and would stay that way for the rest of the day.

My wife's son drove the first thirty miles in his truck, toting everyone's water and food. Then he wanted a turn on his bike, so the Runner and I took a turn driving; this worked out perfect; since the Runner and I would be doing the Ironman one week from that day, we weren't interested in biking the full 100 miles.

Lisa[83] drove, I relaxed, amazed at how much easier it is to ride around the White Rim in a day when you don't do any pedaling.

Then a cyclist rode by, going fast. "How's it going?" he said, as he went by.

Strangely, I knew the voice and the face.

"I'm pretty sure that Tyson Apostol from *Survivor* just went by," I told The Runner. Later, others would confirm it. So there you have it: Tyson is polite to strangers and is fast on his bike.

FORESHADOWING AT HARDSCRABBLE

Eventually, we turned the truck back over to Lisa's son, then she and I got back to riding. We both marveled at the perfection of the day, how good

---

82   And, let's face it, probably murdering them too.
83   Also known as the Runner, the Hammer, my wife, as mentioned earlier. You are keeping up, aren't you?

the trail conditions were, and how much better one feels on the final third of a mountain biking century if one skips the middle third of it.

I felt strong enough, in fact, that when we got to Hardscrabble Hill, one of the iconic climbs of the trail, I rode nearly the entire thing, only needing to put my foot down at one point.

Of course, this left me very hot and thirsty, so I refueled with an unwise number of caffeinated beverages.

"This," I thought to myself, as I polished off my third caffeinated drink, "is unwise." But my tolerance for caffeine is high and I was thirsty. I wasn't really concerned.[84]

I should have been concerned.

URGENCY BECOMES EMERGENCY

The Runner and I pedaled along at an easy pace; our objective wasn't to finish this ride fast, it was to finish it comfortably and to have fun. Thus, we were riding toward the back of the group though not at the very back.

But I was starting to feel a little bit upset in my stomach.

We stopped to pee at one of the trailside latrines. I considered taking a little bit of extra time and pooping, but it's just such a hassle when biking with bib shorts on.

So we kept going.

Within another few minutes, I was starting to not feel so great at all.

We rode through one of the very few (this year) sections of deep sand. I lost power and fell over. Normally, this wouldn't be a big deal. In fact, falling in deep soft sand is kind of awesome, because it just doesn't hurt at all.

But as I lifted my bike back to upright, I felt something shift, and I knew that I was a time bomb.

And the fuse was lit.[85]

At an optimistic guess, I would say it was a seven-minute fuse.

"Do you remember," I asked Lisa, casually, "whether there are any outhouses coming up?"

"No, we've gone by the last one," she said.

---

84 Cue ominous music.
85 Do time bombs have fuses? I confess to not being well-versed in bomb-related activities.

CHRISTMAS MIRACLE

I tried to picture a reality in which I would not be pooping within the next three minutes. But I couldn't imagine such a reality. As it turns out, it's much harder to use *The Secret*[86] when you have an urgent need to take a crap.

So I began to try to think of what materials I had on hand and to look around for a place where I could take care of business, which an excess of caffeine had made into *urgent* business.

But I could tell that what I needed to do would require toilet paper. Lots and lots of toilet paper.

"Do you have lots and lots of toilet paper?" I asked Lisa.

"No, but I do have one ActionWipe,"[87] she replied helpfully.

I squirmed. This next fifteen minutes or so, I could see, was going to be a remarkably nasty episode in my life.

I looked around, more desperately, for a place to conceal myself and dig a hole.[88]

And then, off in the distance, on the horizon: an outhouse,[89] the most beautifully well-located outhouse in the entire universe.[90]

"I'll see you in a while," I said to Lisa, as I broke into a sprint.

A LITTLE TIME ALONE

By now you have of course figured out that I was the lucky owner of the explosive diarrhea mentioned at the beginning of this story. Which means I don't need to[91] go into a lot of detail here, except to say that if the outhouse had been another fifty feet away, this story might have had a rather horrible section where I tried to cleverly describe how I managed to clean my shorts well enough to put them back on.

Instead, I get to say that I have never been so grateful for a stinky, hot, tiny room with a seat that leads to a hole in the ground.

Sadly, my business was such that it did not end quickly. Also, thanks

---

86   That book that tells you that if you think about something a lot, it happens. Sort of a universe-as-fairy-godmother philosophy. See Chapter 4 in this very book.

87   A really nice, well-made moist towelette, usually used for cleaning up after a long bike ride.

88   A large hole.

89   Cue chorus of angels.

90   Thanks and acknowledgment should go, I guess, to *The Secret*.

91   Nor (honest!) do I want to.

to the vents in the outhouse, I could hear Lisa as she talked to people as they rode by:

"Go on ahead, we're going to be here for a while."

"Fatty's got diarrhea, don't wait for us."

"Yeah, too much caffeine, he just barely made it here."

As she talked, I stood up at least three times, thinking I was done.

And, at least as many times, I quickly sat back down again. I was not done.

"Hey, are you really the last rider?" I finally heard her say. "You'd better give me that daisy."

She continued, "No, not for me. For the guy inside."

I began to contemplate: how would I know, *for sure*, when I *could* leave this toilet? It seemed like it would be never.

Finally, eventually, shakily, I stood up and felt like this time I really could step outside.

Thoughtfully, Lisa had already affixed the daisy to my handlebar for me.

AFTERWARD

As we rode, the daisy looked up at me. Smilingly, encouragingly. And I, considering the disaster that could have been, smiled back. I climbed Horsethief, feeling light as a feather, and twice as relieved. (How relieved is a feather, you ask? Easy: half as relieved as I was.)[92]

I guarantee you, had my stomach begun rumbling, I was ready to turn around and head back to that outhouse. But I made it to the finish line without needing to stop again. Last, but with my shorts unsoiled and the daisy proudly displayed.

Victory is sometimes measured in curious ways.

COMMENT BY WENDY
I'm going to leave the "White Rim" joke to someone else.

COMMENT BY DRDAVE
Very graphic mental note made. DO NOT EVER, OVER-CONSUME CAFFEINATED BEVERAGES ON A STOMACH FULL OF BRATS! Thanks.

---

92   It's simple math, really.

COMMENT BY PHILLY JEN

Wow. Gives a whole new meaning to "fresh as a daisy."

COMMENT BY RICK SUNDERLAGE (NOT MY REAL NAME)

Think how nice that daisy would have felt instead of that cheap toilet paper.

3.

Introspection and Fart Jokes

I AM AN EXTREMELY INTROSPECTIVE, DEEP-THINKING PERSON. I AM AGGRESSIVELY AND COMPETITIVELY INTROSPECTIVE, AND I AM WILLING to go toe-to-toe with any introspector out there. Just give me a topic, any topic at all, nothing is too ridiculous. I'll go full-bore introspective on it.

How much pain, on a scale of 1–10, should you assign to common injuries? **Pondered.**

How is a favorite bike trail like a lover? **Contemplated.**

Why is it nice to sometimes ride alone? **Examined at a deeply personal level.**

Boom. Yeah, that's right. I've introspectified **all** those things and more. So read on, if you're not afraid of the depth and poignancy of my deeply personal insights in this section of the book.

Come on. You're not afraid are you?[1]

---

1   Please note that there is nothing of which to actually be afraid. Unless you're afraid of absurdity.

PAIN LEVEL: FIVE

Everyone has their little secrets, things they'd prefer other people didn't know about them. I'm not talking about the big "where the body is buried" secrets. Just the little, embarrassing things about ourselves that we'd prefer, if at all possible, to keep quiet.

Mine — one of mine, anyway — is that I am very bad at handling pain. I do not handle it stoically. I do not handle it at all. When I'm hurt, my pain owns me and I thrash around on the ground, yelling and screaming.

It has its own beauty, to be certain. When I'm hurt — really hurt, like when I've popped my shoulder out of its socket (again) — I'm not self-aware, monitoring my behavior and filtering my words and actions for the occasion.

When I'm hurt, I am at my most pure, raw, and emotional. And that's pretty darned embarrassing.

All that said, it had never occurred to me to try to assign a value or some kind of stack-ranking to my pain. I either hurt not at all, pretty bad, or am in the process of being murdered.

This story is about when I visited the hospital and was asked to rank my visceral, bloody, oh-please-can't-you-see-what's-happening pain.

I hope you enjoy it.

I have many endearing qualities and one of them is that I get very excited about things most people wouldn't. Last Friday, for example, I was excited because I had bought a new cable lock for locking bikes to a hitch rack.[2]

But before I could use it, I would need to cut the zip ties that kept the cable bound into a tight coil.

Luckily for me, I am never without my Leatherman Micra. I figured that the fold-out scissors would do the job nicely.

"Wow. That is one tough zip tie," I said to myself as I held onto the coiled cable with my left hand and applied increasing pressure to the scissors blade with my right hand. "The stupid...thing...just...won't...cut!"

And then, as I put my weight into it, the zip tie cut.

Hooray!

---

2   I know: a cable lock!!!

Except, not really *"hooray,"* because, suddenly deprived of the resistance from the zip tie, my scissors shot forward, the blade coming to rest once it was buried, up to the hilt, in the flesh of my hand between my forefinger and thumb.[3]

There was a lot of blood.[4]

THE ONE THING I REMEMBER FROM BOY SCOUTS

Here's a surprising fact you probably don't know about me: I am an Eagle Scout.[5] Here's another fact you probably won't find surprising: I remember hardly anything at all from my two years as a scout (I got my Eagle as quickly as was allowed by the program so my mom would stop pestering me about it).

As blood gushed everywhere though, I did remember: *apply pressure.*

And whaddaya know, *it worked.* I brought the bleeding under control. The only problem is, this meant that both my hands were now fully occupied: one hand with being a bloody gushing mess and the other hand with being a makeshift cork.

I was outside (I have a bloody sidewalk that shows exactly where) when this happened, so now had the problem of getting inside to ask my wife to drive me to the hospital. I was absolutely certain I'd need stitches for this.

It's not easy to knock on the door when your hands are occupied as mine were. But if you're willing to kick your own door, it is totally possible to convey some urgency to your door knocking.

FRIDAY NIGHT DATE

My wife, sadly enough, had seen me bloodied up quite a few times.[6] The good thing about this is that by this time, she'd had enough experience with my clumsiness-induced injuries that she effectively and resignedly just got to work.

---

3   Sadly, this pre-dates Instagram and iPhones, so I have no photo, nor slo-mo video, to show you. I apologize.

4   And also, quite a bit of high-pitched screaming.

5   Or at least I was. Does being an Eagle Scout have an expiration date?

6   The most awful was when I tore my upper lip in half while mountain biking, or rather, while crashing after failing to mountain bike. The second most awful was when I failed to clear a curb while rollerblading fast, downhill. Yes, *rollerblading.*

First things first: she ran across the street to see if our neighbor, the EMT, was home.

Nope.

So she then went next door to see if our other neighbor, the fireman/paramedic, was home.

Nope.

While she was checking to see if there was anyone who could lend a hand (no, not literally), I lifted my right hand in order to sneak a peek at the damage on my left hand.[7]

The renewed gushing of blood started immediately, and the startling realization dawned that I have never seen the inside of me so clearly before.

You know, I don't think I've ever mentioned this, but the sight of my blood makes me very queasy. Which is to say, I nearly passed out.

With the possibilities of neighbor-supplied medical assistance exhausted, my wife drove me to the emergency room. As she did, I apologized over and over. "Sorry about this," I said, still lightheaded about being able to see so much of my blood all over the place, but also recognizing that this was the first day I'd been home in two weeks. The dinner and movie my wife had planned for the evening had turned into no dinner and a trip to the hospital.

All because I, a middle-aged man, evidently do not know how to properly handle a pair of scissors.

AN INTERESTING QUESTION

In a twisted sort of way, there's something satisfying about being a bloody mess when you walk into a hospital emergency room. You've got yourself a real emergency here. You're applying pressure. You're making a mess on the floor. You feel like it's your right to blow right by the people who look like they came here because they were feeling slightly disconsolate.

"What seems to be the problem?" asked the person whose job it must be to not pick up on obvious clues.[8]

---

7   Or, to be entirely truthful, I was looking at my hand in the hopes of discovering that it really wasn't all that bad. It was.

8   I mean, "seems" to be the problem? I distinctly remember picking up on that word and wondering why she would use it. Which means my agony hadn't reached the point where I would stop finding offense where none was meant.

"I've been cut long and deep. My left hand. I'm bleeding a lot."

So I'm escorted to what is labeled the "Triage Room." A nurse then applied a gauze bandage and wrapped it up tightly. While she did this, she asked me an interesting question:

"On a scale of one to ten, what would you say your pain level is?"

Hm. Well, that's a poser of a question.

I thought about it, then said, "Five, I guess."

After which I immediately regretted not saying, "Eleven! No, *fourteen*! **Give me morphine!**" because she said, "ok, go sit down."

And there I sat, for 45 minutes or so, while a number of people who came in after I did, sporting what looked like nothing more painful than a modest case of ennui,[9] got ushered in ahead of me to see doctors.

I'LL STICK WITH FIVE

During this 45 minutes, I had plenty of time to contemplate how embarrassing it is to have the most serious wound of your life[10] be from a self-inflicted scissors cut at the age of forty.

Eventually though, they rummaged up a doctor for me. Before he unwrapped the now quite bloody bandage, he asked me the same question:

"From one to ten, how bad does it hurt?"

I stuck with five.

He then unwrapped the bandage, and said, "Well. This...looks like more than what I'd usually expect from a *five*."[11]

He then spent several minutes cleaning me out, sending the nurse to go get a tetanus shot, talking with me about mountain biking on the White Rim, testing my fingers to see if I could feel anything, testing my thumb to see if I could move it, expressing surprise that I could because it looked like I had gone deep enough to sever some working parts, and then sewing me up.

By the time I left, I was thinking it'd be fun to ride with this doctor.

---

9   You have no idea how much it pleases me that the word "ennui" just occurred to me like that, unbidden, without the help of a thesaurus or anything.

10   Except for maybe the concussion I got from the first time I went mountain biking.

11   Which, believe me, made me feel like a complete badass. It was all I could do to not start making stories up about my incredible pain tolerance and whatnot.

WHY FIVE?

On the way home, my wife asked me why I had said this ugly cut hurt at only level five. The answer is easy. I told her I've got a pretty good basis for comparison.

Level 7: While riding the Brian Head Epic 100 one year, I crashed at mile 70, bruising my hip, separating my shoulder, and breaking off my saddle. I rode the next 25 miles of uphill without a saddle, during which time both my calves cramped up solid and my kneecap actually fell off and rolled back down the mountain.

Level 8: While riding the Leadville 100 one year, I crashed on a downhill section, completely dislocating my shoulder and getting a nice road rash. I re-socketed it on my own and then finished the race while dry heaving, completely exhausted and dehydrated.

Level 9: At 0.1 miles per hour on a technical move on Porcupine Rim, I fell on my side once, catching all my weight on my right arm. This tore my rotator cuff and started my ever-growing, internal transshoulder lesion. This is also what caused the "Elden Scream" my friends still talk about to this day.

Level 10: I watched my wife go through six months of chemo. That stuff sucks.

So the next day, the nicest day of the year so far, I didn't go on a ride. As I said, I'd been out of town and off the bike for two weeks. I couldn't put weight on the hand and for sure couldn't use the brakes.

From an emotional pain perspective, I'd put that at about a...five.

Oh, and here's my hand, 48 hours later. Looking much better, I'd say, though still very puffy.

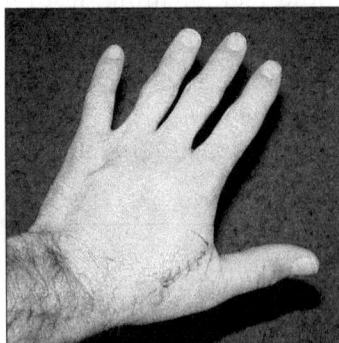

COMMENT BY SEVEN22

Level five seems appropriate. Lacerations are generally not that painful. Honestly, the amount of hair on your arm is more interesting than the wound.

COMMENT BY SEAN

I've made a couple of ER visits and they certainly expect you to be a wuss. I just go ahead and cater to that, as I sure hate to disappoint people.

COMMENT BY JON

I'm an ER nurse and I think five was about right, well maybe six or seven. I use the scale of zero being no pain while ten is being set on fire while having your testicles crushed. Get well soon and watch out for infection.

COMMENT BY THE WEAK LINK

As a physician I feel extremely qualified to clarify common usage of the Pain Scale, based on my careful observations:
10 — Having EKG electrodes ripped off someone's hairy chest.
9 — Getting a TB test (that's me, actually. I'm not sure why I hate intradermal injections so much).
8 — The blood pressure cuff inflating to about 400 psi.
7 — Getting a rectal exam.
6 — Getting the EKG electrodes applied. The gel coating on the electrode can be so frightfully cold.
5 — Getting my bill and discovering that the insurance company has retroactively denied coverage for everything.
Frankly the scale is worthless. I've seen people with a pain level of nine head outside so they can smoke. On the other hand, I once collapsed in my office because I had a gallstone attack and I rated the level as a six. I'm guessing that getting a limb amputated without anesthesia would make a ten rating.

GROUP RIDE (EXCEPT FOR THE "GROUP" PART)

I'm not sure if I've mentioned this before, but I'm extremely famous. Here, let me give you an example. Just the other day I was at a grocery store, where I paid with my debit card. Now, I had never met the lowly clerk there before, but as she rang me up, she said, "Did you find everything you need, Mr. Nelson?"

Yes, that's right. She knew my name.

I tell you, being known everywhere is crazy sometimes.

With fans clamoring to be around me day in and day out, you may be surprised to learn that I often do not ride with a large group. Indeed, you would be as likely to see me riding by myself, effectively camouflaged with helmet and glasses and a fake nose, or with a small group.

"Why," I hear you ask, "would you not go riding with your adoring throngs on a daily basis?"

Well, this story will explain.

I love going on big group road rides. And last Saturday I got in a fantastic five-hour ride with an incredible group of guys.

And you know what really made it great? I didn't go with a group.

As it turns out, a group ride of one can be exactly the right number sometimes.

START TIME AND PLACE

The original reason I had for not calling anyone or going to the bike shop for the weekly organized ride was that I had no idea what time I'd actually be available to ride on Saturday.

Amazingly, however, the start time for my solo group ride was at *exactly the same moment* I got the go-ahead to go out. 9:47, I believe. Equally wonderful was the way that every single one of us was ready to go at *the same time*. No dawdlers finishing a last-moment tuneup. No impatient Type-A's jumping down my throat for not being ready to roll right when he was.[12]

Better yet, everyone was accommodating enough to start the ride from my house. Nice!

---

12   I'm making a pointed, cutting comment to a couple of specific people here. And I can do that, because I have never kept anyone waiting. Ever. In my whole life.

THE COURSE

With most group rides, choosing the route is a difficult and complex series of negotiations. Is it long enough to challenge the hardcore riders, but with bailout points for those who need to get home earlier? Is there enough climbing? Or is half the group's idea of the right amount of climbing a little too much for the other half of the group?

My group was considerably more relaxed about the course we'd be riding. I suggested, "Hey, let's see how high we can go up on the Alpine Loop before we hit snow. Then we'll come back down and decide what we want to do from there."

You'll find this hard to believe, but everyone I was riding with thought that was a fantastic idea.[13]

THE PACE

I've got a fairly major family crisis simmering right now,[14] and one of the things I wanted to do on this group ride was push this problem out of my head for a while. As I started the climb up American Fork Canyon, it occurred to me that a really good way to do this might be to shift into a high gear, stand up, and crank away as hard as I could until my head was filled with nothing but the sound of my legs yelling at me to cut it out.

The group obliged and joined me, which was really great of them, considering that they all knew we were only twenty minutes into our five-hour group ride.

Of course, within twenty minutes I was totally blown, but everyone else in the group was too, so nobody was very bothered by the fact that I was now going at a snail's pace. In fact, we all thought it was now a good idea to shift into our granny gears and just survive the rest of the climb.

It's like the group was *reading my mind.*

---

13   And while I was, as I believe is now clear, alone, I am confident that any group of any size would have agreed that my ride plan was pure genius.

14   I am not really talking about Susan's battle with cancer in this book. That deserves, and will get, a book of its own. But yes, that was the crisis I was talking about here.

A PERFECT PLACE

Once we got past the gate that stops cars from going on the Alpine Loop road in the winter, there was a lot of gravel and scree in the middle of the road. These were easy to thread around, though I realized the traditional group race down this part of the mountain was out of the question with all this junk in the road.

Once we turned around and got back onto the part of the road that's maintained during the winter, I had an epiphany: the section of road between the Tibble Fork turnoff and the mouth of American Fork Canyon is the perfect working descent. Here's why:

- **Grade**: The road is just steep enough that you can — and should — get into your biggest gear and pedal as hard as you can. It is not so steep, however, that you will spin out in your biggest gear.
- **Twists and Turns**: The road is constantly twisting gently, just enough to keep you leaning slightly through the banks, but not enough that you ever need to touch your brakes.
- **The View**: American Fork Canyon is beautiful. Always. While you don't have time to look at the details as you descend (you had plenty of time for that during the climb), you still get this impression of a green and granite blur buzzing by your peripheral vision.

I was thinking about how much I love this descent and how much it felt like flying and what a joy it was to be on a bike when I briefly saw Dug, riding up the mountain in the other direction. For a second, I felt a little bit bad for him. Unlike me, he wasn't riding with a group, and I thought about turning around and riding up with him. By the time I completed that thought, though, I was another half mile down the road and would never have caught him if I had turned around.[15]

CONSENSUS

Coming out of American Fork Canyon, my group now had to decide where it wanted to take the ride. I suggested that we head up and over Suncrest, then ride along Wasatch Blvd. That's a ride with lots of rolling and climbing, and has been a personal favorite lately.

---

15 Later that day, Dug sent me this text message: "I saw you coming down AF canyon. You had a goofy grin on. Were you telling yourself jokes?"

Now, for the first time since the ride began, however, there was dissent in the group. "You go over Suncrest several times per week," I said. "Let's go south for a change."

"How about something simple, like a ride out to Cedar Fort and back?" I replied. I had to admit, the idea had merit. It was a nice, direct ride on a road with a wide shoulder and a consistent-but-moderate climb.

And just like that, we had come to an agreement.

What a fantastic group I was riding with.

DECISION AND REVERSAL

When riding with a group, I usually don't bring an iPod. For this ride, though, I did. The nice thing about riding with an iPod is that you can listen to it when you feel like rocking out, and turn it off when you feel like thinking.

It's almost like you have choice in the matter.[16]

As far as I know, the road out to Cedar Fort goes on forever. However, I have always turned around at one of two points: at the Cedar Fort gas station (the only store at Cedar Fort) or at Camp Lloyd, where the road loses its nice wide shoulder.

The group argued about which we should turn around at today. Finally, we decided on the gas station.

Then, however, a strange thing happened. I got to the gas station, turned around, and then changed my mind. I felt like continuing on for a few more minutes. So I turned around and continued on to where the road loses its shoulder. And you know what? Not a single person in the group complained about the way I overrode the plan like that.[17]

Although, to be honest, I think I might have heard someone grumble about how stupid we looked riding in a circle on the highway.

By now I had been out 3:15. I knew that my ride back should take about 1:15, which would give me a nice 4:30 ride.

Except I didn't account for the headwind. Or for the fact that I was pretty well cooked. So by the time I pulled into my garage, I had been out for about 4:50.

---

16   For those of you who believe that riding with headphones is wrong, please accept my apology. I will never do it again. Honest.

17   I think it's pretty obvious that I'm the alpha male in the group.

I would have got home sooner, but those bastards I was riding with would simply *not* take a turn pulling.

COMMENT BY RICK

This is exactly why I almost always go on group rides of one. Nobody else wants to get up at 4:30 in the morning to ride. To be honest, neither do I, but with an 18 month-old at home, that's the only good time to do it.

SEVEN PERFECT INSTANTS

I ride, more or less, pretty much every day. And almost every day, I love the time I'm out there. But only occasionally will I have a moment that is truly perfect.

Here, I'm going to detail a few — today, a few equals "seven" — perfect moments, perfect instants most cyclists have experienced.

But first, you've got to understand what I mean by "instant." An instant is an incredibly brief moment. So while your first springtime ride in buff, tacky alpine singletrack was almost certainly perfect, it was not a perfect instant. Perfect ride, probably. Perfect memory, certainly. But not a perfect instant.

A perfect instant is a moment that hits you suddenly and often unexpectedly. It's there and then it's over. And if you don't think about it, you may lose it.

I don't know why I'm flogging this description so shrilly. Sorry.

I'm more than happy to admit the possibility that seven is perhaps too small a number of perfect instants that can happen on a bike. In fact, the number of perfect biking instants may not even be finite. By all means, list your own in the margin of this book.[18]

Here, though, are my seven.

A PERFECT CARVE

You're flying down a nice, straight downhill, rolling at a fast-but-not-freaky 38 miles per hour. You've got to make a left turn, but you don't have to stop. You've got the right of way. You could hit the brakes, but instead you bring the inside pedal up and just lean for all you've got. Your bike tracks smoothly, Your tires grip fine, and you exit the corner as fast as, or maybe faster than, you went into it.

Tell me you aren't grinning.[19] You know why you can't tell me you aren't grinning? Because you *are* grinning, that's why.

---

18   Unless you're reading it as an e-book, in which case that's probably not a fantastic idea. I'm sure you'll come up with a good solution of your own. You're smart. I trust you.

19   Go ahead, try.

CERTAINTY OF SUCCESS

When trying a technical mountain biking move, I have had to suspend the "three tries" rule,[20] oh, krazillions of times. Friends are usually good about letting me wear myself out trying the same move, over and over and over, until I eventually give up.

But then, once in a while, everything lines up just right. Right as I get to the crux of the move, I somehow *know* I'm going to clean it. I don't know how or why I know it, but I do know it. That moment of certainty, that I'm somehow doing it right and will shortly be celebrating at the top of the move, is the very essence of a perfect instant.

DISASTER AVERTED

Have you ever brought too much speed into an exposed corner, panicked, locked up your brakes, and then, just as you were about to plummet to your certain demise, managed to ease up on the brakes just enough to get your wheels to start turning again?

You stop skidding, your wheels hook up, and you roll out of the corner, safe, with the rubber side down. The adrenaline kicks in. You are alive!

And evidently, invincible.

DISASTER CONVERTED

One moment I will never ever forget is the time I was bombing down the Powerline trail in the Leadville 100. The trail is riddled with wheel-eating erosion ruts, and I managed to drop my front wheel into one of them. Of course, the front of the bike stopped immediately, and the endo that immediately followed should have planted my face firmly into the ground.[21]

Instead, unbelievably (but believe it anyway, OK?), I managed to click out of my pedals as the bike flipped over, stepped over the handlebar, and landed on my feet, coming to a shuffle-stop. My bike slid to a stop just a foot or two behind me. I picked up my bike and, doing my best to look nonchalant to the astonished onlookers lining the trail, continued on.

---

20   This is the universal rule in mountain biking whereby any person may call a halt to the forward progress of the ride in order to retry a move at which that rider has failed. And in fact, any rider may try as many as three times, and nobody can complain about it. In this way, we become better, more technical cyclists.

21   At, if my calculations are correct, roughly twice the speed of sound.

No more than a couple seconds lost. No damage to me. No damage to my bike.

Perfect.

NEW CLEATS

You know how your mountain biking cleats, especially Eggbeaters and Time ATAC cleats, wear down over the course of the season until they're nothing more than misshapen blobs of brass? It happens so gradually that you don't even really notice the increased pedal-to-shoe sloppiness until it's pretty much too late.

But then, when you finally replace your cleats and step into your pedals the first time, it's like you've just bought a brand new bike. That solid *click* tells you you're locked in solid and ready for anything.[22]

LAST SUMMIT

Nobody's making me do tough climbs. I'm seeking them out. I'm getting what I asked for. Fine. But still, every time I reach the top of a hard climb, I experience a perfect sense of exultation. First, I'm so happy it's over. And second, I'm so happy I stuck it out. It's just about enough to bring tears to my eyes.[23]

NOT EMPTY AFTER ALL

You've been chasing someone in your group. You've been doing fine, staying right with him, but now you know it: you're completely blown.

Then, just as you're about to sag and let him go, you notice that he's dropping his pace. He's cooked, too. Realizing this, you find something in yourself. You stand up and power by him.

Turns out you've got a little bit more in you than you thought.

These moments of perfection, well, they're rare. And I'm not bothered even in the slightest on rides where I don't have even one of them.

But I sure like it when I do.

---

22   I'm leaving this in as a perfect moment because I obviously felt that way when I wrote this, long ago. Now, however, I would dispute it, saying that any perfectness experienced when clicking into pedals with new cleats is completely negated by the horror of not clicking *out* of your pedals in time, because you're not used to needing to exert so much force when twisting your heel out.

23   Except I'm far too manly to ever actually cry.

COMMENT BY BIG BONED

The moment the sun reaches above the horizon Sunday morning as you race the 24 hours of Moab solo (or any 24 hour solo). All your doubts, worries and cares evaporate in that instant and you know that you've got this one in the bag. The temperature somehow magically rises about 15 degrees in that instant too.

COMMENT BY DUG

When you're racing for the city limit sign, you're in a perfect draft behind another cyclist or three, pushing 50 mph, and at just the right moment, you come around, stand and push the pedals like you've never broken a chain at speed in your life, and you take the sprint by a half wheel.

Also the moment you stop at the gas station after a long hot mountain bike ride, and you get a 44oz Diet Coke, and take that first unbelievably satisfying sip. It's like crack.

COMMENT BY MOCOUGFAN

I did a 60-mile road ride last week, my personal longest. When I got home my wife smiled and asked how many miles I did. I told her 60. The smile changed to instant admiration and respect. My chest stretched out a bit. Definitely a cool instant.

COMMENT BY SPBARNES

This never happened to me until pretty recently...it is THE BEST. You have been climbing through varied terrain and your legs are totally spent. Down a short stretch, flat for a while, and then yet another climb. Afraid you can't possibly make it up one more. But you do. And the one after it, too. You keep getting more and more tired, but you know that it doesn't matter. The energy may get lower and lower, but there is always a little more. And always a little more than you thought there would be. It is the feeling of being an athlete, not just some clown with a machine.

COMMENT BY MEHERA

You are outside in some wild beautiful place and you have the fleeting realization that "at this moment in time, there is nowhere on the planet I would rather be!" Rare and profound.

STRANGER IN A STRANGE BIKE SHOP

Racer's Cycle Service is my favorite bike shop. I am perfectly comfortable there. Sometimes I will go there just to sit around and ask Racer questions while he works on bikes.

I'm certain that's quite a treat for him.

I've had other favorite bike shops, ones where I'm comfortable asking novice-level questions...in spite of the fact that I've been riding for just about half my life. Or where I can butt in front of all the other customers and ask for expedited service on my bike (because my cycling needs are always critical).

Racer's is, essentially, a place where I am treated like I own the place. Which makes sense considering how much I've spent there over the years.

So my question, the overarching question behind this entire story, is: is it really too much to ask for me to want to be treated this way everywhere I go?

I hate going into foreign shops. And by "foreign shops," I don't mean "shops in a foreign land." I mean "any shop besides the one where I don't have to tell them how to set up my brakes or what height to set my saddle, because they already know."[24]

I have my reasons. As you are no doubt aware, I am a famous and beloved figure in the cycling community. I am regarded as both insightful and witty. Knowledgeable and self-deprecating. Gruff yet tender. Well-known yet easily accessible.

As such, I am comfortable in practically any bike-related situation. I am happy to join a group ride even if I don't know anyone. I know I will either hang and find someone with something interesting to say or I will get dropped and turn on my iPod.

I am comfortable meeting strangers on the road and trail. After all, we're doing the exact same thing at the same place at the same time, so we must have other stuff in common.

I am comfortable giving directions to cyclists, both on the road and

---

24   Yes, Racer really does know my bike fit by heart. Or he's got it written down somewhere. In any case, I don't have to adjust anything after having him build a bike for me. The grips are cut down how I like them, the brakes are at the right angle, the seat is where it should be.

off, although I am usually quite certain that my directions are wrong.[25] I figure that even though I am probably giving people directions to a place other than where they want to go, once they arrive at the place to which I have directed them, they will be glad of the journey. Plus, there's relatively little chance I'll run into them ever again.

I am not, however, comfortable going into a bike shop where nobody knows who I am.

ESTABLISHING CREDIBILITY WITHOUT COMING OFF AS A VAIN, BORING TURD

When I walk into a bike shop, I don't really need much. I just want to be revered as the famous and beloved cycling personality that I am. Would it be too much, for example, for the senior staff to drop whatever they're doing, including helping other customers, and come attend to my needs? (That question was rhetorical. You shouldn't feel compelled to answer it.)

Also, a comfy chair and a backrub while I wait for my bike would be nice. And I wouldn't mind it if someone would come up and revere me a little bit. You know, ask for an autograph, beg me to tell some of my favorite biking stories, that kind of thing.

Instead, for some reason, I think I give off a strange "I don't know anything at all about bikes" vibe to bike shop employees. Maybe it's my gut. Maybe it's the Dockers. Maybe it's the male pattern baldness (yes, I shave my head, but you can still tell I have male pattern baldness). But they always act like I don't know anything about bikes.

When I moved to Washington a few years back, for example, there was a bike shop about a mile away from my home. I came in, figuring this was destined to be my home away from home.

Instead, when I said I wanted some advice on a good lube for riding in Washington, they gave me a look that was specially designed to make me feel like I was an idiot.

Of course, I wanted to explain that I actually know quite a bit about bikes. That I've been riding for years and years and years. I am not just a guy who casually and occasionally rides, either. I ride all the time. I

---

25   This is, sadly, not even close to a joke. I have given horribly misleading directions several times. I don't mean to. I'm just really bad at giving directions. See "Mr. Helpful Directions Person," p.313.

talk about bikes all the time. I'm the guy in the neighborhood everyone asks their bike questions to. I'm bike shops' favorite kind of customer.

And I would have liked to explain this to them. But I just couldn't find an opening. For some reason, it's not easy to go into a bike shop and announce, "Hi, I'm a really experienced cyclist, so please accept me into the pack. You may, in fact, want to treat me as the alpha male."

So I'm working on a couple introductions to make it clear that I'm really into cycling the next time I go into a strange bike shop. Tell me what you think:

- **The Casually Hardcore Opening**: "Hi, how's it going?" (Wait for response.) "Oh, good. Hey, I was thinking of doing an easy century today, and wanted to know if you had any route suggestions." (Wait for response.) "Oh, I'm sorry, I wasn't clear. I meant an easy *mountain bike century*. You know, something with no more than 14,000 feet of climbing."
- **The Know-it-All Opening**: "Hey, how's it going?" (wait for response, but don't appear to pay attention.) "I see, without needing to walk around or glance at any of the price tags, that most of your bikes here are in the $400 to $1200 range. Is that what your customers tend to want? (Don't wait for a response.) Where do they go to get their *second* bike, when they fall in love with riding and want something nicer than what you've got here?
- **The Put-Them-on-the-Defensive Opening**: "Hey, this is a cute shop. You got anyone here who isn't just doing this as his summer job?"

Some of these are still a work in progress.

FREQUENT BUYER DISCOUNT, OR LACK THEREOF

When I go into my local bike shop (LBS), I know that I'm going to get the best deal possible. Better than the best deal possible, even. If that's possible.[26]

Anyway.

Here, nearly word-for-word, is the conversation I had with Racer when it was time to settle up and pay for my new Lemond Fillmore.[27]

---

26   Which, when I think about it, is *not* possible.

27   A very inexpensive single speed steel road bike. One of very few bikes I look back at with nostalgia. The other two are my first real mountain bike (a Specialized Stumpjumper) and my Ibis Ti Mojo, which was a work of titanium art.

I'm not saying what the actual numbers were, because I have a feeling Racer's wife would not approve.

Racer: "That will be $xxx."

Me: "What?"

Racer: "OK, I'll drop it by $50."

Me: "That's not what I meant. I don't mind if you make a little bit of profit when you sell me a bike, Racer."

Racer: "Whatever."

Me: "Charge me $100 above that price. That's the lowest I'd feel good about paying."

Racer: "I'll add $25."

Me: "$75."

Racer: "I'll add $50, but that's my final offer."

Me: "This has been a very weird transaction."

I don't expect this kind of discount from anywhere but my local bike shop, but I'm pretty sure that non-local bike shops (NLBS) make up for the discounts they give to their friends by overcharging interloper customers.

Last week, I'm pretty sure I paid $72 for a tube, for example.

I FEEL OLD

I realize that bike shops tend to hire younger people. They work for cheap and they don't have to feed a family. But I swear that when I go into most bike shops, they are staffed by teenagers *exclusively*. Looking for a light setup for the Kokopelli Trail Race last year, I went into a shop near where I work and — I swear I am not making this up — the kid in the shop tried to get me to buy a couple of commuter lights.[28]

He simply didn't have a point of reference for any kind of riding that didn't involve mad skillz on the halfpipe while wearing Vans and a BMX helmet.

I realize that I am 41.[29] But please, bike shop owners who have never met me, have the courtesy to do the following:

---

28   I still look back on this moment from time to time, and have never puzzled out to my satisfaction whether he didn't understand what night riding is, or whether he thought I don't.

29   Did I really write this post seven years ago? I must have, because now I'm 48. Weird.

- Have someone at the shop who is older than 20. Otherwise, I feel like I've somehow managed to stumble upon a boy scout troop.
- Forbid all your employees from ever calling anyone "sir." I don't know anyone who likes to be called "sir." I understand the military is considering no longer using the word "sir."
- Tell your employees that not everyone over 40 will necessarily want a hybrid, cruiser, or recumbent.

THE SOLUTION

Of course, I wouldn't gripe and gripe and gripe if I didn't have a solution. What I'd like to propose is a universal LBS members card. This is not something you could apply for, but when an LBS owner/manager feels you have become a truly loyal customer, she or he could issue you this card in a super-secret ceremony involving things like taking oaths, reciting slogans, and swearing to obey the law of the pack.[30]

Then, whenever you're at an NLBS, you could just show your card, therefore avoiding the posturing and hint-dropping. The card, in effect, would say, "This guy rides. Treat him/her like one of your own." And then the NLBS employees could relax, joke around with you, call you by your first name, and give you the good buddy discount.

Oh, also, there would be a super-secret-bonus version of the card that tells the NLBS that the carrier is a much-beloved cycling celebrity, and that, as such, a comfy chair and backrub may be in order.

COMMENT BY HELLKITTY

Try going into the LBS being a female. They NEVER take you seriously, no matter what.

COMMENT BY DUG

I think I see your problem. You should never under any circumstances go into anything other than your LBS. It's very much like infidelity.

---

30   That's a cub scout reference, for those of you who have never had the pleasure of having to memorize Cub Scout oaths, mottoes, laws, and whatnot.

COMMENT BY AXEL

My technique is to start the shopping by asking for spokes. Spokes are perfect in that they are not expensive, they indicate that you take your bike seriously and they are not available on a rack in the middle of the store, but back in the shop. Anyone who confidently orders three 235mm spokes will immediately be recognized as a serious rider and treated with the proper respect for the price of less than $2. If you are not in the mood to get more spokes, turn down the ones they have as 'low quality' and proceed with the rest of your shopping....

PHASES OF A RELATIONSHIP

Yeah, I like riding my bike. But it's not like I'm weird about it. Well, yes, I did pick the house I live in because of its proximity to mountain and road bike rides I love. And I did marry my wife near the trailhead of one of our favorite mountain bike rides.

And I have not gone more than two or three days without riding a bicycle in more than twenty years.

And sometimes I give my bikes names. And sometimes I talk to them. And sometimes when I can't go on a ride right at that moment, I go in the garage and stare at them.

And when I've thought I had one of my bikes stolen, I felt like I was stabbed in the stomach. A very real, personal loss, going way beyond how other types of property theft feels.

So, what I guess I'm saying is: yeah okay, maybe there is something weird about me and bikes and riding.

In fact, upon going back and reading this story I wrote a few years ago, maybe it's time I seek help.

One of the most gratifying experiences human beings can have in a lifetime is a deep, abiding relationship. You never know when such a relationship might begin, and it's not always easy to tell whether you've come across a relationship that's got enough staying power to last a lifetime, or merely a few days.

Once found though, there's no denying it's worth it. As the two of you learn more about each other, discovering depth and quirks you would never have suspected when you first met, you can't help but say to yourself, "this is what gives my life joy and meaning. This relationship, truly, is sublime."

I am talking about, of course, the relationship between a cyclist and a mountain bike trail.

FIRST DATE

Does the relationship between trail and rider spring to life fully formed? Do you know every waterbar, every spur, every ledge drop the first time you ride a trail?

No, of course you don't. You wouldn't want to even if you could, because that would take away the joy of early courtship, the rapturous early days of mutual discovery.

And that would be sad indeed.[31]

So when you first hear about a trail, take it slow. Don't just rush to the top of the trail in a car and bomb down it. Shuttling a trail is like introducing yourself to a beautiful woman by grabbing her butt. Sure, it's been done — all too often, really — but you can bet that the trail will not respect you for it.

No, instead find out about the trail. Ask friends what it's like, what its best qualities are. What days are best to ride it? What you should wear, baggies or lycra? Should you bring bottles, or is a Camelbak in order? Should you be riding full suspension, front suspension, or does this trail prefer the old-fashioned rigid singlespeed?

Remember, this is your only chance to make a first impression with the trail, so make it a good one.

Next, introduce yourself to the trail by riding the whole thing. Do the uphill first. Acknowledge the trail's fine characteristics, but don't be too effusive. Excessive flattery sounds false, and the trail can tell the difference between honest appreciation and a tacky come-on.

SECOND DATE

Oh, the heady moments after the first ride on a new mountain bike trail! In your euphoria, you will want to tell all your friends about it: it's clever switchbacks, its teasing false summits, its rambunctiously fast and daring descent.

Can you sleep the night after such a ride? No! All you can think about is riding that trail again, if only it will have you. Sleep is kilometers — nay, *miles!* — away.

"Please, please, please," you pray to St. Eddy,[32] who watches over cyclists. "Let that trail like me as much as I like it."

And then, at last, the moment of the second ride arrives. Sometimes this second ride reveals flaws you didn't notice in the rush of the first ride. Perhaps the trail is usually crowded and you were just lucky the

---

31 I'm being very understated here.
32 Yes, I know that Madonna del Ghisallo is supposed to be the patron saint of cyclists. To which I respond, "St. Eddy is funnier."

first time you rode it. Perhaps it is not as technically challenging as you remember from your first ride. Maybe it's one of those master-it-and-move-on trails.

Perhaps it turns out that the trail is infested with mosquitoes, ticks, and angry, mutant wolverines, some of which appear rabid.[33]

Hey, it happens.

More often, though, the second ride is your opportunity to notice exquisite, charming details you didn't notice during the first ride, because you were taking in the big picture. "This trail has three distinct kinds of terrain!" you might find yourself exclaiming excitedly. "All in one ride! How is that even possible?"

"And here is a spur that takes me on a quick downhill jaunt over roots and ledges, and through four switchbacks, before rejoining the main trail. I can't decide which way is better, they're both so good!"[34]

You may find your emotions welling up, getting the best of you. In which case: pull yourself together, man. Trails don't like people who can't control themselves.

At the end of the ride, if you find yourself astounded to note that you somehow — impossible as you would have thought it just one day ago — like this trail *even better* now, well, you're on the way to a long-term relationship.

GOING STEADY

Before long, you find yourself telling all and sundry that this trail is the best trail in the world. You can't help yourself. And when it's time to ride, you don't even think about where to go ride. It's a foregone conclusion. Why would you ride anywhere else?

The more you ride this trail, the better you get to know it. Now totally comfortable with the main features of the ride, you begin to explore different lines. Maybe try blasting up a difficult pitch in a harder gear or perhaps seeing if you can ride the entire trail without ever putting your foot down.

You begin to notice even subtle things about the trail. You can tell the difference between how it rides in summer and autumn. You come up with names for certain moves on the trail, little in-jokes that have

---

33 Because angry mutant wolverines that *aren't* rabid isn't bad enough.
34 I am, of course, describing actual experiences I have had with actual trails here.

meaning only you and the trail would ever understand.[35]

Eventually, you stop calling the trail by its proper name. In your head, at least, it's "my trail."

OL' BALL AND CHAIN

Then, one day after riding your trail, you realize: you just did the entire ride without noticing a single thing. Your mind was elsewhere the entire time.[36]

And don't think the trail couldn't tell, Buster.

Soon, you're wondering if maybe you've outgrown this trail, if maybe you've seen all it has to offer.

And then, one day, a riding buddy tells you about a trail that's just been cut. It's still a little rough and the line's definitely evolving, but it has real potential.

You go ride it, you know, just to see what's out there. Suddenly you're no longer interested in "your trail." All you can think about is this latest piece of singletrack. You don't even feel guilty, because hey, it's just a trail, right?

You heartless bastard.

REUNITED

Months go by, during which you rarely, if ever, ride your trail. You make feeble excuses for not riding what used to be your favorite trail. "It's out of my way." "It's winter and it's covered with three feet of snow." Oh, sure, from time to time you run into each other and you half-heartedly promise yourself you're going to go riding there sometime really soon.

But you never do, do you?

Until one day. For some reason, you wake up with your old favorite trail fresh in your mind. You've been dreaming about it. Your dream has brought it all back to you: the intensity of the climb, the rush of the descent, the joy of a perfectly realized series of switchbacks.

How could you have been *such a fool?*

---

35 "Blair Witch." "The Crux." "Endless." "Bob's Bane."

36 I'd like to make the case here that this isn't necessarily a bad thing. It's only while riding a trail you're truly comfortable with that you can think, let your mind wander, and introspect a little bit. A trail that truly understands you knows that this doesn't mean you don't appreciate it. It just means that you trust it enough to let it take care of you for a little while.

You rush back to your trail, for you now realize that this is truly the best trail in the world. You ride it again.

And it's just as you remember. It's like you've never been apart. It's perfect.

But some day, some day *soon*, as you're bombing the descent and a heretofore unseen exposed root end expertly threads your front wheel's spokes and brings the wheel to an immediate halt, launching you up and over as if your bike were a trebuchet, propelling your body twenty feet toward a welcoming boulder field, you will finally understand the gravity of your sin.[37]

Sure, the trail was willing to take you back. But you were a fool to think you had been forgiven.[38]

> COMMENT BY TRAVIS
>
> Alas, my favourite trail is in another country, and it will be some months before I can ride her again.

> COMMENT BY MYTZPYK
>
> For a minute I thought I was going to need a cigarette.

> COMMENT BY ERIC D
>
> I heard that people in Utah sometimes have multiple trail relationships. Is that true?

> COMMENT BY KEITH
>
> I'm getting a little worried: I reach satisfaction/exhaustion long before my trail does. Do you think my trail might be looking for a stronger, more experienced rider?

> COMMENT BY LEROY
>
> But how do you explain a road rash you didn't pick up on your trail? I don't need the explanation. It's for a friend.
> Really. Why are you looking at me like that?

---

37   Once again, based upon real events.

38   When I originally wrote this, I wondered if I had ended this piece on too harsh a note. Now, years later, I know for *sure* I ended it on too harsh a note.

UNCHAINED

Take a moment to consider the bike chain. Picture it in your head. Got it? OK, now picture how it works. Holes in the chain, meshing with the teeth in the cog, pulling the wheel around.

Whenever you're pedaling, every single one of those tiny little parts is in motion. Moving, bending to a greater or lesser degree, while supporting and propelling all of your weight and momentum.

It's too much for me. I can't hold it in my head. I can't believe chains don't break all the time.

Which brings us to this story...

I don't like to think about my bike chain. It's just too unsettling. While the rest of my bike is made of big, solid pieces (except my spokes, which I also don't like to think about), the chain, the part of the bike that is responsible for transferring all the power from my (massive and well-defined) quads to the dirt, is made of plenty-six thousand teeny tiny pieces.[39] You've got the figure-8 pieces, the cylinders that go between, and a teeny tiny pin, thinner in diameter than a human hair, that holds each link together.

When you consider the near-infinite number of moving parts in a given bike chain (plenty-six thousand, as I've already made clear), it's not surprising that this is the part of the bike that requires the most maintenance and is the second-most-likely part of your bike to fail.

What's surprising, really, is that the bike chain works at all. Ever.

Oh, and since I know you're going to ask: the part of the bike that is most likely to fail is the tire. Which is not much of a surprise when you consider that a bike tire is a piece of soft, easily punctured rubber containing pressurized air that constantly rolls over sharp rocks, broken glass, porcupine quills, and razor blades.

Seriously, it's amazing we ever get out of the driveway on these things.

Anyway, back to chains.

---

39   I just Googled "how many individual pieces in a bike chain" so I could impress you with actual research I have conducted while working on this book. The answer wasn't immediately obvious in the first page of results, however, so I lost interest and wrote this footnote instead.

CHAINS ARE EVIL

By and large, I am able to successfully avoid thinking about the physics of the bike chain.[40] I just pedal and the bike goes forward. End of story.

I think the chain resents this taken-for-granted status. So, from time to time, the chain will break.

Here's the thing about the way chains break, though: they never do it at a good time. They never break while you're coasting downhill or riding along, seated, on the flats.

No.

Chains always break while you are climbing,[41] cranking uphill and straining as hard as you possibly can. And you are standing. With your face over the front wheel, chest over the stem, and crotch over the top tube.[42]

That is when the chain decides it's had enough.

With an audible "ping,"[43] one of the pins lets go. At which point all of the following happen simultaneously:

- Your chest gets core-sampled by your bike stem
- You get crotch-filleted by your top tube
- One of your knees crashes into stem or handlebar
- One of your calves gets gored by your pedals
- Your face gets a tire burn
- Your chain gets sucked into your drivetrain

Oh, and if you happen to be lucky enough to stay on your bike when this happens, it will be because the bike has sensed you are on a 40% incline or are in the middle of a ledge move, and now have no way to go forward. At which point, gravity is more than happy to show that it's not such a "weak force" after all.

---

40 And don't even get me started on trying to picture how the rear derailleur works. You pull or release a cable, and a bunch of pulleys and springs move up and down and sideways all at the same time, somehow keeping the chain tensioned and aligned. It makes me queasy, just trying to picture it. I think I need to go lie down.

41 Most likely in a tricky, technical move or in an all-out bunch sprint for a summit finish line.

42 What could possibly go wrong?

43 A sound I now associate with horrible pain.

CHAINS ARE PSYCHIC

Do you want to know the very best way to ensure your chain will never break? No, it's not to clean and lube your chain at regular intervals. No, it's not to replace the chain before it stretches beyond a certain point.

The best way to ensure your chain won't break is to carry a chain tool and an extra link or two when you ride.

I have never, in my whole riding career, ever had a chain break when I was carrying the stuff I needed to repair a chain.[44] I have, however, had chains break seven times (that I can remember) when I wasn't carrying a tool.

The only possible cause? Chains are psychic, in addition to evil.

For those of you getting ready to comment with stories about how you've had chains break while you were carrying a tool, I have the following to say: they do this to maintain plausible deniability. Have you never watched *X-Files*? Sheesh.

CHAINS ARE A PSYCHOLOGICAL MESS

Answer this set of questions, if you please:
- Which part of your bike requires the most frequent maintenance (cleaning, lubing)?
- Which part of your bike is most likely to damage another part of the bike (e.g., score your chainstay)?
- What is the part of your bike is never regarded as beautiful or elegant?

The answer to all three questions is, of course, the chain. And it knows it. I think the chain has an inferiority complex (it's ugly and gets dirty), compounded with a superiority complex (it knows it's the part that makes the bike go), compounded with good old-fashioned insecurity (it's always demanding more attention, and complains loudly and incessantly if you don't give it that attention).

And they leave an embarrassing mark on your calves.

---

44   Seven years later, this remains true. In the seven years since I originally wrote this, however, I have had chains break exactly zero times. Chains have gotten really, really good.

COMMENT BY DUG

Two weeks before LOTOJA last year, Sunderlage and I were doing some final training rides up AF canyon, and, like always, we were sprinting the final quarter mile to the summit. Just as we got up to speed, my chain snapped, and everything on your list happened, and then some. After I ran through the six options on your list, I started a new list and flipped over the bars and down onto the pavement, cracking my helmet in two, grinding my right elbow and hip and knee, and breaking two ribs. At least you can coast down from there, 11 miles and 3000 feet.

COMMENT BY AL MAVIVA

Look on the positive side of breaking a chain. Even though it fileted your crotch and left your teeth scattered on the trail, a busted chain is still really handy if you happen to get in a fight with The Hell's Angels on your way back to the trailhead.

COMMENT BY EL ANIMAL

You know what Fatty? I love chains. Chains are mechanical marvels that were invented a lot of time ago, and still we have not found another thing to replace them. Chains are strong enough to transmit power in an efficient, flexible, and very light way. Chains (not the wheels, not the frame, not the tiny saddles) are the workhorse of a bike. There are not evil chains, there are only poorly maintained bikes.

COMMENT BY CHARLIE BROWN

I've had exactly one chain break in all my years of riding. Of course it was at an absolutely fantastic time—about a quarter way up the Powerline Climb at Leadville the year before last, right in the middle of a downpour. I did have a spare quicklink, but in my dazed and confused condition, I threaded the chain perfectly through the rear derailleur, hooked up the quicklink, only to find out that I missed the front derailleur. Did you know quicklinks are not quick to unlink when coated with grit and it's cold and rainy and you're seeing spots?

WHY I CLIMB

If I were good at going downhill really really fast, this story would be called, "Why I Descend."

But I don't descend well. I descend cautiously, at best. Comically badly, at worst. I think this is because I am just too good at picturing what could go wrong as I descend. And when I descend, since my brain isn't occupied with trying to force my body to do something it would rather not be doing, I have plenty of time to vividly picture everything that could go wrong.

I could hit an oil patch. A deer could jump out at me. My front tire could burst into flames.

When I'm climbing, on the other hand, my mind is perfectly and fully occupied with one single image: the summit.

Having your mind so focused is both rare and beautiful and, quite possibly, addictive.

As such, over the years, I've gotten good at climbing.

Once in a while, you'll have a day where things are so busy that you have no realistic expectation of getting in a ride. You've just got too much to do. Optional stuff[45] is going to have to wait for another day.

And then, almost by magic, a "ride window" appears. An appointment falls through. You finish the errands before you expected to. Your spouse takes pity on you. Whatever. The important thing is, you've got maybe 70 minutes. Not enough time for a *long* ride, but certainly enough time for a *good* ride.

The question is, what kind of ride should you do?

The answer, for me, is obvious and easy: *climb*. And with the amount of time I have, I climb the nearest major climb: Suncrest. I then drop down the other side, turn around, and come back.

Two four-mile, 1500' climbs. Takes just over an hour, if I really push hard. Which I do.

---

45   Also known as "stuff you enjoy doing."

OBVIOUS?

I say the decision to do a climbing ride was obvious and easy, and I mean it. I just love climbing rides. So far, this week, my rides[46] have been:

- **Monday**: Up AF Canyon to Alpine Loop Summit, down to Cascade Springs, and then back again: about 6500' of climbing
- **Tuesday**: Up the South side of Suncrest, down the North side, and then back again: about 3000' of climbing
- **Wednesday**: Repeat of Monday
- **Thursday**: Up AF Canyon to Alpine Loop Summit and back again: about 3500' of climbing

Nobody's forcing me to select these rides and I'm not doing them because I'm training for a race.

I just like to climb.

But, and I get this question pretty often from friends and neighbors, why do I choose these routes, when I don't have to?

That question isn't as easy to answer.

WHY DO I CLIMB?

As I was climbing up the north side of Suncrest, I was pondering that question. "Why am I climbing? Why do I seek this out?"

Because, climbing seems like a good idea except when you're actually doing it. This is the grand paradox of climbing.

Another rider turned onto the road, about 75 yards ahead of me. He looked strong. Good legs, nice bike. A worthy opponent.

"Hewwo wabbit," I said, in my best Elmer Fudd voice. You know, because Elmer chases Bugs Bunny. And because he's bald. And short.[47]

I stepped up my pace, the pain easier to endure now that I had a more exciting objective than merely to survive the climb.

I had prey. A carrot. A rabbit.

By the time I was 50 yards behind him, the guy I was trying to catch had seen me. He knew what was going on. He stood up and picked up his pace.

Ha. He had sacrificed any legitimate claim to not caring whether I caught him. He cared, all right.

---

46   These are all road rides, because at time of writing, my right shoulder was injured.
47   Look, let's just say I identify with Elmer Fudd and leave it at that, OK?

In fact, he cared *deeply*.

Each time he looked back and saw I was closing the gap, he'd stand and put on a burst of speed. A foolish tactic. Bursts like that cost more than they're worth. Ullrich-like, I remained seated, staying in second gear. I knew that, to him, it would look like I'm going slow because my cadence is low.

I also knew that he wouldn't get a look at my tell-tale quads until it was too late.[48]

HEY, HOW'S IT GOING?

Eventually, inevitably, inexorably, I caught him. And by law,[49] that meant we were required to exchange pleasantries.

I went first.

"Harsh climb, isn't it?" The subtext, of course, being that while the climb was indeed harsh, I handled this harshness with greater alacrity.[50]

"Yeah," he replied. "And it's just too hot to climb well." A lame excuse, because we were both cycling in the same climate.

"Have a good ride," I concluded, pulling in front of him. And then, ten seconds later, looking back to see if he had cracked.

He had.

My victory was complete.

MY ANSWER

"This," I thought to myself. "*This* is why I climb." Because it's the closest thing I've got to a superpower. And by "superpower," I don't mean some lame freebie superpower you get because you were born near a red sun or bitten by a spider, for crying out loud.

"Acquired by lottery" superpowers suck.

I have the kind of superpower Batman has. And don't believe for a second Batman doesn't have superpowers. He has tons of superpowers. It's just that he's earned them all.[51]

---

48   I am truly insufferably vain about my legs. In my defense, I say that since these legs are my only attractive feature, I get to talk them up whenever I want.

49   The law of the JUNGLE.

50   And aplomb.

51   I am fully aware that Batman doesn't exist in our universe, but I'm making a point here.

I climb because I can roll up beside someone on a bike, and unless climbing is also *his* superpower, I can surprise him.

Eventually, it all comes down to this: I climb because I can.

COMMENT BY MARK

Fatty, if it were me you were chasing, I would let you catch me, then try and hang on, only to surprise you at the end. That way, when you did inevitably pass me, it would have been obvious I was not trying to prevent it, thus diminishing your satisfaction with the feat. Moreover, on the off chance that I did hang and pass you at the end, you'd have had that to live with, without first having had the satisfaction of beating me when I was trying. That is how we non-climbers deal with the smugness of you climbing types.

COMMENT BY LEROY

My beard grows in white.

You want to demoralize someone on a climb? Pass them while sporting a white beard. And if they pass you... well, hey, way to go, racing an old guy.

COMMENT BY TERI

I climb because Rainier and St. Helens are right in my own backyard. I climb for the jaw-droppingly gorgeous views, the sound of snow-melt streams, the fragrance of newly-opened wildflowers, the thrill of smooth, black-ribbon winding descents, the chill of tall snow banks that I glide past in the heat of a summer day. I climb because I'm a middle-aged woman with a fast bike and most people think I shouldn't...it's not proper, you know. I climb to show them I can, I will, and I do.

COMMENT BY BIKEMIKE

So, are you Batman or Elmer Fudd? I know there's a fine line but I'm confused.

THE SLOW GUY

You know what the problem is with tying your identity to being a really fast cyclist? It's when you stop being a really fast cyclist. And go back to being a fat cyclist.

Is it grounds for an identity crisis?

You bet it is.

I haven't been on my bike much, lately. And by "much," I of course mean "hardly at all." And by "hardly at all," I actually mean "twice this month."[52]

I have my reasons. Good reasons. Convincing reasons. Reasons so excellent-sounding that you will want to use them yourself the next time you find yourself with no will to ride. In fact, my reasons are so good that they are very nearly true.

I will detail these reasons at a later date, and will license their use for a reasonable fee.[53]

Right now, though, I don't want to talk about the fact that I have not been riding much (at all). I want to talk about what has happened on the couple of times I have been riding recently.

But first I want to take a little walk down memory lane.

HOW I DECIDED I WANTED TO BE A FAST GUY

My friend Dug was the person most responsible for getting me into mountain biking. He was, so to speak, my shepherd.

Nowadays, Dug is a mellow rider. He rides for fun, and for no other reason. He spurns racing, or when he does race, he races with irony. This makes him a fantastic shepherd for new riders.

Long ago, however, back when I was learning to ride, Dug was a different kind of shepherd. At the time, he was into racing, and so he and his fast friends would regularly drop me, making me the guy everyone had to wait for at the top of the climb.[54]

---

52 I know, I say elsewhere in this book that I haven't missed more than a couple days of riding in twenty years. It's possible I was exaggerating.

53 Several years after writing this story, I have still not enumerated these reasons. This may be because whenever I try, these very good reasons start reading a lot like excuses.

54 And the bottom of the descent. And at major junctions. And, in short, everywhere.

And so I had to put up with the reality of riding up to the group at these regroup points and seeing them in various stages of relaxation: some straddling their bikes, some sitting on their top tubes, some laying on the ground, feigning sleep.[55]

As I rode up during one of these regroups, Dug once derisively said (and I remember this clearly, because it scarred me for life), "Did you have a flat back there or something?"[56]

At that moment I decided that I would become a faster rider than Dug.

And I did, too. It took about three years, but I'm really, really good at holding a grudge. Oh, and also by then Dug had stopped caring about racing. Coincidentally.

So anyway, that's how I decided to become a fast guy: spite.

It occurs to me that I need to come up with a better "origin" story for myself. Something noble, with a really cool training montage. And maybe a car chase.

IT DOESN'T TAKE LONG TO BECOME THE SLOW GUY

It took about three years for me to go from being the slowest guy in the group to being one of the fastest (I never got even close to being as fast as Brad and Kenny, but I never expected to, either).

It seems singularly unfair, then, that it has taken me only two months to become, once again, the slow guy.

"Oh, Fatty," I hear you saying. "You're exaggerating; you haven't *really* become the slow guy in just a couple months. Have you?"

"Yes," I answer, my head hung with shame. "Yes, I have." And I don't mean that I am *one* of the slow guys. I mean that I am verifiably, literally, *the slowest* guy in the group. And I don't mean that I'm just riding at the back of the pack.

No.

I mean that I am off the back and out of sight. The slow group tries to ride extra slow to let me stay with them, but they can't go that slow.

In truth, people marvel that, so slow is my speed, I am able to remain upright.

---

55   At least, I hope they were feigning. I never asked.
56   No. No, I had not had a flat.

RUMINATIONS OF THE SLOW GUY

Here is the example that is seared in my mind. I was riding with a large group — about fifteen of us — last weekend. As we began the first climb, a couple people were behind me. And by "behind me," I mean right behind me, and fighting the impulse to yell "onyerleff!" and ride by. So I did the right thing: I pulled over, mumbling something about needing to adjust my derailleur and catching up in a few minutes.

And then I was alone.

Utterly alone.

QUESTIONS TO MYSELF

As I slowly (oh so slowly) rode up the trail, turning the granny gear on a climb I have done countless times on my singlespeed, I contemplated the fact that I am, indisputably, the slow guy in the group again. I asked myself deep, meaningful questions about being slow. Obligingly, I also answered these questions. Here's how the interview went.

Q: How do I know I am slow?

A: Well, my perceived exertion is just as great, maybe greater, than ever. I don't feel like I am moving a lot slower. And yet, people I have always been faster than are now way ahead of me and they aren't working hard. So unless everyone is pulling an elaborate hoax on me by having trained incredibly hard and taking EPO for the past couple months without telling me,[57] I am definitely slow.

Q: Is it bad to be slow?

A: No, of course it isn't. The only speed that is bad on a bicycle is the speed at which you are not enjoying yourself. If you enjoy riding your bicycle slow, then it's good to be slow.

Q: Do I enjoy being slow?

A: No. Decidedly not.

Q: How is it possible I got so slow so fast?

A: I don't want to talk about it.

Q: OK. But it hardly seems fair that it takes so much work for so long to get fast, and it takes no work whatsoever for a remarkably short period of time to get slow.

A: Tell me about it.

---

57   That would be a pretty weird joke.

THE DREADED REGROUP

As (ever so eventually) I approached the top of Clarks, I had to consider the probability that everyone would be waiting for me there. They would be in various states of repose: some snacking, some chatting, some napping.

No doubt they would expect me to explain myself when I reached them. I considered several things I could say:

- "It's opposite day! I win."
- "When I write about this in my blog, I'm going to leave this part out, OK? I've got $5 for everyone who promises not to leave a correcting comment."
- "I'd have gotten here sooner, but I had to swap out my bottom bracket about halfway up the trail. Oh, and I discovered a hiker in shock with a broken leg; it was a compound fracture. It took a few minutes for me to set the leg correctly and form a good hard cast using nothing but the materials around me."
- "I hate all of you." (Sometimes the best offense is to be really offensive.)

In the end, though, I chose none of these. Instead, when I rolled up to the group I said, "Man, I am so *fast!*"

Stunned by my audacity and confounded by the contradiction of my assertion to their direct observations, they said nothing.

COMMENT BY DUG
So seriously, did you get a flat?

COMMENT BY 29ER
You have to admit, your friends are faster than most people's friends. "Slow riding is better than no riding." I'm going to be chanting that from now until probably May.

COMFORT RIDES

I love it when someone takes me out on a new ride. It can be a mountain bike ride or a road ride. It can be close to home or out of state. Adding a new place to be on my bike is always great.

That said, I think there's a good reason why, 95%[58] of my rides are on the same trails and roads I've ridden and known for years.

The fact is, the more I know a route, the more I love it.

Why? Well, the first reason is because the better I know a route, the better I am at riding it. I have a sense of how to mete out my effort. I know when I need to conserve energy on a climb because it ends in a false flat and when to let it all hang out. I know the best, cleanest lines. I know what's around the next corner without ever seeing it.

But the real reason I love the rides close to home is because they're piled high with memories.

Yesterday afternoon, The Hammer and I got out our mountain bikes. I admit I was giddy, because it was the first day the whole year I felt like I could wear a short-sleeve jersey.

Not that I'm giddy about the prospect of short-sleeved jerseys in general, mind you, but it had been a long winter and I was giddy about finally having a day when wearing a short-sleeved jersey wasn't an act of defiance.

"Should I bring an iPod,[59] or are we going to be talking during this ride?" The Hammer asked.

It's a fair question. While I'm normally pretty talkative, when I'm riding I often stop talking altogether; I get absorbed in the ride and stop thinking in words.

"Leave the iPod at home," I hazarded, not really sure I'd be able to back up the promise of being a good conversationalist.

Turns out I didn't need to worry. I talked pretty much nonstop during the ride, just narrating things that had happened on the same route over the course of years and years of riding.

---

58   Of *course* I keep home-away statistics for my rides. Don't you?
59   This ride happened before The Hammer had fully figured out her phone and the miracle of Pandora.

A FIRST

As we climbed up Hog Hollow, a long, moderate dirt road that becomes narrower, steeper and more technical as you go up, I recalled that this was the first "away" mountain bike trail I had ever been on. By which I mean, up until then, the only trail I had ridden was Lower Frank, near my house in Orem.

Dug had persuaded me to come try out something different, to go out to Hog Hollow, climb it, and then drop down the other side to the Sliding Rock.

All I remember from that ride is the climb. At the time, it just seemed impossibly steep and unbearably long. And ridiculously technical. I recall telling Dug that I needed to stop and take a break three times on that two-mile climb.

It's strange, I thought, how your perceptions change. Now I think of the Hog Hollow climb as nothing more than a convenient on-ramp to get to the real attraction: Corner Canyon Park. It's a good warm up, but hardly taxing, even on a single speed.

But it's still a good memory of branching out for the first time, along with the feeling of triumph when I reached the saddle.

I told The Hammer about the many times the group of us would race to the top of Hog Hollow, and how I never tried to hang with the group. I was too slow.

I could have also told her about the time Jeremy filled Dug's inner tube with water for one of those races, to slow him down. But I decided to keep that one to myself. A story to be told another time, on the same climb.

ANOTHER FIRST

Being at the top of Hog Hollow doesn't mean you're done climbing. Not at all. It just means you get a one-minute break before more climbing Jacob's Ladder.

As The Hammer and I got to the top of Jacob's Ladder, I started thinking about another first: my first descent down Jacob's Ladder.

Now, Jacob's Ladder is about three parts jutting rock, four parts packed earth, two parts erosion ruts, and six parts pea-sized gravel. All on a sharply descending, often off-camber fin.

Yeah, it's kind of technical. But nowadays, I love the descent. Even though I've crashed hard on it, I know that (almost) every time, I can fly down. The thrill's worth the risk.[60]

But it hasn't always been that way. I remember the first time I rode Jacob's Ladder, I was with a group of riding buddies, and as they disappeared off the front and I looked at the rocky ledges and loose sandy gravel in front of me, that I had a long walk in front of me.

And I took my time about it, too. Muttering the whole way, angry at them for showing me a trail that, eventually, I would come to love.

A THIRD FIRST

A drop down Ghost Falls brought us to Clark's, one of Corner Canyon's main arteries. My first time up that trail was also the first time I had ever ridden a single speed. I remember Rick Sunderlage (not his real name) happily chatted (meaning that he wasn't working hard at all on the climb) the whole way up, talking about how much he loved single speeding and how this was a perfect trail for it and wasn't it awesome the way you had to stand and rock the bike for big chunks of the climb?

Or at least I think that's what he was saying. I had a hard time understanding everything he said, what with the sound of blood pounding in my ears.

Meanwhile, I was wondering if Rick would be offended if I vomited on him.[61]

A STUNNING EPIPHANY

And here's the thing: just about every section of every road or trail I normally ride is like this for me now: I've got an anecdote for pretty much every little bit of everywhere I ride.

Which means, I suppose, I'm becoming that old guy on the group ride.[62] You know, the one who's always going on and on about the good ol' days.

I shall now punch myself in the throat.

> COMMENT BY GRIZZLY ADAM
> You've been "that guy" for a long time. We just never had the heart to tell you.

---

60 Except, of course, when it isn't.
61 I certainly hoped so.
62 Or, more accurately, "have become that old guy on the group ride."

4.
Valuable, Practical How-To Guidance You Can Use *Right Now*

HAVE YOU EVER CONSIDERED HOW HARD IT MUST BE TO BE IN AN EDITO-RIAL MEETING FOR A BIKE MAGAZINE LIKE *Bicycling*? TO COME UP WITH a magazine's worth of bike-related articles, month after month, year after year?

All about a sport, which, when you think about it, is nothing but sitting down and moving your legs in tiny little circles.

How do they do it? I'll tell you how. With "How-To" articles. These tried-and-true magazine sellers follow a very specific, reliable pattern:

1. **State a problem.** It's perfectly fine for the problem to seem like a non-problem to anyone who has any sense at all. For example — and I am not making this up — the first five results I get when searching for "how to" at bicycling.com are (with my one-sentence solution in parentheses):
   - **How to Ride in Hot Weather** (Put on sunscreen; wear light, wicking clothing; drink lots of water)
   - **How to Ride Alone** (Get on your bike and ride it, without other people)
   - **How to Lock a Bike Strategically** (Run the chain through both wheels, the frame, and something that is fixed to the ground)
   - **How to Snap a Mid-Ride Selfie** (Don't)
   - **How to Lock Your Bike** (See the third bullet above, but

feel free to ignore any of the steps, because apparently this time you're not going to be strategic about it)

2. **Describe the problem in detail**. And make sure it seems much more complicated and important than it actually is.

3. **Describe a multiplicity of solutions**. It's perfectly fine to come up with some that are stupid. You've got a word count to hit.

4. **Don't tell them which solution is best**. Leave it up to the reader to choose one that "works for you."

5. **End with a vague promise of increased happiness, and improved riding experience**. Or a stupid pun.

My how-to guidance, on the other hand, is practical, necessary, compelling stuff that you MUST READ RIGHT NOW OR YOU WILL NEVER ENJOY RIDING YOUR BIKE AGAIN.

You're welcome.

HOW TO PAY FOR YOUR BIKE STUFF

When I want to buy something bike-related, I simply go to the bike shop and buy it. It doesn't matter whether I need it or merely want it. I just buy it.

I can do this because I am a manly man, and, as such, have complete control of the family finances. My purchase decisions are made with confidence and authority, and are never questioned.

Nor are my choices ever ridiculed.

At all.

I'm that masterful.

Sadly, most of the rest of you are not as dominant as I am, so you must resort to cajoling, subterfuge, and other mealy-mouthed machinations in order to support your biking habit.

I pity you.

As long as you're going to be so desperately sad about the way you purchase your bike gear, you may as well at least improve your technique, so you can beg, lie, and steal with some style.

I'll do my best to help, even though — since I never, ever, ever have to resort to such underhanded techniques — I find the entire business intensely distasteful.

HOW TO BEG

Begging is the correct technique to use when you believe your case for making a purchase is strong: your bike is old, your shorts are nearly worn out, your helmet is unbearably stinky,[1] but you do not really, when it comes right down to it, have the money in the budget to cover the expense.

What you are looking for here, is a reprioritization of fund allocation, an agreement that it is more important for you to buy a new headset than it is to buy new shoes for your children.[2]

The best way to achieve this aim is to beg without *seeming* to beg.

---

1   Or broken, I suppose, though I've found that I rarely if ever have to beg to get a new helmet when I can prove the old one won't do the job. That said, I'm about twenty-five times more likely to buy a new helmet because I want my helmet to match my frame than I am to buy a helmet because my old one cracked.

2   As if it's not self-evident.

Follow these steps:

1. **Identify the non-essential item(s) currently in the budget which you want to replace with your very-essential bike-related item.** The items' prices must be approximately equivalent.

2. **Make a good case.** Approach your significant other with an explanation of how you've been thinking it might be a financially sound move to hold off on purchasing the currently-in-budget item. "You know, dear," you might say. "If we buy shoes for Junior this month, that means he's going to wear out of these new shoes *one month sooner.* Suppose we waited an additional month. It's been a mild winter and the holes in his shoes aren't that bad. It's not like it'd kill him to curl his toes under in order to fit in those shoes for one more month, either."

3. **Look at both sides of the story**. Once you've made your case, make the opposing case as well, *but make it poorly.* "On the other hand, maybe we should go ahead and buy those shoes for him now. I'm sure he won't become a selfish, snobby kid just because we're constantly buying him new clothes before he's had a chance to wear in what he's already got. Hey, in fact, he's asking for a motorcycle. Maybe we should look into buying that for him, too."

4. **Avoid Direct Association**. Once you have made your point, do *not* immediately say some boneheaded thing like, "Oh good, now with that extra money I'm going to buy new titanium axles for my pedals." Wait thirty-six hours, and then say, "I've been needing[3] new pedals for about nine months now, and it looks like there's finally room in the budget. I'm going to go buy those today." Note the assumptive close, and further note that there is no easy-out provided for your significant other (e.g., some mealy-mouthed phrase like "if it's alright with you" tacked on to the end of the sentence).

5. **Stay Cool.** When this works, you may be so amazed that you'll be inclined to start falling all over yourself with expressions of gratitude and promises of future favors. Don't do

---

3   Never, ever, *ever* say you've been "wanting." You *need.*

this. If you do, your significant other will realize that s/he has been hornswoggled and will reverse her/his decision, and the game is over.

HOW TO BEG ABJECTLY

Sometimes, what you want may be really silly, and you know it is. You may want a fourth road bike, for example. Or a power meter, in spite of the fact that the reality of what you need to do to improve performance is startlingly obvious.[4] Or perhaps you want to buy a pair of Assos shorts, just to find out if they really will give you a Luxury Body[5] (please let me know how that turns out).

In cases like this, the best thing you can do is beg, in the classic sense of the word. Take your sweetheart by both hands (this is required), look her deep in the eyes (I'm saying "her" because I really can't even picture a woman begging like this), and lay it all out on the line.

"Sweetheart," you should say, "I have no rational reason why I should get a power meter. I don't need one. I'm not even sure what they do. And yet, I want one. Desperately. I can't sleep. I can't concentrate at work. Please, indulge me."

This will work. Once. So choose your item of abject beg-worthiness wisely.

Also, don't tell anyone about your abject begging episode, because it will creep them out.

HOW TO USE THE TURNABOUT TECHNIQUE

If you live with a selfish person, or someone whom you suspect could become selfish given the proper stimuli, the simplest and most direct way to get what you want is to offer an exchange. "Hey, you know how you've been admiring that new Toyota Sequoia? I bought one for you today. Oh, and I also bought myself a new set of Shimano xtr disc brakes for my singlespeed."

Note that with this tactic, you must spend noticeably more on the "turnabout" item than you did on yourself.

---

4   Lose eighty pounds.
5   About eight years ago, my analysis of an Assos ad and their promise of a "Luxury Body" went semi-viral. That is what this particularly weird in-joke is in reference to. You can find this analysis on my blog, or you can buy my first book, *Comedian Mastermind*. The latter would be my preference, naturally.

Also note that this tactic will quickly drive you into the poorhouse, since you must always plan on spending more than twice the cost of the item you want, every time you want to buy something.

BLACK BUDGET

This is the most underhanded[6] of all possible methods of purchasing bike-related gear: buy it with money that your significant other doesn't know you have.

In order to purchase items from the Black Budget, first you must create a means to acquire money without your significant other's knowledge, such as:

- **Lunch money**: Don't eat lunch. Save your money. In cash.
- **Cook the books**: When purchasing groceries, always ask for cash back. Report your grocery spend as if the cash back were part of the grocery spend.
- **Donate blood plasma**. You can make a secret $20 a week doing this. I know a guy who actually did this. I won't give away who it was, but his first initial is D. You know, as in "Dug."

You must also have a place to secretly store this money. An envelope at work. A bank account at a different institution than where you normally bank (be certain that the monthly statements are sent to your email address, not to your physical address).

You must be careful when purchasing items with the Black Budget. Put simply, you must never purchase something obvious. For example, you cannot purchase a new bike with the Black Budget unless you already have so many bikes that there is no way your significant other will be able to tell you've added one to the collection. If you buy a new helmet with the Black Budget, buy one the same color as your old helmet.

Bike shoes are a safe Black Budget buy, because all bike shoes look the same to non-bike people.

All of this, frankly, is deplorable. You should never do any of this. Ever. At all.

I certainly don't.

---

6   To me, it also seems like the easiest, most-sensible, smartest way. I'm not sure what says about me, but I'm sure it's something good.

COMMENT BY BIG MIKE IN OZ

That reads more like my biography than a cautionary tale. Tips on getting caught: Don't! You will suffer for periods of time not measurable with mere calendars.

COMMENT BY BIKEMIKE

Been working in a bike shop for almost 20 years now and there is no way I could have afforded half of the stuff I have, had I not worked in said shop. That being said, I could curl your pretty Sidi shoes right up into the back of your Luxury Body shorts with some of the stories about men (yes, all men!) hiding money and out and out lying, just to get their swag fix.

COMMENT BY GRAHAME

Here in the UK, there are some very friendly bike shops that are prepared to supply a "wife receipt." This acts as proof that the £600 wheels really were a bargain at £300. This helps a great deal.

HOW TO BE LIGHT

I'm pretty sure that cycling is better at encouraging eating disorders than any other sport. While every other sport that I know of, which isn't many, focuses on athletes training their bodies and minds to be the most capable instruments possible, in cycling we demand that our bodies be both incredibly powerful and light as a feather.

Our legs should be massive and powerful. Lungs and heart: same deal.

The rest of us, on the other hand, we only begrudgingly allow to exist at all.

Indeed, we resent any effort required that does not contribute directly to the turning of the cranks. So much so, in fact, that electronic shifting, which is only trivially easier than regular shifting, has become regarded as an only somewhat excessive purchase.

We've got to be light. It's not good enough to be strong; the strong light guy will beat the strong almost-as-light guy up the hill every time.

Cycling, you know I love you, but you put the "func" in "dysfunctional."

Many people have noticed, lately, that I am an excellent climber. Fast. Focused. Featherweight. Also, I am very, very handsome, but that is the subject for another story on another day.[7]

It is not uncommon, truth be known, for me to receive requests for climbing guidance from professional cyclists, though I am contractually obligated to not mention these cyclists by name. Considering the remarkable sums of money these people are paying me, I am more than happy to respect their need for privacy.

Because I value you, dear reader, above all my very, very high-paying clientele and because I know that the only reason you do not gladly pay a $49.95 monthly subscription to this site is that I do not ask it of you, I shall today offer you the same guidance. At no charge whatsoever.

Today, I shall tell you how to fly up the hills. Today, my friend, you shall be transformed.

---

7   But hopefully, one very soon, and written by someone else, so I can be all aw-shucks about it.

SECRET TIPS

There are three crucial components to being a magnificent climber. No, of course you cannot expect to be as magnificent as I am, but you can become at least relatively magnificent, and you should be satisfied with that.

These are my secret tips. Share them with nobody.

First, you must *pedal*. Some fools believe that they can simply coast uphill, through the medium of offering promissory notes to gravity against future descents. And while I have patented this idea and have built a prototype drivetrain that successfully implements this theory, it is not yet available for sale.[8]

It is not enough to pedal, though. You must pedal in sine waves. Yes, I know: conventional cycling wisdom would have you pedal circles. But conventional cycling wisdom doesn't get paid ridiculously large sums of money by the top pro cyclists in the world, now does it? Consider the motion of a pedal as it goes by you. Is that pedal going in a circle? *No.*

It's oscillating up and down as the bike moves forward. A sine wave. How will this help you pedal better? Well, to be honest it won't, but it's still true.

Second, you've got to stop braking as you climb. It just slows you down.[9]

Once you've got the basics down, you're ready for the vital third step in becoming a climbing powerhouse.

You must become light.

Many cycling pundits *think* they understand this vital technique for being a world-class climber, but they don't. Not really. All they know are the crude basics: lose weight, ride a light bike. Sure, that's fine as far as it goes, but the details — how do you lose weight? how do you make your bike light? — are where traditional givers of advice will fail you.

I, dear reader, will not fail you. The following strategies will help you become the climber you have always dreamed of becoming.[10]

---

8   "Why have you not put this miraculous invention into production?" you ask? The reasons are technical, but basically boil down to a problem with the elastic bands breaking.

9   There, see how much faster you are already?

10   Unless, of course, you have been dreaming of becoming as good a climber as I, because that would be laughable. Set your sights on something attainable, you charlatan!

TECHNIQUES FOR MAKING *YOURSELF* LIGHT

Most cyclists believe they already know that diet and exercise will make themselves light and that the only variables are time and willpower.

Nothing, I am happy to say, could be further from the truth.

This is all you need to do:

- **Shave**: This has been considered good practice among cyclists for years, but the full extent and reasoning behind shaving has never been fully explained. Shave everything. Head to toe. This includes your eyebrows and eyelashes. No decorative facial hair (you too, ladies). Not only is hair non-aerodynamic; every single little hair has weight. In fact, don't just shave. Wax. That way you can get the hair beneath the surface of the skin.[11]

- **Exfoliate**: I'm not talking about using a mildly abrasive skin cleanser here. I'm prescribing a twenty-minute session, top to bottom, with 80-grit sandpaper. Some people might call this torture. I call it the cost of greatness.

- **Avoid Sunscreen**: This one's easy. You know all that sunscreen you rub onto your skin? Yeah, you think it doesn't weigh anything? Well it does. Stop using it; it's weighing you down.

- **Fingernails and Toenails**: I know, you already trim your fingernails and toenails nice and tight. That's a good first baby step. Now finish the job. All the way to the cuticles, champ.

- **Liposuction**: Some people call this unnecessary surgery with no demonstrable long-term benefit. I call it the shortest route from fat to fast.

- **Remove unnecessary body parts**: Do you know what your tonsils are good for? How about your appendix? Nothing, that's what. So what are you carrying them around for? And while we're having this discussion, answer me this: do you really think you'd walk any worse if you removed your pinky toes? And don't even get me started on the dead weight everyone dangles around by keeping their earlobes.[12]

- **Remove unnecessary decoration**: Got a tattoo? You think that ink doesn't have mass? Ha.

---

11 *Special note to Tinker Juarez:* You could be fourteen pounds lighter if you got rid of all that hair.

12 I'll bet you anything that the racers at Team Sky, with their "Marginal Gains" philosophy, are shaking in their saddles over this very thing right now.

- **Dehydrate**: Many cycling authorities encourage you to stay hydrated if you want to ride well. I'll let you in on a little secret: they tell you that because they're coaching someone else they want to beat you. The truth is, water is incredibly heavy. While I recognize it as a necessary evil (my kidneys sometimes fail when I let my water mass dip below 40%), I'm not going to lug any more up the hill than I have to. You shouldn't either. I recommend going without fluids for at least 36 hours before a ride of any significance. Then, during the ride, spit. A lot. And don't drink anything.
- **Bloodletting**: This got a bad rap because it was invented back in the medieval ages, but just because something was invented a long time ago doesn't mean it was a bad idea. I mean, wheels were invented a long time ago too and I don't see you rushing to eliminate *those* from your cycling rig.

TECHNIQUES FOR MAKING YOUR BIKE LIGHT

Many people spend thousands upon thousands of dollars to make their bikes light. I heartily endorse this behavior. In addition to purchasing lighter parts, though, you should also consider making your bike lighter through the medium of *removing* bike parts. For example:
- **Remove the rear brake**: Everyone knows that most of your stopping power is in the front brake. So why incur the expense and weight of that redundant rear brake? A good modern front brake has enough stopping power and then some. You know how much weight you'll save by getting rid of the rear brake, cabling, and levers? Fourteen pounds, that's how much. Most people don't realize how heavy rear brakes are.
- **Remove the bottle cages**: Since you aren't going to be drinking when you ride anymore (see "Dehydrate," above), you won't be needing those bottle cages anymore, will you? Nor the bottle cage bolts.
- **Sand the paint job off**: I've heard that some bike manufacturers put between 2–5 coats of paint on their bikes, and then seal the job with a high-gloss finish. For those manufacturers, I have a question: Do you also insert lead weights into the tubes? Because you might as well.
- **Never carry any tools**: You know, I have ridden hundreds of times without any tools or flat-fixing supplies without ever missing

them. In fact, the only time I have ever missed not carrying stuff to do bike field repairs is when my bike breaks or flats. And that's hardly ever.

- **Never let your sweat drip onto your bike:** You're going to sweat when riding, although if you've done your dehydrating properly, you won't sweat much. Just don't sweat on your bike. That leaves a salty residue, and salt has mass.

- **Helium:** Fill your tires with helium. Fill your bike tubes with helium. Before rides, breathe a helium/oxygen mix, which is 30% lighter than conventional air. I do not understand why so few people understand this.[13]

TECHNIQUES FOR MAKING YOUR CLOTHING LIGHT

Over the centuries, cycling clothing manufacturers have refined their wares to the point where cyclists can be comfortable in the saddle all day.

But being comfortable isn't the point, is it? Being light is the point. Here is how to customize your bike clothing to get rid of that ungainly bulk:

- **Get rid of the pockets:** You're not carrying anything in your jersey pockets, are you? Of course you're not, because anything in those pockets is going to weigh something. And since you aren't using those pockets, you may as well get rid of them.

- **Get rid of the armpit fabric:** Cutting a gaping hole in your jersey directly beneath the armpit serves dual purposes. First, it makes the jersey lighter. Second, it has a cooling effect, which is useful since you won't be sweating much anymore and will be more susceptible to heat stroke.

- **Get rid of the collar:** Are you going to wear a tie with that jersey? No? Well then, what's the collar for? I mean, besides to weigh you down?

- **Shorten your shorts**: When you get right down to it, the primary function of the bike short is to hold the chamois in place. So why do they go all the way down onto your thigh, sometimes almost to the knee? Chop them off higher and you'll get rid of several unsightly tenths of an ounce. And you'll get a nicer tan on the tops of your quads.

---

13   I really do know a guy who, in real life, keeps a nitrogen tank in his car with which to fill his tires.

FINAL ANALYSIS

Do I expect many cyclists to follow my advice? No, I do not. And why will most of you snigger and ignore me? Because most of you are not truly committed climbers.

Just you wait, though. In a few short days the Tour de France will be on TV and you will see cyclists with the healthy glow of freshly sanded skin, the dull gaze of people who have not had a drink in two days, sporting sheared short shorts on brakeless and paintless bikes. Then you'll know that not everyone has been laughing off my (very, very) wise (and, frankly, expensive) counsel.

And then you too will do what it takes to be light.

COMMENT BY SPROCKETBOY

This all seems pretty reasonable to me. I have also found success by reducing the number of spokes in the front wheel. You can also do this yourself by removing one spoke at a time until the wheel collapses, then putting one back.

COMMENT BY 2LILTIME

I find a good colonic reduces weight also. Although it is highly advisable to wait a sufficient amount of time AFTER the colonic before resuming riding. Lesson learned.

COMMENT BY TIM D

You don't need both those kidneys.

COMMENT BY CRASH

I actually prefer pedalling in cosine waves. I find it more effective. Pedalling in sine waves is so old school.

COMMENT BY WILLIE NELSON

You only need one eye (depth perception is overrated during a climb), no false eyes or patches.

COMMENT BY JOSH

You may want to start charging us as I think you might have to spend some time in court fending off lawsuits of varying degrees. By the way, I am a mathematician, and the motion in this case wouldn't be a sine or even a cosine wave. In fact, the motion would closer resemble, ironically enough, a cycloid. It would not be an exact cycloid, as a perfect cycloid is dependant upon both rotary motion (pedal) and horizontal motion (bike travel), this because the rotary motion of pedaling is not in sync with the horizontal motion of the travel of the bike itself due to gear ratios. Only in the case of a fixed gear with a 1-1 ratio of pedal travel to wheel travel would produce a perfect cycloid.

I hope you are thoroughly nerded out right now. If not, the basic equation of a cycloid is defined as a parametric equation as follows:

$x = t - a \sin t$

$y = 1 - a \cos t$

Do I win the Nerd Award?

HOW TO JUSTIFY BUYING YOUR NEXT BIKE

I swear, anytime I even consider buying a new bike, someone will appear out of nowhere and say, "N+1!"

Where, of course,[14] *if for any cyclist, "N" is the number of bikes that cyclist has, "N+1" is the number of bikes that cyclist needs.*[15]

It is the single most tired cliché in the cycling universe. It's irritating. It's aggravating.

It's also distressingly accurate.

We cyclists are simple folk. We don't need much to keep us happy. Really, all we need are clear skies, a road or trail, and some free time.

And a helmet, of course. And gloves. And shorts with a special anti-microbial chamois insert. And form-fitting shirts. And very stiff-soled shoes, preferably Italian-made. And specialty sports drinks, with an incomprehensible combination of carbohydrates, proteins, electrolytes, and a lemon-lime flavoring that for some reason makes one think of furniture polish.

Oh, and we need a bike, naturally. More specifically, we need *another* bike. Always. And that means we need to pay for another bike.

Now, it's not the paying *per se* that's difficult. We can always find a way to get the money we need for bike stuff: take a second job, sell a kidney, money laundering, whatever. You wouldn't think it to look at us, but we cyclists can be downright resourceful when it comes to acquiring gear.

What's difficult is justifying the expense of yet another bicycle, whether it be to our wives, our parents, our co-workers, or, less often, to our own nagging conscience.

Sometimes we fail in our justification, and then where are we? We're in the Purgatory of No New Bikes, that's where we are. That's a bad place. A bad, bad place.

We should never have to be in that place.

And if you will follow these techniques, you will never be in that place again.

---

14   Insert heavy sigh here.
15   By which I mean "want."

IT WILL SAVE MONEY ON GAS

This may surprise you, but bikes can actually be used as transportation. There are some people who, oddly enough, actually use their bikes to get around from place to place, instead of driving.[16] Explain that with this new bike you will be saving *serious transportation costs* and doing *your part for the environment.*[17]

Caveat: Do not explain that the new bike you're considering costs approximately the same as three years' worth of fuel. Do not explain that any of the bikes you already have would work as transportation, too. If brought up as a counterargument, explain — dismissively — that your other bikes aren't really for that kind of thing.

IT'S LESS EXPENSIVE THAN A HUMONGOUS TELEVISION

This will take a little bit of preparation, but is well worth it. For about three weeks, don't mention the new bike you want.

At all.

Instead, with increasing intensity and frequency, begin talking about how you're thinking about getting a giant high-def television. Eighty inches, at least. And a Blu-Ray DVD player. And a subscription to high-def cable/satellite (or both). And a serious sound system to go with it. Be very, very open that this will cost about three times as much as the bike you want.

Argue convincingly (not too convincingly, though) and loudly about why you ought to get this massive entertainment system.[18]

About the time your boyfriend/girlfriend/spouse/parent is at wit's end, capitulate. Right in the middle of an argument, act like a light's just come on in your head. "You know, you're right!" you say, catching them off-guard. "It's outrageously expensive and it would just rot my brain, *especially when a new bike would cost me less than half as much!*"

They'll be so relieved — not to mention pleased at having clearly won an argument with you — they'll just let that remark go. Next day, you come home with the new bike, as the two of you agreed.

Bonus: It's possible this technique will backfire on you and your

---

16   I know. Weird.

17   My goodness, but you are a responsible human being.

18   Be careful; I used this technique and found myself switching loyalties. Have you ever watched *Game of Thrones* on an 80" TV?

significant other will really get into the idea of buying a home theatre system. That's the beauty of this technique: even if you lose, you win!

YOU WILL EASILY RECOUP THE COST OF THIS BIKE IN PRIZE MONEY

Did you know there's big money in bike racing? There is! Just ask Lance Armstrong; he's made a very comfortable living by racing his bicycle.[19]

Do you think Lance Armstrong won the Tour de France seven times[20] riding a piece of crap like the one you ride? No, he most certainly did not.

If you're going to start winning races and making millions of dollars like Lance, you're going to need a better bike.[21]

The prize money will follow naturally.

THIS BIKE WILL COST HARDLY ANYTHING AFTER THE TRADE-IN

Thinking of trading in an old bike for the new one? Excellent. You'll want to get out your soft math skills for this next strategy.[22]

First, find out the suggested retail for the new bike you want. Reduce that figure by 25%, because nobody pays MSRP for anything these days. Then take another 10% off because you're friends with a guy at the shop. Take another 5% off because you're a sharp negotiator. Tell your significant other that's how much your new bike will cost.

Next, estimate how much your current bike is actually worth. Add 10% to that, because I can tell you've taken really good care of your bike.[23] Add 5% because I think you're just being too modest. Then add 15% to that figure because you want some negotiating room. Tell your significant other that's how much you'll be selling your old bike for.

If you're any good at all with creative math, you should actually be able to make a case that you may well be pocketing some money when all is said and done.

Note: When it turns out that the actual cost of the new bike is much higher and the amount you sell the old bike for is lower than you expect, I highly recommend shrugging and blaming taxes, shipping,

---

19   Sure, complications came later.
20   Hey, can we just skip past this part of the story and pretend I never wrote it?
21   Among other things.
22   I'm really awesome at math that doesn't require me to do any arithmetic.
23   Seriously, that thing looks brand-new, and you can quote me on that.

and the fees the online site charged. "Man, everyone wants a slice," you can say, resignedly.

THIS BIKE IS THE BIKE TO END ALL BIKES

This approach is dangerous, but desperate times call for desperate measures, as I think all of us who have ever had a carbon fiber jones can attest.

"I know I have a lot of bikes already," you should say (it's good to start with a true statement, because that fools people into thinking other things you say may also be true). "This one, though, is different. It fits me unlike any bike ever made. It will never break. It is both beautiful and functional. It weighs ten pounds, fully loaded."[24]

Continue with, "This is the ultimate expression of a bicycle. I shall never need another."

Look her/him right in the eyes as you conclude, "Hey, it's not like I'm talking about buying a Ferrari here, but how often in my life will I have a chance to own something that is truly perfect?" (**Note**: Do not say this if you own a Ferrari.)

Try to mist up a little as you say this.

It adds impact.

---

24   When I originally wrote this story about five years ago, I wrote "fourteen pounds, fully loaded." Times have changed.

HOW TO TALK TO NON-CYCLISTS

The fact that you are reading this tells me all I really need to know about you. You're a cyclist. I'm a cyclist.[25] *We therefore both know what's really important in life. We see the world as it truly is. If we were each to answer the question, "What would you do with a million dollars?" our answers would vary perhaps in what equipment we'd buy and where we'd go to ride, but in little else.*

If we were to have a conversation, we'd have an understanding of how each other thinks. Maybe you're a Cat 2 roadie and maybe I'm a cross-country endurance geek, but we both know that turning the cranks in a perfect circle is the ultimate form of self-expression.

Sadly, not everyone is like you and me. I am sad to say that there are people out there who rarely, if ever, ride bikes at all.[26] *It's possible you even know someone like this. A coworker. A family member. You'd be surprised at how common non-cyclists are, actually. You probably encounter them several times per day and simply don't notice them, because they aren't interesting.*

Mostly, you can safely ignore these people, simply by riding away from them. Sometimes, though, it is impossible to avoid non-cyclists. Surrounded, you have no choice but to communicate with them.

Don't worry. I'm here to help. Just follow these five simple rules.

RULE 1: UNDERSTAND THEIR BIZARRE WORLDVIEW

You need to understand that non-cyclists don't realize that cycling is the most important thing any person can be doing at any given moment at any point in the universe. Non-cyclists' eyes and minds are shuttered, leaving them to believe that things like friends, community, work, and even family supercede what they naively call "just exercise." It's sad,[27] but true.

To appease non-cyclists, when asked about what matters to you, you must from time to time mention friends, family, the environment, or some other such nonsense. Otherwise, they'll never leave you alone and it will be hours until you can get away, back to the comfort and kinship you feel with your bicycle.

---

25 Or, possibly, you're my mom. In which case, Hi Mom!
26 I know, it makes no sense at all.
27 Pathetic, really.

RULE 2. USE METAPHORS FROM "REAL LIFE"

Non-cyclists aren't ready to hear about your exquisite existence in its unadulterated perfection. No, you will need to translate the sublime cycling experience into terms they might be able to understand. Naturally, you and I know that the following metaphors don't do the actual cycling event justice, but they'll have to do.

- **To describe how it feels to ride down perfectly banked, twisty forested singletrack on a cool autumn morning**: "It's like that scene from *Return of the Jedi* where Luke and Leia are zooming on their flying motorcycle things. Except you're the one powering the flying motorcycle. And you're not being chased by stormtroopers. And you don't have to tolerate the constant chattering of Ewoks."

- **To explain why you gladly get up at 4:30am each weekday morning to ride your road bike for three hours on an entirely unremarkable road**: "You know how you have to drive your car in stop-and-go traffic to get to work every morning? Well, imagine if you didn't have to stop. And imagine your car going as fast as you can make it go. And imagine starting the day feeling perfect. It's kind of like that."

- **To explain why you pay $200 to participate in a race you have very little chance in winning**: "Ever play the lotto? It's like that, except much, much more so."

RULE 3: PRETEND TO BE INTERESTED IN THEIR LIFE

This one's going to knock you off your feet. Believe it or not, non-cyclists sometimes think they have something interesting to say, have an interesting hobby, or an intriguing experience to relate.

This, of course, is utter nonsense.

Still, for the sake of propriety, you must act as if you care. Feel free, as they talk, to pleasantly daydream about biking. Just smile and say, "absolutely," from time to time.

Warning: It's entirely possible that a non-cyclist will say something with which you disagree. When this happens, do not engage. If you do, you will have unwittingly stepped into a non-cycling conversation, and who knows where that will lead, or when it will end.

Always remember: Be polite, be brief, be gone.

RULE 4. ACT LIKE THEIR THEORY ON DOPING IS VERY INTERESTING

A tactic non-cyclists will often employ, once they have discovered you are a cyclist, is to try to talk with you about cycling.[28] This usually takes the form of trying to talk with you about *doping* in cycling.

You will, no doubt, be tempted to gouge your ears out rather than hear their simplistic, uninformed opinion, i.e. "doping is bad," to its rambling, incoherent conclusion. After all, as a cyclist, you have no doubt been pummeled with story after story after story about doping. You have heard so much about doping that you could now be called as an expert witness at the next doping trial. Or open a lab. Or be the next president of WADA.[29]

But if you point any of this out to your non-cyclist "friend," he will no doubt take that as a sign that you are interested in continuing the conversation. So, instead, repeat this simple phrase: "Yeah, doping sucks."

Your friend will feel like he has made his point, whatever it was.

RULE 5. DON'T EVER TELL THEM HOW MUCH YOUR BIKE COST

Few people ever own anything that works, fits, or looks so beautiful as a truly well-built bike. And yet, when they find that your bike costs as much as their high-end computer or mid-range stereo, they will fake a heart attack, guaranteed.[30]

The solution? Tell non-cyclists you paid $499.95 for your bike, no matter how much you really paid for it. This number has been scientifically formulated to sound like more than a non-cyclist would pay for a bike, without otherwise drawing attention to itself.[31]

No matter how you try, you can't always avoid non-cyclists. All you can hope to do is minimize contact with them so you can get back to what's important.

And I think we both know what that is.

---

28 Did you just roll your eyes? Because I did.
29 I hear they're looking.
30 Go try it. I promise: they will fake a heart attack. If you're feeling a little resentful, you can then show them this footnote.
31 Which is why this book has been priced at $499.95.

HOW TO GET RID OF UNWANTED FITNESS

I have an annual tradition, one that is very important to me. I never let a year go by without observing this important ritual. In fact, I can't even imagine my life without it.

I am talking about, of course, putting about twenty pounds on as soon as fall begins.

Part of this tradition is to act like this year will be different. "This year," I tell myself, "will be different." And then I laugh and laugh, and then I cry a little.

Because I know it won't be different.

I'll start eating Halloween candy about three weeks before Halloween, I'll build fat-gaining momentum that I won't be able to halt (nor will I even try) before Thanksgiving, and after that, it's just one feast after another until after the new year begins.

By which time...well...you don't think I call myself The Fat Cyclist ironically, do you?

This story is about the very helpful tips I have learned over the years. Tips that will help you quickly put on weight that you will have to fight tooth and nail to get back off later.

Like me, I'm sure you've worked hard through the winter, spring, and summer getting yourself in peak physical condition. Whether you've been working toward excelling at racing, touring, or just want to be able to ride as much as you like, you've been true to your goals. You've dieted right, trained smart, and now you're in great condition.

Which leads up to a very important question: now that it's mid-autumn,[32] how can you lose this fitness as *quickly as possible*? After all, you can't claim drastic gains at the beginning of the year if you don't start working on your stunning fitness reversal right this instant.

Obviously, you've got important questions on your mind. Questions like, how can you gain that weight back? How can you lose the definition in your legs? How can you completely reverse the gains you've made in your aerobic capacity?

---

32   I wrote this in fall, and I meant for it to be read in the fall. If you're reading this in any season but the fall, please bookmark this story, skip it, and move on to the next story. I'll see you in a few months.

And, most importantly, how can you do all this in the shortest time possible?

I'm here to help. Just follow these simple techniques.

TECHNIQUE 1: COAST

The first thing you want to do is tell yourself how important it is not to overtrain and burn yourself out. Your important races for the season are over. So now's maybe a good time to cut back on your ride intensity, duration, and frequency.

Start avoiding hills, too.

As you ride less, you'll find that before too long, your body adapts. It's really quite surprising[33] how quickly it adapts to not going on those hard rides. You'll notice within just a few weeks that you're just as tired from a one-hour cruise as you used to be after a two-hour interval workout.

Isn't it great how efficient your body is?

You'll find that the weather and daylight patterns are more than happy to oblige as you work on this technique. As the days get lighter later and darker sooner, ask yourself this question: "Is it really necessary for me to go riding when it's cold and dark outside?"

The answer, just in case you're not sure, is: "No, it's not a great idea to go riding when it's dark and cold. You'd better go for a ride during lunchtime."

Of course, you know that you won't go riding during lunchtime, because you'll be eating *lunch*. For some strange reason your appetite has increased, even as your riding time has decreased. But that's neither here nor there.[34]

TECHNIQUE 2: KEEP EATING LIKE YOU'RE RIDING
100 MILES EVERY DAY

Even though you are riding less, you should by no means start eating less. That would be foolish. Instead, continue to inhale pasta[35] at the same desperate rate as when you were burning 6,000 calories per day. The reasoning goes like this: "Well, when I was eating 2,100 calories per day and exercising three hours per day, I was losing about two

---

33   Horrifying, really.
34   It is, however, both here AND there.
35   And any of your other favorite carbohydrates.

pounds per week. So if I eat 4,000 calories per day and exercise each Saturday for an hour, my weight should about hold steady."

My math is correct. Trust me.

As long as you're still eating all that pasta, you ought to mix it up a little. You know, start adding a little cheese. Just enough for flavor. And maybe a little more, for texture.

It's not like you don't have months until the next riding season begins. You should live a little.

Oh, and you know what else goes with pasta? Alfredo sauce. That stuff is *delicious*.[36]

Humans have a hibernating instinct, just like bears. It's a scientific fact. Or at least it seems like it should be a scientific fact, because as days get shorter and cooler, all I want to do is eat and sleep.[37]

It is very important to not fight this instinct. Those instincts are put there for a reason. And that reason is: you'll soon be either sleeping through the winter or walking across a glacial expanse with occasional penguin meat as your sole source of nutrition.

Okay, maybe not. Still, you never know. Better safe than sorry.

Eat up.

TECHNIQUE 3: DO IT FOR YOUR FAMILY

You know what's going to happen if you keep eating and training like that? Friends and family are going to stop wanting to hang out with you altogether. They've been patient, they've been supportive. So, you should tell yourself, it's time you reward them by going out to eat with them from time to time.

And by "from time to time," I, of course, mean "two meals per day, and perhaps making an occasional run for ice cream or beer."

And by "occasional run," I of course mean, "nightly run."

Follow these simple techniques, and I guarantee you will lose that unsightly fitness in a surprisingly short time. Less than a third of the time it took you to gain it, usually. At least, that's how it always goes for me.

Before you know it, you'll be back in your winter pants, the ones that are two sizes larger than what you've been wearing during the summer.

You know, the ones you swore you'd never need again.

---

36 And you know what goes well with any extra alfredo you have left over? Breadsticks.
37 And I assume you are the same or I hate you.

POSTPONE RESUMING YOUR DIET

Using these tried-and-true techniques, I generally hit a very important personal landmark each year around Christmas time: I finish gaining back all of the weight I had worked on losing during the spring and summer.

Generally, on the day after Christmas, I'll say to myself, "OK, now I've had my fun. It's time for me to get serious about losing weight and getting ready for next year's racing season."

And then I'll say that exact same thing to myself for close to a month, without losing a single pound.

OK, to be honest, I'll generally gain a few pounds after Christmas, too.

"How," I'm certain you're asking yourself, "is it possible for you to tell yourself, in all earnestness (because I promise you that I am oh-so-earnest), every single day, that you're going to get back to an athlete's diet, and then gain weight?

I'm glad you've asked.

HOW TO LIE TO YOURSELF

The truth is, I've got an elaborate system that lets me tell myself, for any given moment, that now is not quite the right time to get started on a diet. Any efforts I make right now will fail, whereas the efforts I will make at the next point on the horizon are just perfect.[38]

This system, I'm sure, is entirely unique. Which is to say, I'm positive that those of you who, like me, fight the losing battle, will not have a similar system already in place, and so are therefore trapped into rigorously observing your diets, because you just can't find a good excuse.

Well, I'm here to help. I personally guarantee you can have diet-postponement success identical to mine with the following easy 5-Step Program (©2015[39] Fat Cyclist Enterprises, all rights reserved):

1. **Realize you don't have the right kind of food on-hand.** Really, you had planned to eat nothing but egg whites, wheat bread, and grapefruit for an entire calendar year, but you forgot to go to the store last night and it turns out that you don't have any of those things on hand. What to do?

---

38   Somehow, between now and then, I'll pick up willpower and discipline. Meanwhile, these frosted cookies aren't going to eat themselves.

39   Original copyright: 2008. Nothing has changed.

2. **It's OK, because it's early in the day.** It's a well-known fact that breakfast is the most important meal of the day and that anything you eat early in the day doesn't make you gain weight, because you're going to work that off during the day. It's the afternoon and evening calories that you have to watch out for. Therefore, the doughnut, omelette, and batter-dipped, deep-fried Twinkie I'm eating are fine, as long as I don't screw up for the rest of the day.

3. **I'll exercise a little extra when I get home.** The great thing about having a heavy lunch, apart from the wonderful siesta it brings on, is that it gives you great motivation to really work out when you get home from work/school/whatever. You're going to need that energy; better fuel up.

4. **Well, it's too late to do anything about it today.** OK, so you were feeling kind of hungry when you got home from work. Strangely enough, you can still feel hungry just a few hours after a big lunch. You grazed around the kitchen for a while, which basically means you eat whatever's front and center in the fridge and pantry. After that, you didn't exactly feel like exercising. And now suddenly you realize: you've blown today. You ate heavy for breakfast and lunch, then had a snack instead of exercising. May as well call this day a loss and plan on doing better tomorrow.[40]

5. **This is my last hurrah.** You know what you should do? You should go ahead and live it up a bit tonight: eat pizza for dinner, have some chips and dip for a snack, then maybe a bedtime bowl of cereal. You're accomplishing three important things by doing this. First, you're getting it out of your system. Second, you're getting rid of that bad food so you won't be tempted by it tomorrow. And finally, you're drawing a line in the sand. Tomorrow morning you'll be able to look back and say, "That was it. That was the last time I'll eat like that for the next year." Maybe eat a little extra, just because you're angry at yourself. As you know, that will erase the appeal of food for the foreseeable future.

Tomorrow? Repeat.

---

40 Honest. For reals this time.

COMMENT BY BOTCHEDEXPERIMENT

You forgot another benefit of having a big dinner: carbohydrate loading for the next day's vigorous exercise. I mean you don't want to start tomorrow's killer workout all glycogen depleted, right?

COMMENT BY MIKE

It's frightening how dead-on your program resembles my own, except you forgot my personal Rule #1: If a coworker that weighs less than you is eating it, it must be a health food. After all, that coworker weighs less than I do, right?

COMMENT BY MASHER GNASHER

Because I jog a mile and do 10 pushups and 10 situps everyday in winter, I blame the weight gain on bone-mineralization and muscle gain. That is how I account for the 10 to 15 lbs.

HOW TO BE POPULAR

As you are no doubt aware, I am, in addition to being almost ridiculously handsome and athletic, quite popular. It may be safe to say that I have the second most popular blog in the fiercely competitive and rapidly expanding "Cycling Lifestyle & Satire" niche of the blogosphere. I am currently 85.1% less popular than Bike Snob NYC, in large part due to the negative TV spot about me he ran last week in Iowa and New Hampshire.

What will no doubt astound you, however, is that my extraordinary popularity in the world of blogging is only half the story. For, you see, I am popular in the real world too. People will often call, email, text, or instant-message me, asking if I would like to go on a bike ride with them. Or have lunch with them. Or return things I have borrowed to them.[41]

If I am not otherwise engaged and am reasonably confident they will not ambush me with demands for yet another autograph,[42] *I'll sometimes have my assistant arrange a riding appointment.*

This is the story of how my company has become so sought after and desirable.

THE SECRETS OF MY SUCCESS

I know, I know: you are confounded by, and not just a little jealous of, my extraordinary popularity. And you no doubt are saying to yourself, "Fatty, I want to be invited on bike rides! I want to enjoy the company of others! I want to be perceived as a boon companion! Is it possible for me to be popular, like you?"

The simple answer is, "No, you will never be as popular as I am. Stop trying. You're only setting yourself up for failure."

But that does not mean you cannot be popular. At least somewhat popular, anyway.

Today I will share with you my secrets on how I have become so magnificently popular.

---

41   Sometimes they'll even ask me to pay back loans to them! Ah yes, I am a very popular person indeed.

42   Or demands for repayment of loans.

BE PREPARED

As you likely know, the Boy Scout Motto is, "Try to set everything on fire."

Oh, I'm sorry. That's the *secret* motto, the one you're not supposed to know about. The other motto,[43] the one they want you to know about, is "Be prepared."

It's a fine motto, one which cyclists should apply in their own lives, in spite of the fact that the Boy Scouts might come after us with a trademark violation lawsuit in hand.

Luckily, the bicycle is a lightweight and relatively simple machine, so it's easy to be prepared for most common problems. You only need to bring a few things with you on a ride to be adequately prepared to take care of the nutritional, health, and mechanical needs for yourself and those with whom you're riding. Specifically:

- Water
- Energy bar
- Water filter
- Chlorine tablets to treat microbial agents or make a pond safe to swim in
- Sterile dressing
- Latex gloves to keep blood and gore from other people's gross injuries off you[44]
- Antibiotic ointment
- Burn ointment (in case you come across a Boy Scout)
- Bee sting ointment[45]
- Adhesive bandages
- Duct tape
- Thermometer
- Cell phone
- Tweezers
- Aspirin
- Ibuprofen
- Any other painkillers you can dig up
- Antacid

---

43   Or is it slogan? Or law? Quote of the day?

44   Or to keep the grease from chains off your hands, I suppose.

45   At this point I'm just looking for excuses to write the word "ointment," because it's such a strange-sounding word.

- Laxative (in case you need to pull an emergency practical joke)
- Chain lube
- Anti-seize compound
- Hex wrench set
- CO_2 cartridges (10)
- CO_2 valve
- 26", 27.5", and 29" tubes — two of each
- Bottom bracket tool
- Bike cleaning brush set
- Crank pullers (both square spindle and spline types)
- Cable cutter
- Assos Chamois Creme (when only the very best will do for your chamois-lubricating needs)
- Chain tool
- Cheese (aerosol)
- Digital scale, to resolve heated discussions about which bike is lightest
- Spoke tool
- Freewheel remover
- Extra spokes
- Extra derailleur
- Matches
- Gasoline (1 qt)
- Portable welding torch and goggles
- Headset wrench
- Bearing cup press
- Pliers
- Lasagna
- Pedal wrench
- Hacksaw
- Cyanide tablets
- Tire levers
- Utility knife
- Batarang
- More duct tape, because one roll might not be enough
- Flare pistol with extra flares, because you just know you're going to want to shoot off a flare or two just for fun.
- $20 to buy a ride home

I may have left a few things out, but you get the idea.

As important as it is to have these things for your own use, if you want to be popular,[46] you must also be prepared to happily loan any or all of these items out, without complaint or condition, even if it leaves you without. Once, for example, I gave my friend Kenny a trailside bone marrow transplant, because his bones had become dangerously brittle that afternoon. I did not ask him to return the marrow. Rather, I offhandedly said, "Forget it. There's more where that came from."

That's just the kind of person I am. Which means, naturally, that this is the kind of person you should aspire to be.

BRING SNACKS

Most cyclists bring something to eat and drink for the ride. But energy bars and Accelerade are not what I'd call sumptuous fare.

They are, on the other hand, what I would call "nasty-tasting."

Imagine the surge in your popularity when you, at a stop in the ride, bring a small red-and-white checked tablecloth out of your Camelbak,[47] followed by napkins and salt and pepper shakers.

I guarantee, your riding buddies' surprise will be matched only by their delight.

But you're just getting started.

Next, remove a roasted chicken (or, if you really want to be fancy, a pheasant) and a Ziploc bag full of salad. One of your water bottles will now be revealed to contain ranch dressing.

Tip: Ranch dressing goes bad in just a couple hours, so be sure you brought those first-aid supplies I mentioned earlier.

Of course, your friends will think this is extraordinary, but you've only just begun. Next, you will reveal that your Camelbak bladder is actually full of a delicious malt beverage, which you will be happy to distribute.

After this, perhaps you break out the mashed potatoes. Don't worry about gravy, though. That's going too far.

After the main course, your guests will certain be expecting dessert. I recommend pie, because everyone likes pie.[48]

---

46   Like me.

47   Camelbak paid me $1.84 for this product placement. Thanks, Camelbak!

48   From time to time you'll run across someone who claims to not like pie. They're just looking for attention.

I leave it to you to figure out how to carry the pie, but I will give you this hint: a few inexpensive bungee cords combined with the holes in your helmet give you carrying capacity well beyond what most people would expect.

Now, I know a few of you are thinking, "Fatty, that sounds like an awful lot of work."

To which I reply, "That's fine. Some people aren't really cut out to be popular. Enjoy your solitude."

BRING A GOOD CAMERA

What cyclist doesn't want to be filmed and/or photographed?[49] Unfortunately, few of us ever bring anything but a simple point-and-shoot camera with us.

You can, and should, go the extra mile by bringing a high quality SLR camera, an assortment of lenses, a good flash, a couple of reflecting umbrellas, and a tripod.

And since cycling is, after all, an active activity, be sure to bring a good hi-def camera with you. And not one of those cheesy camcorders, either; your filmwork will look hopelessly shaky and unprofessional unless you use a good shoulder-mounted camera or steadicam.

And for the love of all that's good in the world, don't forget to bring enough batteries.

WAITING FOR STRAGGLERS

It is a sad fact of life that not everybody on a bike ride is going to go at the same speed. Someone's going to have to wait up and someone's going to have to catch up.

Of course, you could just stop and wait when someone is behind you. And you just try to catch up when you lag behind. But those won't help your popularity skyrocket the way the following techniques will.

- **If you're the person who is waiting up**, it is your responsibility to not look like you have been waiting around for very long when the group arrives. They all know you're faster than they are. Don't rub it in. Please be aware that if you glance at your watch, ask questions like "Fixing a flat?" or are straddling

---

49 This is a rhetorical question; do not feel obligated to send me a letter containing your reply.

your top tube, resting your forearms on your handlebars as people arrive, they have the legal right — nay, the *obligation* — to punch you in the throat.

- **If you're the last person to arrive,** you need to understand that you owe nobody an explanation. If you feel you must give an explanation, it had better be interesting. You should know, by the way, that any explanation that sounds like an excuse *is* an excuse, and is automatically not interesting. So, if you're last to arrive, simply say, "Thanks for waiting up," immediately followed by a comment on what a great road/trail this is. In short, nobody minds a slow guy. Everybody minds a sad-sack, hang-dog whiner.

Oh yes, I should also say one last thing on this matter: I am assured it is impolite to turn around, ride back to the group, and then ride back with them. This message has been conveyed to me through the medium of a punch in the throat.[50]

MECHANICALS

Sometimes bikes break, which is why I always have my full-time pro mechanic ride with me. You, on the other hand, probably do not have mechanic on staff, so must fix your own bike. How sad for you.

As you repair your bike, you should first offer to take care of the problem on your own. "Go on ahead, I'll catch up when I can," is the proper phrasing. If your riding group has any ethics at all, they will decline. If they take you up on that offer, that's either a statement about you or the group, and it's not my job to figure out which. I can't do *everything* for you. Sheesh.

As you work on your bike, you should be careful to accept offers of help, but only if the offers of help come from competent people. Which is to say, not everyone who says they know how to true a wheel has the same technique in mind. i.e., one person may get out a spoke wrench, the other may get out a very large rock.[51]

As you repair your bike, stay focused. Don't be chatty; it's not the time.

---

50   Yes, I used to do this. I'd get to some natural regrouping point, then I'd double back to the group, turn around, and travel at their (much slower) pace. This, I should note, did not improve my popularity.

51   That said, I've seen some people do some pretty amazing field repairs using a rock.

If you start talking up a storm, your co-riders are permitted[52] to observe that you may want to spend more time fixing and less time talking.

On the other hand, anyone standing around while a mechanical issue is allowed to offer observations and advice. This advice does not need to be practical, helpful, nor even relevant to the situation. I, for example, like to offer the following observation when others are fixing their bikes: "This wouldn't have happened if you had been riding with a song in your heart."

If the person repairing the bike complains that they, in fact, *did* have a song in their heart, I like to first offer the advice that it's clearly time to choose a new song, and then observe that they might get done fixing the bike a lot sooner if they'd spend more time fixing their bike and less time talking about whether or not they had a song in their heart.

INJURIES

Occasionally, you will fall off your bike and get hurt. There's no getting around that fact. So the question is, when you fall and sustain a compound fracture to your femur, will you scream like an idiot, or will you be prepared with a witty, self-deprecating phrase that will defuse the tenseness of the situation?

Of course, you *want* to be able to say something funny and interesting when you're injured, but the fact is it's not easy to come up with clever witticisms when you're writhing in agony.

The solution? Think of what you'll say when injured *ahead of time.*[53] For example:

- **If you're suffering waves of nausea due to blunt force trauma**: "Hey, I think I'm going to barf. Can I borrow your helmet to catch it in?"
- **If you've sustained a large puncture wound due to a large-diameter impaling object**: "Cool, I've been core-sampled! Now I'll always know how old I am!" [*Note: Use this line only if your co-riders are intelligent enough to intuit the connection*

---

52   Encouraged, really.

53   And since you'll probably be in shock, you might want to have your thoughts written down on a 3 x 5 laminated card that you can keep in a jersey pocket against these situations.

between the large hole in you and the fact that a tree's age can be determined by being core sampled and having its rings counted.]

- **If you've sustained a concussion:** "Darn! Now I can't seem to remember where I've buried all the treasure!"
- **If you've sustained a compound fracture:** "Before you ask, yes, that's my femur poking out of my shorts, although I am also happy to see you."

These are just a few samples, although you could be forgiven for thinking they are so good that you might just go out and get yourself intentionally injured, so you can try them out. This is not a great idea.

And remember, there are lots of other injuries you can, and most likely will, sustain as a cyclist. I can assure you there is a clever quip that can be made for every single one of them, if you're willing to apply yourself.

ATTIRE

Wear a clean jersey and shorts, for pity's sake. And for my sake. I'm begging you.

THE ROUTE

Of course you have a great idea for where the group ought to ride today. But sometimes the group will want to ride somewhere else. When this happens, you should pout and make observations at every opportunity about how you'd all be having a better time if you had gone on the ride you had in mind. Example: "We wouldn't be riding into this headwind if we were riding the Wasatch Boulevard loop." Your friends will love you for that.[54]

You should be aware, however, that your friends may choose to express their newfound love of you through the medium of avoiding you and never inviting you on another ride.

There are many kinds of love, after all.

GIVING ADVICE

When you ride with others, bear in mind this simple axiom:

*"Every rider is allowed to give three pieces of unasked-for advice **per lifetime**."*

So make them count.

---

54 I'm being sarcastic.

I, of course, am the obvious exception to that bit of universally-understood wisdom.

Right now I can picture you, flush with excitement. "Now I know how to be a popular cyclist!" you say, your voice welling with joy.

And yes, if you will follow these rules and best practices with utmost care, you will indeed be a popular cyclist.

But not as popular as I am.

COMMENT BY TIMK

I tried the whole prepared meal thing and found that it was nice and all, but I needed more respect.

I recommend getting yourself a proper BOB Yak trailer to haul a Lodge Hibachi Grill and cooking steaks for your fellow cyclist. You will of course wish to substitute a nice red wine for that malty beverage in your Camelbak.

COMMENT BY LIFESGREAT

Velveeta is easier to carry and can be used for some simple repairs. :)

COMMENT BY STAN

When I was younger, I always used to be the first to the top of every hill. Then I'd turn around and ride down to meet the group and then beat them to the top again. It was not intended as a polite move. Heh.

COMMENT BY CLYDESTEVE

Elden, there is something that has been bothering me. I really do not think you should store the quart of gasoline right next to the welding torch.

HOW TO SUCK IN YOUR GUT
FOR PHOTOGRAPHS

There are few things in the world that make me happier than having someone say, "Why is your nickname 'Fatty?' You don't look that fat."

Sure, it eats at me a little bit that practically everyone says I don't look "that" fat. But a backhanded compliment is still a compliment, right?

I owe a lot of my success to exercise and diet. But I owe much, much more of my success to a concentrated and serious study of the art of holding my gut in when pictures are being taken of me.

By holding my stomach in just so, I have found that I can fool the entire world into thinking that I have no paunch at all.

And it's not like that illusion vanishes the first time I take a breath or something, either. Nosirree.

I am happy to, in response to numerous requests, now reveal my secrets on how to properly hold in your stomach.

What is the purpose of the book you hold in your hands? To entertain? To make me unfathomably rich? To help you pass the time as you wait in a grocery line or use the restroom?

Yes to all of these. But is that all? No. No indeed. This book is meant to educate you, offering practical tips and advice regarding all aspects of the cycling experience, from the least important to the very most important, here and now, the art of hiding your gut while being photographed in a skin-tight cycling jersey.

BASIC TECHNIQUES

Observe the following photo as a simple illustration of a group of friends about to participate in a ~~fight to the death~~ friendly race.

To the casual observer, this looks like a poorly-composed snapshot from someone's phone camera.[55] When you look closely, however, it is more. So very much more. This photo, in fact, demonstrates many simple, yet elegant, techniques you can use to hide your gut.

Starting at the left, let's review.

---

55 Which is exactly what they *want* you to think.

- **Dug** (far left) is using two of the most common techniques to hide his burgeoning middle-age paunch. First, he is wearing outlandish clothing — plaid shorts and knee-high black socks — to distract you from his stomach. More importantly, he is turning his body in such a way that his right hand, evidently just casually gripping his handlebar, partially obscures his stomach. This is called the "Handlebar Obfuscation Gambit," or "HOG" for short. Further, he hopes to distract you by putting a ridiculous object on his bicycle: a wicker basket. Nice work, Dug.
- **Adam** (second from left) is showing considerable ingenuity by using three separate gut-hiding tricks. First, he is performing the simplest[56] of all possible gut-obscuring techniques: "Back of Photo," or "BOF."[57] Next, Adam is successfully executing the HOG, but has furthermore paid Dug $9.82 (an amount negotiated by both parties) to obscure his midsection with Dug's

---

56   But, without question, it is also one of the most effective. Just so long as there are enough people in the photo that you can get behind someone. As you may well imagine, the back-of-photo technique doesn't work so well when there are just two people in the photo. Unless it's an engagement photo, I guess.

57   Why is the acronym for "Back of Photo" BOF instead of "BOP?" It just is, that's why.

left arm. This is called the "Proxy Handlebar Obfuscation Gambit," or "PHOG." Well played, Adam!

- **Fatty** (third from left) is brazenly sucking in his gut, a fixed grin hiding the fact that he is seconds from passing out. You're not fooling anybody, Fatty.
- **Sam** (back, fourth from left) is using the BOF to such a great degree that it is impossible to tell how much he weighs. This is for the best, because Sam weighs 809 pounds.
- **Brad** and **Rick** (rightmost and second from right) are using the rather tedious ploy of *not being fat* for the photo. Not cool, guys. Not cool at all.

EXPERT TECHNIQUES

Once you have mastered the basic techniques of hiding your stomach while being photographed, you're ready for these advanced tips, as demonstrated in this photo.

- **Always face front.** If you turn sideways, you expose and emphasize your personal topography. And trust me: you do not want your topography exposed.
- **Always wear bib shorts.** Bib shorts help minimize and distribute the otherwise unfortunate transition[58] from your waist to your upper body. A good pair of bib shorts can compress an otherwise massive muffin top.[59] And yes, Dug is wearing bib shorts under those plaid shorts. Dug's no fool. Though he can play that role.[60]
- **Wear an appropriate jersey.** I recommend the Fat Cyclist jersey,

---

58   AKA "unsightly bulges."
59   Every bit as well as Spanx, if you buy them small enough.
60   This is an allusion to one of my favorite novels, *Nobody's Fool*, by Richard Russo. JFYI.

which, due to its dark sides, is very slimming. It is only when you look *very carefully* at Fatty[61] here that you recognize he is much wider than the pink section of his jersey shown here.

- **Be photographed in the dark.** When you're photographed in the dark, you can be confident that there is only one light source: the camera flash. You are therefore much less likely to be ambushed by shadows from unfriendly light sources (e.g., the sun), which generally have the effect of emphasizing your man-boobs and/or other unsightly bulges.[62]

THINGS TO AVOID

As with any acquired skill, being well-photographed in a bike jersey is as much about knowing what not to do as knowing what you should do. Don't forget these "Don'ts," or suffer the consequences.

- **Don't puff out your chest.** When you suck in your gut, that mass needs to go somewhere,[63] but a puffed-out chest is a sure sign of where you've temporarily relocated your stomach. Suck in your stomach, but roll your shoulders forward to counteract your now-protruding chest. Avoid, if at all possible, puffing out your cheeks and turning blue.
- **Never exhale until the photographer has put away the camera.** After the flash has gone off and/or you've heard the shutter noise, you may be tempted to relax. Don't do it. The photographer may seize upon the opportunity to take a candid photo.[64]
- **Do not allow yourself to be photographed while breathing hard.** It's difficult enough to keep your stomach in place when you're relaxed. When your lungs are working at capacity, it's practically impossible. If someone wants to take a picture right after you've gotten off the bike, say, "Just a sec," and then find a reason to work on your bike, use the restroom, eat a snack, or whatever, until such time as you feel you can hold your breath again for up to 45 seconds.

---

61   I.e., me.
62   Come to think of it, are there any bulges that aren't unsightly?
63   I'm pretty sure this is due to the law of conservation of mass. Man, I hate that law.
64   Remember: The only **safe** camera is a **stowed** camera.

- **Never allow anyone to photograph you while you are on the bike.** You're hunched over, you're breathing hard, and you're otherwise not controlling the situation.

Is this a lot to remember? Of course it is. But is it worth it? Absolutely. Because between learning these techniques and actually becoming thin, which do you think you are more likely to accomplish?

COMMENT BY CAT

Dear Fatty, thank you for the tips. Unfortunately, as a female cyclist, sucking in my gut isn't going to get rid of the wide load in the rear.

COMMENT BY LORI

My personal favorite trick is to be the one with the camera — thus, never being photographed. And/or get really good with Photoshop.

COMMENT BY THE D

As a soft, middleweight roadie, I scrupulously observe the following three-part cycle:
1) Hang with the clydesdales, who make me appear thinner than I am in photos,
2) Draft the clydesdales, which makes me seem faster than I really am at the rest stops,
3) Thanks to the "efficiency" of the above, never actually get any thinner or faster.

COMMENT BY SWEDOZ

The joy of living in Sweden where the weather is always so crap you can have enough clothes on to hide your gut.

HOW TO USE *THE SECRET* IN CYCLING

Like most everyone else in the world, I have heard of The Secret, the book that promises untold wealth, health, and perfectly-styled hair on a daily basis...as long as you buy the book. Like most everyone else, I was curious what secret The Secret contains.

And like most everyone else, I looked on Wikipedia to find out, where I learned that the secret of The Secret is that if you think about something in the right way, whether it be an event or an object or the removal of the letters "C" from the English language, the universe attaches other similar thoughts and forces to your thought, your thought gathers force like a giant thought-snowball, and then the thing you thought about will happen.

Which is really awesome. Because I hate redundant letters.

However, since — to my dismay — I did not master the secrets of The Secret by reading the Wikipedia article, I went ahead and downloaded the Kindle version of the book to my phone, and read it as quickly as possible, provided "as possible" means "whenever I was in line at the grocery store, or whenever I needed to use the bathroom for an extended period of time."

And you know what? You can probably do just fine with reading the Wikipedia article.

Which is not to say, however, that The Secret does not work. It does! For example, I am going to, right now, think about eating the Twix Bar I have here.

And now I am eating it.

Freaky, isn't it?

But The Secret has a dark underbelly. Yes it does. And that dark underbelly is that if you don't formulate your thoughts correctly, you may get the opposite (or worse, a strange tangent) of that thing for which you hoped so much.

I call this "The Universe as a Trickster Genie" principle.

Specifically, The Secret tells us that the universe is a little bit stupid, in that it doesn't understand negatives. And I don't mean that it doesn't get double-negatives, which would be understandable, because who doesn't have trouble with those from time to time?

I mean that it actually doesn't hear negatives at all.

So, for example, if I were to think to myself, "I am not going to eat another Twix bar," the universe just picks up on the "eat" and "Twix bar" part. And — get this — right now I am eating another Twix bar.

Oh, it is so delicious.

Thanks, universe, for making me eat another Twix bar even when I thought I shouldn't.

And also, now I guess I understand why I'm seeing more of the letter "C" than I used to.[65]

Like everyone else in the whole world, I am utterly convinced that *The Secret* is a powerful force in my everyday life. However, unlike most cyclists, I have spent hours, or quite possibly days, considering, "How can I use *The Secret* to become an extremely awesome cyclist? And how can I be certain to formulate my thoughts correctly, so the universe doesn't go pulling some wacky prank on me?"

The universe has rewarded me with the answer (because I used *The Secret* to tell it to give me the answer), and I will now teach you the things you must and must not think in order to leverage *The Secret* in your riding.

TO WIN A RACE

- **Do:** Imagine yourself going very fast, crossing a finish line. And be sure to also imagine nobody else in front of you, and lots of people behind you. And be sure to imagine yourself crossing the correct finish line, or you might wind up winning a completely different race.[66] And you might also want to imagine a calendar nearby with the current date on it, or you might win the race, but as the sole participant in the octogenarian category, 55 years from now.
- **Do NOT**: Imagine the problems you might have that might obstruct your win.[67] For example, do not imagine yourself with a mechanical. Do not imagine yourself with a show tune running endlessly through your head. Do not imagine yourself being passed by me. Except now I have already made you imagine all of those things, and I am going to totally beat you when we race.[68]

---

65   In fact, my middle name now starts with a "C." Curse you, *The Secret*!

66   I once accidentally won a NASCAR event in this way. I am not complaining, because they let me keep the trophy.

67   You're imagining those problems right now, aren't you? Well stop it! Stop it *this instant!*

68   Furthermore, now you are imagining me beating you (just as I am), and so now you've been double-whammied by *The Secret*!

TO AVOID A CRASH

- **Do**: Think of yourself riding upright, in every possible terrain. Think of the road being empty. But do not think in terms of "devoid of crazy drivers," because then you're still thinking about — and therefore attracting — crazy drivers. Just think of a nice empty road.[69] And go ahead and imagine ice chests on the side of that empty road, spaced every 100 feet or so and filled with the beverage of your choice. Oh, and imagine ice, too, because the universe needs you to be specific.
- **Do NOT**: Think of the word "crash." Ever. It doesn't even matter if you think of the word "Don't" before you think the word "crash." You still thought of crashing.[70] Also, you should probably not stop wearing a helmet. Because there may be someone out there who *is* thinking of you having a crash, and maybe that someone is better at *The Secret* than you.[71]

TO HANDLE A CRASH IN THE EVENT THAT YOU'RE HAVING ONE EVEN THOUGH YOU THOUGHT YOU HAD DONE A PRETTY GOOD JOB OF IMAGINING NOT HAVING A CRASH

- **Do**: As you fly through the air toward the tree, boulder, road, or cinder block wall, imagine pillows. Lots and lots and lots of fluffy pillows. And it may not be a bad idea to imagine an ambulance on its way, just in case the pillows don't arrive on time.
- **Do NOT**: Imagine yourself hovering in the air, magically defying the laws of gravity. The universe is totally not cool with people flouting[72] its laws, and will slap you down even harder. Don't go upsetting the universe, people. Also, do not imagine yourself lying in a broken, crumpled heap, because that's counterproductive. Besides, you'll have time for that later.

---

69   With very occasional, very polite, drivers. Who are giving you a thumbs-up out their sun-roofs as they go by.

70   Oh for crying out loud. You're thinking about crashing, aren't you? You are hopeless.

71   It's not me thinking about you crashing, though; I promise. I want to beat you in races, but I don't want you to get hurt in the process.

72   Flout (verb): To openly disregard a rule, law, or convention.

TO GET A NEW BIKE

- **Do:** Imagine yourself with a new bike. Be really specific about the bike though. Know the brand, the model, the year, the size, the color, the components, wheels, and tires. Everything. Also, imagine that you obtained it legally, because otherwise the trickster universe might just plop one in your hands, but it's stolen, and some of your local authorities may not really understand *The Secret* as well as they should. Also, imagine that it's yours, and not that you're just washing it for a friend or something.
- **Do NOT:** Imagine what your significant other is going to say when s/he sees you coming home with yet another new bike. In fact, you may want to do some pre-emptive counter-imagining around that scenario.

TO LOSE WEIGHT

- **Do:** Imagine yourself thin and ripped.[73] Imagine yourself buying all new cycling clothes. Imagine yourself a blur of motion as you climb your favorite killer hill.
- **Do NOT:** Imagine yourself not eating. Because the universe will ignore the "not" part and will make you eat. But also, don't imagine yourself eating, because, of course, that's where the problem began in the first place, isn't it? But remember, you should not stop eating altogether, because that brings problems of its own. Like starvation, for example. Wow, this *Secret* thing is turning out to be pretty darned tricky.

TO GET AWESOME QUADS

- **Do:** Imagine yourself with my quads.[74]
- **Do NOT:** Imagine me wearing a big floppy sombrero, because that would be a mean trick to play, especially since I'm letting you have my quads[75] and stuff.

---

73   Or, if you're a road cyclist, imagine yourself thin and well-muscled for your lower half, and terrifyingly emaciated for your upper half.

74   But not literally my quads. Imagine yourself with quads very similar to mine. Neither of us is going to be happy if you have my quads.

75   I mean, quads similar to mine.

Really, I'm just getting started here. I also have very useful tips I can give you on what to think and what to not think on how to spin circles, how to ride a clean line, how to keep your chain lubed, and how to avoid broken glass. And much, much more.

But to get that, you're going to need to buy my upcoming book, *The Secret and Cycling*, for which I am right now imagining getting a big fat publishing contract.

And I'm imagining it already being written, too.

PS: Whoever it was that imagined me wearing fake elephant ears, an orange tutu, and these clown shoes, *cut it out*.

COMMENT BY BILL

I don't want your quads. I want your Twix bar. I have been doing real good this week about not having candy bars and I read your blog for educational and entertainment purposes and now I am craving Twix bars! Thanks a lot.

COMMENT BY TINA Z

Damn, I really want a Twix bar now. Thanks Fatty.

COMMENT BY IAN

So if I imagine myself not having a crash and someone imagines away the letter C, will that also keep me from getting a rash? Because that would be great if I could not keep getting this rash. It's bright red and located right under my... wait... I've said too much haven't I?

COMMENT BY JENN

Huh. Turns out, I look a little weird with men's quads. They don't match my butt. Or my calves. Kalves? Alves?? I'm so confused.

HOW TO BEHAVE WHEN A CYCLIST OF THE OTHER GENDER IS HURT

We were just riding along. Honest, that's all we were doing. My wife — The Hammer — and I were mountain biking on Little Creek Mesa, near St. George, Utah. And she crashed. A juniper bush grabbed one of her handlebars and just wrested the bike from her grasp.

The Hammer went down, hitting her tailbone[76] *good and hard against a sharp rock. I could tell that it had hurt, based on the way she hopped around and then ran in place, crying and swearing a lot.*

Luckily for everyone involved,[77] *I had my GoPro going at the moment and caught it all on tape. Which is what I told her.*[78]

Which was not very clever of me.

Since then, I have spent some time considering how I could have better reacted, thereby hopefully avoiding unfortunate events that transpired for a good long time.

Luckily for you, I will now share what I have learned.

As a cyclist who sometimes rides with a female cyclist, I realize that how one acts may depend on who one is with, and have therefore helpfully segregated my findings into appropriate gender combinations.

IF YOU ARE A MALE CYCLIST WITH AN INJURED FEMALE CYCLIST

- **Refrain from telling her how hot she looks in lycra**. Now is not the time. Trust me.
- **Tell her how tough and awesome she is.** By the way, she is very tough, and very awesome. Just in case you weren't clear on that.
- **Tell her anyone else would be crying harder/acting more pathetic than she is, including you.** But don't use the words "acting more pathetic," because that implies she's being pathetic at all, which she is not.

---

76 Or, as I like to call it, her "buttbone."
77 Except, of course, my wife.
78 I'm sure she'll be happy to know that you can find this video at http://bit.ly/fatsby12. The first crash is at 0:24. Her second crash is at 2:55.

- **Get her bike ready to ride again.** The woman is going to want you to shut up at some point. This is a good time for you to fiddle with her bike and make sure it's good to go.
- **Volunteer to make a tourniquet/bandage out of your jersey.** But not until she's on her feet and seems like she might appreciate your sense of humor again.[79]
- **Describe the events leading up to the injury.** Be expansive and generous with the difficulty of the triggering obstacle and/or event. For example, don't say she went over her handlebars when she hit a rock. It was a *big ol' honkin' **ledge**, and she darn near cleared it anyway.*

I'm not exactly sure why we all start telling the story as soon as the event happened, but it seems to help, and it seems to help more if you get started with the exaggeration right away.

IF YOU ARE A MALE CYCLIST WITH AN INJURED MALE CYCLIST

- **Ask if he's alright.** Depending on how old you are and where you live, you should either end the sentence with "dude," "man," or "bro." It makes the question affectionate and concerned-sounding without being too affectionate and concerned-sounding.
- **Suppress your laughter**, at least until you're certain he's not bleeding out.
- **Lean his bike against a tree.** He won't trust any tweaks, fixes, or adjustments you make anyway.
- **Wait for 30 seconds before asking if he's ready to ride.** If he says he needs another minute, wait another thirty seconds and ask again. Repeat as necessary.
- **Describe the event**, but feel free to trivialize certain aspects, such as the prime cause of the event, and enhance other aspects, such as the high-pitched scream the victim made upon suffering a compound fracture.

IF YOU ARE A FEMALE CYCLIST WITH AN INJURED MALE CYCLIST

- **Tell him how hot he looks in lycra.** For guys, there's no bad time

---

79 If she ever did in the first place. This is not, it should be noted, a great time for you to explore the boundaries of her appreciation of your sense of humor.

to hear this, and even when we're injured there's a small part of us that's wondering if our guts are sufficiently sucked in.[80]

- **Otherwise let us suffer quietly**. We're trying to be manly and stoic.[81] If you begin to describe the event, we're going to think it sounds silly, because you're not exaggerating our manliness sufficiently. If you call the injury on our leg a "nasty little scrape," you're making it that much harder to refer to it as a five-inch-long gushing gash when we recount it later.
- **Don't touch our bikes**. Unless we beg you to help us unclip.

IF YOU ARE A FEMALE CYCLIST WITH AN INJURED FEMALE CYCLIST

- **Honestly I have no idea**. Do whatever it is you women do when you're with each other. Like, talk about how much you miss us men. That's what you do when we're not around, right?[82]

Now, I'm sure some of you are thinking, "Well, how about administering a little first aid?" But that would assume I know what I'm doing and would not be making the problem worse. For example, in my panic, I might have been likely to give The Hammer rattlesnake poison antidote, which probably wouldn't have helped very much.

> COMMENT BY DANESS40
>
> You might want to mention to stand clear of a male cyclist for the first 5–7 seconds after the crash. Sometimes men jump up right after an injury and just want to punch something....you don't want to be that something! EEK!

> COMMENT BY DOWN SOUTH
>
> My husband needs to read this. He's fantastic at annoying the crap out of me asking if I'm ok, but the rest could use some work.

---

80 And whether our accident has made us more attractive to you, somehow.
81 While simultaneously trying really hard to not pass out.
82 Or maybe you forget we exist at all. That is my deepest, darkest fear, and the one I suspect is probably correct.

COMMENT BY KELLY

So wait. You didn't tell us if it would be appropriate in a male/male situation to comment on how hot they look in that lycra.

COMMENT BY HEIDI

You posted a video of your wife crashing (and crashing again) and you're still married? You ARE a lucky man.

Middleword

DAN WUORI

YOU'VE PROBABLY NEVER READ A BOOK WITH A MIDDLEWORD. AND THAT'S BECAUSE THERE'S NO SUCH THING AS A MIDDLEWORD, OR THERE WASN'T until Fatty read my submitted Foreword and told me it wasn't long enough. When I balked, he told me that for every page I agree to write in his book he'll enter my name in a drawing for a tricked-out mountain bike.

I told him that I'd already fallen for that gag one too many times on his stupid blog, but then I remembered two things:

First, I could use a 29er.

Second, I made a promise in the Foreword to keep Elden honest. And after reading merely the first half of this book, it's clear that the guy is full of it. With this in mind, I will devote the remainder my efforts here to correcting just a few of the factual errors and outright lies Fatty has tried to pass off over the preceding chapters.

CORRECTIONS

- *Page 6*: Levi Leipheimer has been bald for quite some time. He did not adopt this style in 2013 in an effort to steal Fatty's wife.
- *Page 18*: America's 19th President, Rutherford B. Hayes, did not in fact coin the group ride warning, "Car back!"
- *Page 33*: Fatty has never successfully performed a tracheotomy using a spoke and a Presta valve.

- *Page 47*: Contrary to claims made here, Elden first shaved his legs to appear in a touring production of The Rocky Horror Picture Show.
- *Page 58*: Despite its name, Nutella should never be used as a chamois cream.
- *Page 73*: Fatty does not hold the Strava KOM up Italy's Mount Etna, or any other active volcano for that matter.
- *Page 91*: Elden's first book, *Comedian Mastermind*, did not outsell *A Tale of Two Cities*. It also was not an Oprah's Book Club selection. Or even very good.
- *Page 109*: Crosby, Stills, Nash, Young, Liggett, and Sherwen did not perform at Woodstock. Phil and Paul actually left the group in late 1968.
- *Page 120*: There is not a Tour of Greece and Italy known as the Gyros d'Italia.
- *Page 126*: The traditional 5th anniversary gift is wood, not a case of lemon-lime energy gels.
- *Page 145*: The grupetto is not Pinocchio's father.
- *Page 164*: "Truing" your wheels has nothing to do with admitting their price to your spouse.
- *Page 172*: The laws of aerodynamics do not support any claim made on this page. Or any other page really.
- *Page 188:* The winner of Paris-Roubaix in 1986 was not named Jean-Luc Picard. Indeed no Starfleet captain has ever placed in the top ten.
- *Page 199*: Stephen King's *The Shining*, is not about a man driven to madness after being forced to ride a stationary trainer all winter.
- *Page 201*: A Bobke Roll is not a traditional German pastry.

I'm telling you, there's something I just don't trust about this guy.

5.

Deep and Insightful
Cycling Industry Analysis

I SUBSCRIBE TO PRETTY MUCH EVERY CYCLING MAGAZINE THERE IS. *Bicycling. Velo. Peloton. Dirt Rag. Bike Monkey. Mountain Flyer.* AND others I can't remember right now and can't be bothered to get up and go look, because I had lasagna for dinner.

If you have a cycling magazine, let me know. I will probably subscribe to it.

That said, I don't usually read the articles. I just flip through the pages, looking at the pictures. And the ads.

Oh, I love the ads. I stare at them for much, much longer than the advertiser expects. And I find that I am captivated. I cannot look away. I'm intrigued at their assertions. I'm drawn in by their colorful images. I'm enraptured by their metaphors and persuasive rhetoric.

And in short, I feel like someone needs to say something here.

May as well be me, I guess.

I AM STILL WORKING ON MY ENTRY IN THE "WIN THE EDDY MERCKX EXPERIENCE" CONTEST

I have given away a lot of bikes in my time as a blogger, dozens of them, all used to help fundraise for causes I care about.

Whenever I do a contest to give away a bike, there's a little piece of me that worries: am I driving people away with this contest? Am I making it too hard? Is there a way I can simplify it, somehow make people more likely to participate?

When, in February of 2009, I saw Bicycling Magazine's *ad for a contest they were running, a contest where you could win an Eddy Merckx bike, I took a closer look.*

This is partly because I was curious about how other, more professional bike publications ran bike giveaways. It was also because I'd be interested in winning a bike for once, instead of giving them away.

But also, I was...well, I was astonished. And not in an awesome way.

I'm reluctant to post this entry, because I don't want to tip my hand. But the fact is, I'm at an impasse and figure that the likelihood of somebody winning this thing because they stole my idea(s) is worth the risk, because I need some advice.

What am I talking about? I'm talking about the contest in the current issue of *Bicycling Magazine*, of course:

Now, I have to say that I found the headline distracting:

The "Eddy Merckx *Experience?*" I asked.

Enter and you could WIN the
EDDYMERCKX
EXPERIENCE

This makes me think that the PR firm that wrote the ad copy for this contest has Eddy confused with Jimi Hendrix.[1] Which is perfectly understandable...unless you know even a tiny little bit about either of them.

Still. Win an Eddy Merckx bike? I'm all over that. So what do I have to do? Well, the ad copy says I need to do this:

"Tell us — in 50 words or less — how riding a bike bearing Eddy's name and inspired by his legend will empower you to channel 'The Cannibal's' greatness and achieve your most ambitious cycling goals."

I don't mind telling you that I panicked a little when I saw that I only have 50 words to do all that. I mean, they're giving me a grand total of 50 words to write an essay that has a *subject matter consisting of 27 words.*

Yikes.

Being an ambitious-yet-thorough sort,[2] I didn't want to merely use the ad copy as my guide for my entry. Instead, I made certain I completely understood what I was being asked to do, by carefully reading the rules.

It turns out that a complete reading of the rules gives an even more daunting picture of what I need to do in those 50 words:

"The essay should tell us, in 50 words or less, what cycling-specific ambitions or goals riding an Eddy Merckx brand bicycle will help empower the entrant to achieve and how the entrant will benefit from the signature features and technology of an Eddy Merckx brand bicycle. The winner will be judged by the following criteria: (1) detailed and creative description of an entrant's cycling goal, (2) description of specific features and technologies offered in an Eddy Merckx brand bicycle that will enable an entrant to make the most of his/her phys-ical talent, (3) description of how Eddy Merckx's personal success as a professional bicycle racer will inspire or motivate entrant to achieve their goals when they ride a bicycle bearing Eddy Merckx's name, (4) organization and development of the ideas expressed, with clean and appropriate examples to support them, and (5) consistency in the use

---

1   "Both 'Jimi' and "Eddy" have two syllables and both 'Merckx' and 'Hendrix' end in 'x.' They're practically the same name!"

2   A verifiable lie, on both counts.

of language, variety in sentence structure and range of vocabulary, use of proper grammar, spelling and punctuation." [3]

That's 162 words, telling me that in my mere 50 words, I need to do each of the following:

- Talk about my cycling ambitions and goals.
- Talk about how the bike will help me achieve those goals.
- Be detailed and creative[4] in my description of these ambitions, goals, and my accelerated achievement of said goals on aforementioned bike.
- Describe the features/technologies of the bike that will assist in the facilitation of my achievement of my ambitions and goals.
- Discuss, presumably in some detail, how the legend of Eddy Merckx ties into all this.
- Develop all of the above fully, and with good organization.
- No naughty jokes.
- Don't stray off-topic in my 50-word essay.
- Be clever and original in my use of language.
- Demonstrate that I own a thesaurus.
- Use commas, periods, nouns, and verbs where they're supposed to be used.
- Run the whole thing through the spell-checker before I fire it off.

I've got to say that upon completing my review of this to-do-in-50-words list, I briefly blacked out. Then woke up sobbing.

Eventually, though — my jaw set, my visage grim, my nostrils flared — I got to work. I am not happy with my work, but here are my attempts thus far.[5]

THE CHECKLIST APPROACH

My first attempts at writing this essay centered around trying to simply satisfy the requirements set forth in the rules. A representative sample of my 50-word essay using this technique follows:

My cycling ambitions and goals are many-fold (not "manifold," which is a completely different word with a distinctly different meaning, and

---

3   This is, word for word, the actual rules. I mean: wow.

4   Detailed *and* creative in fifty words? This is starting to feel like they're just messing with me.

5   Note that I never did send in an entry into this contest.

would severely alter the meaning of this sentence).[6] *First, I would like to win a bike race in my lifetime. Any bike race. I'm not particular about which race, or even about having to sandbag down to a slower category (if there is one) to do it. I just want to be able to say, "I have won a race." An Eddy Merckx bike would help me achieve this goal by intimidating my competition, hopefully to the extent that they would soil themselves and hence be unable to queue[7] up at the start line. And then I would win.*

My second, and more pressing, ambition is to look sassy on a bike. I have purchased several jerseys and bib shorts and a special very aerodynamic-looking helmet that all go very well with the color scheme of the Eddy Merckx bike featured in this contest. If I win the contest, I intend to take this course to its natural conclusion and buy socks and shoes that go with the bike. And then I will look sassy, indeed.

My third ambition is to figure out why anybody would ever eat bleu cheese. It smells terrible, looks awful, and tastes nasty. What is it other people find appealing about this nasty substance? I must know. I confess, however, that I do not know how an Eddy Merckx bicycle would help me solve this riddle.[8]

The Eddy Merckx bike is really crucial to my achieving my objectives, because, unlike other bikes, it is a lightweight carbon fiber road bike with racing geometry and high-end components. This is totally unique in the world of cycling.[9]

To conclude, I would like to describe how once, Eddy Merckx appeared to me in a dream. He told me that if I ever wanted to win a race, I must be certain that as few people as humanly possible start that race.[10] *He told me that I must have confidence. He told me I must look sassy. He told me his bike was exactly what I needed to do all these things. In my dream, Eddy was eating bleu cheese.*

---

6   It's possible I could have reduced the word count slightly by deleting this parenthetical clause.

7   Also, I should win a prize because I know the proper spelling of "queue."

8   Sometimes I write things, thinking they're hilarious. Then I come back later and wonder who wrote them. This is one of those times. And yet, I have left it in this book! Why? I don't know.

9   This may be sarcasm.

10   That's good solid advice, Eddy.

Curse you, bleu cheese, for spoiling what was otherwise a very awesome and topical dream.

This is, of course, a perfectly wonderful essay and would almost certainly win, except it's 392 words long.[11] I tried the trick of hyphenating every word in each sentence, but I knew that the judges would see through this ruse.

Disappointed, I tried another approach.

APPEAL TO AUTHORITY

As many of you know, Eddy Merckx isn't actively involved in Eddy Merckx bicycles. However, I'm sure his opinion still holds considerable sway with whoever judges this contest.

So I contemplated how I could use these two facts to my advantage. And that's when it came to me: I'd just send a photo,[12] showing how *Eddy has already endorsed me as the winner.* Behold:

Really, no additional text is necessary, as far as I was concerned. The judges would see that Eddy is my close personal friend and that he has already selected me as the winner. Really, there's nothing left to do but collect my bike.

And then the rules went and spoiled my party.

"Entry Material/Entry cannot contain the image or likeness of or reference in any identifiable way (for example, by first and last name, or by any part of a name that is identifiable) any person other than the entrant, including, but not limited to, any depictions of celebrities, unless a signed release from such person(s) is submitted to Sponsors along with the Entry Material/Entry."

Man, those guys thought of *everything.*

So I sent an email out to Eddy asking if it's OK for me to use this

---

11   If feels like a lot more, I know.
12   Yes, that's really a picture of me with Eddy Merckx. I've been trying to find a way to include it in this book since the introduction.

photo, but he hasn't replied yet.[13] I'm sure he'll be cool with me using it, but as a "Plan B," I got to working on one more essay.

JUST LIE

I'm probably the only person this has occurred to, but while the rules are really explicit about what the essay must contain, it doesn't say (and believe me, I have checked) that the contents of the essay have to be *true*. So here's my next attempt.

> *I am a committed Cat 2 cyclist with dreams of moving into Cat 1 this year. I win more often than not, and when I train, it is always watching an Eddy Merckx video. I am the only person I know who rates "A Sunday in Hell" as his favorite movie of all time.[14]*
>
> *I want an Eddy Merckx bike because my current bike is a piece of crap. It weighs 24 pounds, which causes me all kinds of difficulty in climbing stages. Eddy Merckx bikes, on the other hand, are the pinnacle of beauty, reliability, and power.*
>
> *Even more importantly, though, would be the fact that as I ride my Eddy Merckx bike, I will feel like The Cannibal is urging me on, reminding me with every turn of the cranks of what he has accomplished...and what I can accomplish, if I will not break.*
>
> *I want an Eddy Merckx bike so I can make him proud, if only in my own mind.*

This is, of course, pure hogwash. Plus, it's more than three times as long as is allowed, which gives you an idea of how impossibly brief my actual entry is going to have to be.

You see why I'm discouraged? This essay contest isn't just difficult; it's impossible.

But I won't give up.

Because I know, in my heart of hearts, that The Cannibal wouldn't.

> COMMENT BY COWORKERALEX
> What — you're not really Cat 2? That's what Fatty's been telling everyone here in the office for like 2 years...

---

13   He never did reply, but that's probably at least partially because I didn't actually reach out to him.

14   Not true.

COMMENT BY RANDOBOY
Channel Eddy. Be brief. Verb noun. Repeat 25 times.

COMMENT BY AARON
I love bleu cheese.

COMMENT BY DUG
Remember how James T. Kirk beat the Kobayashi Maru? Do that.

AN OPEN LETTER TO VELONEWS REGARDING OUR MUTUAL ADORATION OF ASSOS

First things first. This story won't make any sense at all unless you first know that Assos is a very expensive, premium brand of bicycle clothing made in Switzerland. Ferrari, it could be said, is the Assos of the car industry.

Although it's possible that Ferrari doesn't hit the point of diminishing returns quite as soon.

But that's neither here nor there. Before you read this next story, there are a few things I need to clear up.

1. ***Everyone seems to think that I hate Assos.*** *I don't. Honestly, I really and truly do not hate Assos. I've never tried anything they make (except their chamois cream, which was quite an experience). It's too expensive for me. But that doesn't mean I hate them. That said, I do hate some of their advertising.*

2. ***This story, in particular, is not even really about Assos.*** *It's about VeloNews, and what was probably the single most bizarre issue there ever was of this magazine. The falling-over-ourselves-to-praise-an-important-advertiser-ness was, in its own way, a thing of beauty.*

3. ***I also don't hate VeloNews*** *(which is now simply called Velo).[15] But if they're going to lob an easy one like this to me, it would be wrong of me to not take a swing, right?*

Thank you very much for your attention to this matter.

Dear *VeloNews,*

I love Assos. I love it so much. And it makes me happy when other people love Assos, especially when they love Assos as much as I love Assos.

Hence, as a big fan of both your magazine and of Assos clothing, I was very excited to receive the September 2009 issue of your fine publication.

Imagine my disappointment, then, *VeloNews,* to find you chose only the top-center of the cover of this issue of the magazine for a headline proclaiming "ASSOS PRECISION."

---

15   It's my understanding that next year they're going to shorten it even further, to just "Lo."

Why not something more prominent, *VeloNews*? I mean, including Assos in three articles in this issue is a good start, but, don't you think you could have included a photograph on the cover, as well?

Also, you could have added exclamation marks to emphasize the endorsement: "ASSOS PRECISION!!!" Or better yet, "Assos is Very Awesome! And We Love Them Very Much!" This, after all, is pretty much the substance of the articles in the magazine, so why not reflect that sentiment on the cover?

Why so coy, *VeloNews*?

TABLE OF CONTENTS TREATMENT

While I am disappointed with the way you seem to be showing some restraint with your —absolutely justified — love for all things Assos on the front cover, I am pleased to see that you are at least trying to make amends by the time you get to the Table of Contents: "Threading the Needle: Assos means quality in any language."

TECH & TRAINING

78 | AUTUMN ENSEMBLE
Stay warm and look good on the road and trail as the harvest moon approaches.

84 | THREADING THE NEEDLE
Assos means quality in any language

You see, *that's* the kind of language I expect and require from the non-biased journal of competitive cycling. Something that plainly and simply endorses an extra-awesome clothing manufacturer.

And you and I both know Assos is fantastic, so why worry about substantiating that claim in the articles by actually assessing whether the clothing is worth what you pay for it?

Assos is so wonderful, people should just accept its perfection on the face of without question. Like you and I do.

THE FASHION SHOW

I admit to being a little bit concerned when I saw that your first editorial mention of Assos in the September issue was little more than a photograph and blurb.

Here's what I think you should have written instead:

"The trim-fit jersey has reflective detailing, full-front wind protection, and a zippered security pocket, *unlike other jerseys, all of which are made of the heaviest and least breathable burlap sack material on the market. None of them have zippers, and most of them charge you extra for pockets, which Assos invented, by the way."*

Still, I was gratified to see that you did note the vest adds wind protection. It's *about time* a clothing manufacturer realizes that cyclists want their vests to give them wind protection. I swear, I am so sick of all these vests I've got that provide no wind protection whatsoever. Sheesh!

And I'll bet that formed collar doesn't *just* keep out the chill. I'll bet it also looks sexy as heck. You probably should have mentioned that, too. But I'm going to let it slide, because I know you've got to maintain your editorial integrity. Which you're doing a smash-up job of, by the way.

ASSOS INTERMEDIATE EVO LONG SLEEVE JERSEY/ ELEMENTZERO VEST: The trim-fit jersey has reflective detailing, full front wind protection, and a zippered security pocket. The vest adds wind protection, a ventilated back panel, and a formed collar to keep out the chill.

ANALYSIS OF YOUR HARD-HITTING ASSOS EXPOSE

I have to say, *VeloNews*, that I really enjoyed your first story on how much you love Assos: "Threading the Needle: After 33 years, Assos sets the bar for luxury cycling clothing."

I learned a lot of important things from this article, all of which help reinforce my deep and certain knowledge that Assos is the best clothing manufacturer that has ever existed. For example, here are several actual quotes from the ~~ad~~ article you published, along with my reactions:

- *"While many companies have relocated their manufacturing to Asia, Assos has chosen to continue producing clothing locally to maintain quality control."* This reinforces my long-held belief that it is impossible to maintain quality control over things that are produced anywhere but right at home. Shame on anyone who would ever think to manufacture anything non-locally!

- *"The clothing line itself is largely manufactured in Slovenia, Bulgaria, and Italy."* Um, those Slovenians are awesome! Much more awesome than Asia. And it's not really not all that important to have your clothes actually manufactured locally, anyway.
- *"The aesthetic is tidy, modern Swiss, with polished concrete floors, stainless steel kitchen appliances [...] and a white, silver and black color scheme that's applied to everything, a harmonic blend of Italian and Swiss."* It always has been and always will be of utmost importance to me to know the quality of my clothing manufacturer's kitchen appliances. And it's nice to finally know this white/black/silver thing that's so new and fresh has a hybrid nationality. The next time I go to an Ikea, I'm going to let them know that they're actually Swiss-Italian, not Swedish.[16]
- *"The freshly detailed Audis and Mercedes in the parking lot betray stereotypically Swiss sensibilities."* I love knowing that the people behind my favorite clothing line are driving very expensive cars, because that tells me they really love cycling! And that they fit neatly into their national stereotypes!
- *"Roche plays a major role in design and testing, taking new samples out for long rides around Lake Como and critiquing minute details to ensure the highest quality."* That, *VeloNews*, is truly innovative. I am quite certain that no other bike clothing manufacturer actually has people try on and use clothing prototypes. Frankly, my mind is still boggling that this idea occurred to them. What will Assos think of next?
- *"A Gyrowash simulates hundreds of normal washes to see how things hold up in the laundry."* I'm relieved to know this, because, like many (most?) Assos clothing owners, I generally wash my clothes over and over and over without using them in between.[17]

You know what, *VeloNews*? You totally got it right. Assos really does set the bar for luxury cycling clothing. You proved it, by not mentioning,

---

16   And I'm going to tell them to quit stealing ideas from Assos.

17   And believe me, every time I put my Assos gear in the washer, my washing machine (which is black, silver, and white, and was hand-made by Slovenian monks, by the way) feels a little surge of pride.

apart from vague "other company" generalities, where that bar is set, how others compare, or even what "luxury" means in this context.

And I'd go so far as to say that this article sets the bar for luxury journalism.

ANALYSIS OF "TESTED: THE ASSOS SS.13 JERSEY ($319) AND F1.13 S5 BIB SHORT ($359)

One thing I really appreciate about your coverage, *VeloNews*, is that you're willing to stay focused. Hot on the heels of your hard-nosed investigative report into Assos' kitchen decor, you've got...another article about how much you like Assos.

---

tech and training **TECH REPORT**

TESTED

THE ASSOS SS.13 JERSEY ($319) AND F1.13 S5 BIB SHORT ($359)

My mother bought me my first pair of Assos shorts.

The reason for this is twofold. One, it was many years ago. And two, the things were pricey. Having just gotten into racing a few years prior, I had the impression at the time that Assos bibs were the *crème de la crème*.

Fast forward to today. A few things have changed. I'm not dependent on my mom for my cycling wardrobe. But Assos clothing still commands quite the pretty penny, and I still have the distinct impression that the company makes the best bibs going.

I tested the Assos SS.13 jersey and F1.13 S5 bib short, but in unforgiving European white. In their natural habitat in southern Switzerland, white bibs are common on everyone these days, from juniors to men in their 60s and 70s. In Colorado, well...

But the fit of these things is so plush it's worth enduring the chin music from my chucklehead bunch of riding buddies. One

thing I've always appreciated about Assos bibs is the simplicity of the chamois interface. Like a few companies these days, Assos uses some anatomically considered padding, with various layers of thicknesses and materials. Very much unlike other companies, however, the layer that touches your skin isn't a jumbled mess of raised ridges, stiff creases and heat-melted plastic; it's just a single, soft piece of material. Also, the thick padding that goes under your seat bones is actually under your seat bones, not rotated up towards your waist. (I have a few pairs of bibs that are great in construction and fit, but the chamois placement is off, with the thinner material and seams landing where the thick padding should be. This makes me crazy, and renders the shorts useless for their primary function.)

The six-panel shorts fit snugly, but a separate material used at the front crotch area isn't quite as tight, so the compression effect remains where it should be — on your legs.

These shorts come with samples of Assos chamois cream, laundry soap and a laundry bag.

The SS.13 jersey is a perfect complement to the bibs. It feels like a hybrid of the upper part of a skinsuit and a light, mesh jersey. Sound

weird? It works. The front panels and most of the arms use a tight, stretchy Lyrca-like material for a skintight feel. The back panels use a variety of breathable mesh fabrics, with a strip of hugely porous material right down the spine. The cumulative effect is most noticeable when descending — the front does not flap in the slightest, and you can feel the wind on your back more than you can with a normal jersey. Plus, true to Assos form, there are all manner of small details, such as a small, zippered pocket with a hole for headphones, reflective tabs, two small side pockets in addition to the standard back three, and a loop of fabric at the bottom of the jersey to prevent wear against your bibs.

At *VeloNews*, we're always bickering about the right fit — should you go with a jersey that fits in the shoulders but is slightly baggy through the chest and stomach, or one that is tight on the torso but comes up short on the arms, exposing your farmer's tan? With the SS.13, it's not an either/or situation — the thing fits snugly like a race-cut jersey should, with plenty of coverage on the upper arms.

In all, this is a fine kit. So, um, mom?

—B.D.

BRAD KAMINSKI (3)

This time, you help me make purchase decisions by telling me that:

- *"My mother bought me my first pair of Assos shorts."* It is not clear whether she took out a second mortgage in order to make this purchase, but I think we'll just go ahead and assume she did. And I think we can both agree that it was *darn well worth it*.
- *"The fit of these things is so plush it's worth enduring the chin music from my chucklehead bunch of riding buddies."* I'm not even sure what to say here, except that I hope your buddies have learned their lesson.[18]

---

18   Also, who says, "chin music?" And what can we do to make them stop?

- *"...The thick padding that goes under your seat bones is actually under your seat bones, not rotated up under your waist."* Actually, the problem I have is that the thick padding from other manufacturers (perish the thought) tends to drift down toward my kneecaps.[19] Curse them! Let's agree that Assos is the only company that has ever successfully managed to get a chamois between a butt and a saddle. Nobody else has even come close.[20]

- *"True to Assos form, there are all manner of small details,[21] such as a small, zippered pocket with a hole for headphones, reflective tabs, two small side pockets in addition to the standard back three,[22] and a loop of fabric at the bottom of the jersey to prevent wear against your bibs."* What's really amazing to me is that they were able to get the headphones, tabs, pockets, and the all-important fabric loop into that little hole.[23]

- *"In all this is a fine kit. So, um, mom?"* In all fairness, you should probably check with her first to see if she's paid off the first kit yet.

After reading this, I have to ask myself: am I ready to spend $678[24] on this shorts/jersey combo?

And then the answer comes: *Who isn't?*

CONCLUSION

VeloNews, I know you tried your best to give Assos a fair shake with your September issue, but let's face it, you were unnecessarily hard on them, what with all the research, follow-up questions, comparisons, and rigorous testing. Next time, you may want to take it a little easier on them.

---

19 Or sometimes it tries to turn into 80s-style shoulder pads!

20 A serious question here: Is it a common problem for the chamois to not go where it's supposed to go? Cuz for me, regardless of brand, the chamois just goes where it should go. Should I seek help?

21 Small details are better than big details.

22 And another pocket made to hold a pocket contained within still yet another pocket, all encased in a pocketful of pockets. Imagine a Russian doll-style never ending series of zippered pockets and you'll have it just about right.

23 Hey, look! Punctuation humor!

24 Not a made-up price.

I look forward to your December 200-page "Nothing But Assos" issue with great anticipation.

Kind Regards,

The Fat Cyclist

COMMENT BY BIKEMIKE
This post was longer than an entire issue of *VeloNews*... impressive.

COMMENT BY JOSH
I am considering selling a kidney so that I can buy a new Assos kit. Any takers?

COMMENT BY PHILLY JEN
"Threading the needle," eh? At $678 for a full kit (chamois cream not included), one can only assume they are threading it with a camel. A luxury camel, of course.
I suppose we can thank them for making Rapha look downright affordable.

A REVIEW OF MY DAUGHTER'S COLD-WEATHER BICYCLE PLAN

I want to be perfectly honest with you here. The main reason I am including this particular story in this book is because it will allow me to show it to my daughter (age seven when she created the drawing below, now age 13), to remind her what a sweetheart she used to be.

And yes, still is. She has recently turned thirteen, yet has not transformed into the haughty teenager I have been given to understand all children become.

And I'm sure she never will. Right? **Right***?!*

It started to snow, just a little, while I was out on a ride yesterday. This is not a big deal, unless you're a sissy.[25]

I returned from my ride to two worried little girls. The idea of dad riding out in the snow was very troubling to them. And the worry didn't stop, even after I let them know that I was reasonably certain I would keep all my fingers and toes.

By the time I had cleaned up, Katie had designed a solution the problem. She presented me with her invention:

As you can see, it's me, on a fully enclosed bike, happy and comfortable in spite of the fact that it is cloudy and snowing.[26]

As any good cyclist/father would do, I immediately set out to critique her design. I didn't want to seem cold-hearted, however, so I started with the good news.

The primary virtues of her drawing are as obvious as they are practical:

- **Heater Vent**: Clearly labeled, it is blowing nicely at me. I like the way that Katie has thoughtfully placed it behind, rather

---

25 Which I am, but that's not the point of this story, so let's just keep moving, OK? Thanks.

26 The weather's so bad, in fact, that even the (partially obscured) sun is sad.

than in front or overhead. This way, it's not likely to dry out my eyes or leave me feeling uncomfortably hot in front.

- **Roomy, Weather-Tight Enclosure**: As evidenced by the drawing, not a single snowflake is getting through. That's remarkable, but not as remarkable as the fact that the whole contraption is large enough for me to get up and walk around in. I needn't worry about sudden attacks of claustrophobia in this.
- **Easy Access**: The windshield doubles as the device's front door. Multipurpose functionality like this cuts down on weight, and that's going to be important when I use this thing for my next time trial to the top of the Alpine Loop.
- **Two-Wheel Drive**: Once the snow begins falling in earnest, I'm going to be really glad that the chain goes to both the front and rear wheel, making it possible for me to get out of deep snow and over icy patches. Frankly, I didn't expect this kind of functionality in a first-pass drawing from a seven-year-old.

PROBLEMS

All that's well and good, but here at the Fat Cyclist household, I expect a certain level of excellence from my children. And, I am sorry to report, in several key areas, Katie's invention falls tragically short.[27]

- **Moose Antlers Are Heavy**: It's evident that in lieu of normal handlebars, Katie has elected to have me steer using moose antlers. Yes, sure, I am fully aware of how rustic and handsome those look. Further, I find it a unique and clever application of the "reduce-reuse-recycle" mindset. But still: *Have you ever tried lifting those things?*
- **The Seat is Too Low**: I can see why she has the seat in a low position like that: to keep a low center of gravity for riding and enable the weight savings that come with a low ceiling. I admire this kind of thinking in her, I really do. But as is readily evident in her drawing, I am not going to be able to get optimal leg extension with the saddle where it is. Furthermore, if I were to raise the saddle, my head would bump against the ceiling. "You know my axle-to-saddle measurement is

---

27   And don't think this won't affect her Christmas bonus, either.

74.5cm," I said. "Everyone in this house does.[28] Don't go trying to cheat on your designs and build me a fully-enclosed snow bike that won't accommodate that saddle height."

- **The Wheels are Too Small**: I can see that Katie opted to go with 22" wheels. She knows good and well that I don't have a single tube that size and that it's almost impossible to find good, lightweight rims in that diameter. "Go look in the garage," I admonished her. "Do you see any 22" wheels out there? No? Why do you think that is? That's *right*, because it's not a common wheel size.[29] Now go back to the drawing board and re-do this with 700c — or at least 650c — wheels.

- **No Shifting Mechanism**: I appreciate the fact that Katie acknowledges my current fascination with single speeds, but this is ridiculous. There is no way I am going to get that thing up and over a mountain pass with the current gearing. And if I don't miss my guess — and as an internationally beloved and award-winning internet cycling blogger celebrity I rarely do — she's set this thing up as a *fixie*. Not only is that impractical, it's downright pompous.

- **Coaster Brakes**: Oh, get real.

I, of course gave my daughter all of this constructive feedback and sent her on her way, pleased with my parenting skills, and confident that her next drawing will be better thought out.

I am now prepared to accept my "Father of the Year" award.

COMMENT BY CARL

Very cute... and it looks like she did capture your massive quads.

COMMENT BY DALLASBIKR

Forget the quads...check the left Popeye forearm!
Great stuff :)

---

28 As a family, we recite my bike fit measurements every day, before eating breakfast.
29 And good luck finding tires in this size with the right tread pattern for snow riding.

COMMENT BY STUCKINMYPEDALS

It gets pretty hot here so I'm wondering if the box bike come with a summer option package, something with AC and window shades. When the designs for that come through, sign me up.

COMMENT BY BOOMER

Like me, Fatty obviously lives by the motto, "correct them while they're young and they'll be perfect for life." Katie will thank her father someday when she designs and implements the first practical elevator to a space station...complete with moose antlers and powered by single speeds.

COMMENT BY DR. LAMMLER

1. The seat is too low? Have you ever heard of lowering the center of gravity? Katie understands this.
2. Moose antlers are much safer in a crash than, say, caribou antlers.
3. I think the heater vent is behind you to provide a tailwind to help get you over a mountain pass. It's quite clever, actually.
4. Does it come in other colors to match my very expensive Assos SS.13 jersey?

COMMENT BY JILL

Don't forget that she thought about the traction. She put spikes on the front wheel to make sure that you won't slip in the snow. Very smart.

SPECIAL LIVEBLOG EVENT: READING THE SPEEDPLAY AD

I love reading Velo, *for two excellent reasons. The first is to marvel at Lennard Zinn, their Technical Writer.*

Did you know that he now writes the entire magazine, front to back, every single issue? It's true! Sometimes, because he starts to feel a little bad, he uses a pseudonym, but trust me: Lennard is writing it.

The second reason I read Velonews *is for the ads. I love the ads. Like this one from Speedplay.*

The *VeloNews 2010 Buyer's Guide* is chock-full of ads I love. I look at them, learn serious, important things about the world of cycling from them, and move on.

However, there is one particular ad that has defied me. That has not allowed me to observe, snark, and move on.

It is the full-page Speedplay ad:

Yes, that's really the ad.

When I first saw it, I panicked. Then I turned the page. Then I turned back, with my mind filled with questions:

- Is this really an ad with a full page of text?
- And not just text, but white-on-red text?
- And not just white-on-red text, but in a tall, cramped font?
- And not just white-on-red text in a tall cramped font, but all rammed together in a single, extremely wide paragraph?

Yes, that is what it is. Which makes me think: *Clearly, they do not want anyone to read this ad.* It is so dense and horrible to look at that Speedplay must have some reason for not wanting anyone to plow through the whole thing.

Like, maybe buried somewhere in there is instructions on how to find Jimmy Hoffa. Or the location of a vault containing untold riches. Or a recipe for an indescribably delicious key lime pie.

Regardless, I am confident that nobody, to this point, has ever read the entirety of this ad.

But I am going to, right now. And I am going to liveblog[30] the experience.

Wish me luck. I'm going in.

05:30 — I'm settling down with the magazine. I've got a bowl of cold cereal (Honey Bunches of Oats[31]) and half a grapefruit[32] to sustain me. Will it be enough? I do not know.

05:35 — So far, I have discerned that Speedplay is serious about making the best pedals. Which is good news, because I do not want my pedal manufacturer to go about making the best pedals in some kind of absent-minded, devil-may-care fashion.

05:42 — The next sentence has had me scratching my head in confusion for the past seven minutes: "We obsess about speed, power, biomechanics,[33] and security." Who, in this case, is "we?" Do they mean everyone at Speedplay? Or just the guys who created the ad? Or are they trying to draw me in with them, to make me part of their "we?" I'm not ready for that kind of commitment, Speedplay.

05:47 — I just realized that both the Speedplay ad and the bibshorts ad on the previous page mention "biomechanics."[34] Which causes me to think: "biomechanics" is the "ipsum lorem" of the bike ad world.

05:58 — Speedplay evidently, in addition to speed, power, biomechanics and security, also obsesses over user-friendliness, function, comfort, and durability. This causes me to wonder a few things.

---

30 When I originally published this in my blog, I actually did liveblog the event, posting each update in real time. Like an episode of *24*. Just not quite as enthralling.

31 Is there anyone in the world who does not find this to be the very best breakfast cereal in the whole world?

32 To counteract the effects of the giant bowl of carbs and dairy I'm eating.

33 True fact: all bicycling industry ads are required to include the word "biomechanics."

34 See? Told you.

1. Does Speedplay obsess about other things, too? Like, perhaps, having a complete Pokemon action figure set? Or always drinking the same brand of soda, no matter what? Or putting their clothes on in a certain order? The fact that they obsess about this many things indicates to me that they probably obsess about other things too.

2. Assuming (quite reasonably) that Speedplay is in fact obsessing over so many things, have they considered that perhaps it's time to get help?

3. Isn't "function" really just an umbrella term for all the other things they're obsessing about? It seems that they can maybe take this one off the list. This could be an important first step toward being less obsessive.

06:06 — Speedplay has now stopped telling me about the things it[35] obsesses about. Now it has moved on to telling me things it wants me to see, know, feel, and so forth. For example, it wants me to know that it has rethought pedals from the ground up. Which, since pedals don't really ever touch the ground at all, seems to indicate it have more re-thinking to do.

06:09 — My cereal bowl is empty. My grapefruit is nothing but a rind, all juice squeezed from it. And yet I am only 9% of the way through this ad. I shall fetch more cereal directly, and intend to open a two-liter Diet Coke with Lime, which I will drink directly from the bottle.[36]

06:11 — OK, I think I can continue. Where was I? Ah yes. Speedplay wants me to feel how much lighter their pedals are compared to others. But then, alas, they do not actually make any comparisons at all. So I'm beginning to think Speedplay is toying with me.

06:14 — Speedplay is now telling me how aerodynamic their pedal is. Which brings up a question: Is there any cyclist, in the entire world, who is so fast and rides in such a perfect position that his pedal aerodynamics are a factor, but who also is not already sponsored?[37] Honestly, in my entire cycling career, never has it occurred to me that I could have won a race if only my pedals weren't holding me back so much.

---

35 Or is it "they?" All this text and I still am not even sure who is talking to me.

36 As I do every day. I have no manners whatsoever.

37 I'm asking this rhetorically. I already know the answer. But I'm not telling you what it is.

06:17 — I think I should mention, by the way, that I actually do use Speedplay pedals. And I have for more than ten years. They're fantastic road pedals and I highly recommend them. But this ad is making me think of switching.[38]

06:20 — I am now on the fourth sentence in a row that begins with "We want." I'm beginning to develop a mental picture of the Speedplay personality, and the two dominating attributes are:

- Obsessive
- Needy

06:24 — Speedplay now wants me to measure their stack height to see how much closer my foot is positioned to the spindle for better power transmission. Which, frankly, seems like a lot of them to ask of me. Do they really expect me to measure the stack height of their pedal/cleat combination (as if I have the equipment for that), then go do the same thing with other pedal manufacturers and get back to them with my findings? Measure it yourself, Speedplay. I'm busy right now, trying to make sense of an incomprehensibly long, obsessive, needy, and demanding ad.

07:18 — Sorry, fell asleep. I need to start crossing out the sentences I've read so I don't keep losing my place.

07:23 — Speedplay has just told me, and I quote: "We want you to see how much further you can safely lean into a turn without scraping the pedals." Which means, if I understand them correctly, that they want me to corner harder and harder until I either chicken out or crash on everyone else's pedals, and then do the same thing on theirs. And once I've done that — well, of course I'll be dead long before I complete this battery of tests. However, had I survived, the key takeaway would have been that Speedplay let me lean in harder, so that when the pedal finally did clip the ground, I'd be going a lot faster and hence would be wrecking a lot nastier.

Speedplay, I believe you are asking too much of your prospective customers.

07:40 — Been drinking too much Diet Coke. Had to take a break.[39]

07:42 — Oh good, Speedplay has stopped asking me to conduct

---

38 In the five years that have elapsed since when this ad ran and now, I have not yet switched. So that was an empty threat.
39 It's a good thing I don't overshare or anything.

experiments that require sensitive equipment and an engineering degree, are life-threatening and reckless, or both. Now they want me to notice the stuff that is actually really good about their pedals: they're double-sided so they're easy to get into, and they lock in nice and secure.

Which, you know, is what some people might call their "key differentiator." And it might be all the information this ad really required. So it was really clever of them to bury it in the exact middle of the ad.

07:49 — Speedplay wants us to see that their premium pedals use rustproof stainless steel and Ti components "for durability and aesthetics." Which makes me ask: just your **premium** pedals? So your low-end pedals are going to be ugly, won't last, and will rust? Sign me up!

07:59 — Speedplay, now into the final third of its ad, is telling us that the "pedal's engagement edges are made of hardened alloy steel instead of plastic." That's nice, I suppose, but no more reassuring than if Trek said, "our carbon fiber bikes are made of carbon fiber instead of aluminum foil." Saying "we didn't use crappy materials" shouldn't be considered a selling point.

08:05 — I don't think I'm going to make it. This is just too darned hard. Tell my kids I love them.

08:08 — NO! I will **not** quit! I am going to finish reading this ad! *No matter what.*[40]

08:22 — I keep trying to make sense of this sentence: "We want you to see for yourself that Speedplay pedals offer an unmatched package of performance features and benefits but not at the expense of strength, safety, or functionality." I've read that sentence nine times now, and just can't figure it out. Do performance features and benefits usually come at the expense of strength, safety, and functionality? Aren't performance features and benefits part of strength, safety, and functionality?

And most important of all, why do Speedplay pedals come in unmatched packages? Like, do they come with two left pedals, one of which is red and the other of which is turquoise? And maybe they send only one cleat?[41]

Please, Speedplay. Please start providing matched packages.

---

40   Think of me saying this in a *Last of the Mohicans* voice. And also, think of me as having a full head of hair.

41   This paragraph is really the best part in the whole story. It's a shame you had to read so far to get to it.

08:32 — Finally, I am at the last sentence: "We want you to know that we're serious about making the world's most technically advanced pedal systems."

Hey, waitasec. That's what they said at the beginning of the ad, just longer and more obtuse.

08:36 — I did it. I finished the ad. It took more than three hours, but I did it. I pushed through, keeping my eye on the finish line and the glory that comes with it. Sure, there were moments when I thought I was a goner. But I gritted my teeth and kept reading.

Someday, I will tell my grandchildren. And they will be proud of grandpa, and that he — and he alone — read the entire Speedplay ad.

> COMMENT BY ALLAN
> Maybe Lennard Zinn will tackle your suggestions for pedal testing in the next issue.

> COMMENT BY PAUL H
> Advertisement: 415 words, 1930 characters
> Live Blog of advertisement: 1421 words, 6475 characters

> COMMENT BY DAVE
> You are a better man than I, Fatty. I made it to "micro-adjust-able range of float and pinpoint accuracy of cleat setup" and had a nervous breakdown. My doctor has advised me not to finish the ad.

> COMMENT BY KATHY MCELHANEY
> Someday, I will tell my grandchildren. And they will be proud of grandma, and that she — along with many other Fat Cyclist readers — read the entire Liveblog Event of Fatty Reading the Speedplay ad.

> COMMENT BY CARDIAC KID
> You probably could have finished in 2:58 if your pedals hadn't been holding you back so much.

AN OPEN LETTER TO CYCLINGNEWS.COM

I believe I have mentioned, from time to time, how famous and well-regarded I am in the cycling industry. And yet, I am not invited to join them, all expenses paid, when they go to cover the Tour de France.

I know. There is no justice in this world.

In a (spoiler alert: futile) attempt to right this wrong, I Instant Messaged (it's how people communicated before texting) my friend Dug, telling him that he and I should do a liveblog of a stage of the Tour de France[42] and send it to CyclingNews.

Naturally, they would recognize our genius and would purchase first-class tickets to France for us. And luxury hotel rooms. Because we're that good.

To my consternation, CyclingNews did not reply. I am still baffled by this fact.

And after you read this story, you will share in this consternation. And, I hope, send CyclingNews a very strongly-worded email, demanding that they send Dug and me to France.

By the way, when CyclingNews pushes back, feel free to negotiate Dug out of the bargain. We're good friends, but not that good of friends.

Dear *CyclingNews.com,*

First of all I just want to say: I'm a big fan. Especially around Tour de France time each year, when I follow your live race coverage almost religiously. Your coverage is accurate, clear, and up-to-the minute.[43]

But it's also kind of dry.[44]

What you need, *CyclingNews,* is some "color commentary." You know, a couple of guys who can add some personality to the play-by-play. A couple of guys who aren't afraid to say what they're thinking. A couple of guys who can type really fast, nonstop, for four hours straight.

I'm talking about, of course, my friend Dug and me.

You see, *CyclingNews,*[45] I recently went back and watched an incred-

---

42 This was way back before everyone watched it live on TV. It was kind of like live-tweeting, except there wasn't Twitter, either. The world was a primitive and strange place back then.

43 This is absolutely true.

44 This, too, is absolutely true.

45 As I sit here editing, I notice that when I create these "open letters," I invariably use the addressee's name a lot. And now you'll notice it, too.

ibly dramatic moment from the 2003 Tour de France: Stage 9, Bourg d'Oisans to Gap.[46]

Pretty wild, isn't it? But your stage reporting is...um...terse. So, Dug and I took the liberty of adding our own commentary. Kind of like we were Bob Roll, but there are two of us, and we work for a lot less money.[47]

Below, we've taken your reporting, and added our own comments, exactly as we would have five years ago when this actually happened.

CN: 16:39 CEST, 175.5 km/9 km to go — Vinokourov's attack is good, catching and dropping Casero and closing in on Parra and Jaksche, who are now together.

Vinokourov powers up to Parra and Jaksche and attacks immediately. Jaksche tries to hold him, and does.

Fatty: Well, what do you know. Vino's attacking. How unusual.[48]

Dug: I'm pretty sure he just gave Armstrong "The Look."

Fatty: I guarantee you that Armstrong is going to sue Vino for trademark infringement. Nobody gets to give people "The Look" but him.

Fatty: I'll bet you anything that Vinokourov's a doper.

Dug: Why are Armstrong and company chasing so hard? I mean, who is this Vino guy? Isn't he from Kazakhstan?

Hey. I just had a great idea for a movie about a guy from there. It'll be a big comedy hit.[49]

CN: 16:42 CEST, 176.5 km/8 km to go — Armstrong and Heras are leading the peloton in pursuit of Vinokourov and Jaksche, who can't hold the charging Kazakh any more. Vino has 20" with 1 km to go until the summit.

Vino crosses the top of the Côte de La Rochette, as Armstrong steps up the pace behind. Beloki, Ullrich, Basso, Mayo, Zubeldia all go with him. Armstrong's pace making is good, but he's still got 10 riders with him.

Dug: Really? Only twenty inches? That's not much of an attack, if you ask me.

---

46   Really, you ought to go watch it too. Go here: http://bit.ly/fatsby-01
47   By which we mean, "free."
48   Is it OK for me to miss Vinokourov's racing style? I mean yes, I realize now where all that outrageous power-on-demand came from, but the fact is: that guy was fun to watch.
49   I'll bet Vinokourov never gets tired of *Borat* jokes.

Fatty: You know what? I think Beloki ought to check his tire. It looks a little soft to me. And I think the pavement looks kind of oily.[50]

Dug: No, I'm telling you, Beloki is a master descender.

Fatty: Hey, Basso just threw a banana peel onto the road. That doesn't seem right. Someone could slip on that thing.

Dug: No, I guarantee you: Armstrong[51] couldn't pick a better wheel to follow.

Fatty: How about that Basso? Betcha he's a doper.

Dug: I'm pretty sure Ullrich just emptied a bottle full of cooking oil onto the road. Is that legal?

Fatty: Betcha Ullrich's a doper, too.

Dug: Oh, this is terrific stuff. It's like the old days, when riders would do anything to win. I once saw Merckx put a live scorpion down a competitor's jersey.[52]

CN: 16:45 CEST, 177.5 km/7 km to go — Vino hits the descent with a 16″ gap to Armstrong's group, as the yellow jersey himself leads the chase. Beloki is also helping, as he is in second on GC. Bettini is on the back of the group, that contains all the top riders. Even Jaksche is hanging on.

Vinokourov took the points on the climb ahead of Armstrong, Beloki, Zubeldia and Mayo.

Fatty: If Beloki really wants to win, he ought to take the corners really fast. I understand hot pavement is awesome for improving traction.

Dug: Mayo seems a bit, well, temperamental doesn't he?

Fatty: Totally. I bet you anything he's a doper.

Dug: I expect great things from Mayo. You wait and see. He'll be a great TdF GC contender for years to come.

Fatty: Did you notice that Armstrong is riding with tires that have surprisingly robust tread today?

Dug: Like cross tires.

Fatty: Yeah. Weird.

Dug: Seems like a bad move. What could possibly be the advantage?

Fatty: It makes no sense at all.[53]

---

50 Sure I'm joking, but the events that unfold next haunt my every descent to this day.

51 I know, I didn't make the "Betcha Armstrong's a doper" joke here.

52 Please spread this story as fact.

53 This may be foreshadowing.

CN: 16:47 CEST, 178.5 km/6 km to go — Beloki and Armstrong are leading the chase behind Vinokourov, who is flying with 6 km to go. This will be a close finish, but there is a 20" time bonus on the line... Look out for Bettini.

Dug: What kind of name is "Beloki" anyway?

Fatty: Yeah, it sounds like a sound effect. Like the sound a body makes when it hits the pavement at high speed, breaking bones and tangling with metal in the process. I'd rather have a last name like "Winsalot."

Dug: Is Betinni officially a midget? He's like 4 feet tall.

Fatty: I think they prefer to be referred to as "Adorable People."[54]

Dug: Is he riding on 20" wheels?

Fatty: Hey, you know how you can tell when Vinokourov is going to attack?

Dug: Tell me.

Fatty: If it's been at least 3 minutes since his last attack.

Dug: I'm telling you, he should be checked for rabies. Seriously. I think he's foaming at the mouth.

Fatty: Beloki's looking good. That guy's a solid rider.

Dug: Someone should tell those fans alongside the road that you're not supposed to spray Pam all over it.

CN: 16:48 CEST, 180.5 km/4 km to go — This is a very technical descent, and Vino has lost a couple of seconds to Armstrong's group on it. But he's still clear. One mistake will cost him the stage.

Beloki loses it! Armstrong has to go down the grass embankment, taking a short cut. He amazingly gets back onto the group. Beloki is out though. He locked up his brakes just before a corner, and landed heavily on his hip.

Dug: Whoa!

Dug: I mean: Whoa!

Dug: Did you SEE that girl on the side of the road? She was HOT![55]

Fatty: Get up, Beloki. Shake it off. You're fine. You think this race is going to win itself?

Dug: Merckx would be back up already. In fact, Merckx would have

---

54   I feel it is my duty to report whenever one of my own jokes makes me laugh out loud. This is one of those times.

55   I should probably, in fairness, also note that Dug made me laugh out loud with this comment, too. It's possible I'm just in a very silly mood right now.

taken Armstrong down with him, bitten him, then taken his bike and ridden off.

Fatty: I'm just glad there's a cyclist's code, where everyone always stops to help an injured rider.

Dug: Yeah, look for Vino to slow up any second.

Fatty: I think Armstrong is just riding around in that field looking for first aid supplies.

Dug: How on earth did Armstrong manage that little cross country jaunt? No normal human being could possibly have ridden down that field, jumped off the bike, climbed over that embankment, and gotten back on the road. It's like he's had special forces training.

Fatty: My fervent wish is that they will replay this moment on TV over and over for all eternity so that it gets burned into my psyche and I can never ever ever descend down a fast mountain road without having the image of Beloki go all ragdoll play through my brain.[56]

Dug: What's weird is that Tyler Hamilton pulled three muscles just witnessing the crash. And maybe broke a collarbone.

Fatty: Hamilton. Pfff. That guy's totally a doper.

Dug: I'm pretty sure I heard Beloki's femur crack from way up here in the booth.

Fatty: Merckx would have made a splint from one of his teammate's top tubes and would be on the attack now.

CN: 16:50 CEST, 181.5 km/3 km to go — Beloki has two teammates with him, but is still lying there. That was a hard crash.

Vino has 3 km to go, and is certainly not going to wait for the rest.

Fatty: I don't think the crash was *that* hard.

Dug: Yeah, Beloki is just milking it.

Fatty: If Armstrong had fallen, the entire peloton would have come to a complete stop out of respect, then withdrawn twenty paces to await instructions.

CN: 16:51 CEST — Ullrich, Hamilton , Armstrong, Zubeldia, Mayo are all working hard to try and catch Vinokourov. Behind them, Beloki still hasn't got back up.

The gap to Vino is now 30".

Dug: Beloki *still* isn't up?

Fatty: I think he may be napping.

---

56 Wish granted.

Dug: What a baby.

Fatty: No doubt about it. He needs a good talking to.

CN: 16:51 CEST, 183.5 km/1 km to go — Vinokourov has 1 km to go, and is on track for a great stage win in a dramatic finale.

Armstrong will thank his lucky stars that he avoided that crash somehow.

Dug: Armstrong has lucky stars? No yellow moons? No blue diamonds?

Fatty: I'm beginning to think that Beloki's podium finish is in danger for this tour.

Dug: Seems like he could have at least crossed the line.

Fatty: Oh well, I'm sure he'll be back next year, stronger than ever. He's going to be a force to be reckoned with.

CN: 16:53 CEST, 184.5 km/0 km to go — Vinokourov crosses the line, absolutely delighted with his win. Behind him, Bettini flies to take second place in front of Mayo and Armstrong.

Vino will move up to second on GC behind Armstrong, with Mayo in third now at 1'02".

Beloki has been taken away in an ambulance after locking it up on that last descent. A sad exit for him for this Tour, which held a lot of promise. But Vinokourov put them under a lot of pressure with his attack. Armstrong's handling skills were pretty impressive to avoid that, and he was lucky there were no fences when he went cross country. Hamilton even patted him on the shoulder when they passed him after he'd got back in the pedals.

Dug: Hamilton *touched* Armstrong?[57]

Fatty: I just saw the replay of where Hamilton touches Armstrong's shoulder. Hamilton's arm completely fell off.

Dug: That's going to adversely affect his sprint.

Fatty: Oh well. Anyway, that was a pretty good stage.

Dug: Yeah, I suppose.

As you can see, *CyclingNews*, we have a great deal of insight to add to your race coverage. We look forward to working with you as you cover the Tour de France this month.

---

57 Allegedly. Litigation is ongoing.

Kind Regards,

The Fat Cyclist

COMMENT BY BOB

I read this out loud to my wife. I don't think she appreciated it as much as I did.

COMMENT BY MIKE ROADIE

Phil's a doper.

COMMENT BY WILD DINGO

You and Dug are both probably dopers.

6.

Pet Peeves

I AM NOT AN UNREASONABLE MAN. OK, THAT MAY NOT BE TRUE. I PERHAPS AM AN UNREASONABLE MAN, BUT I AM NOT RIDICULOUSLY UNREASONABLE. Although I am, I must confess, both ridiculous and unreasonable. But that's different.

I think I'll start over.

What I wanted to say is that I am, in general, perfectly happy to let people do their own thing. You want to wear a jersey emblazoned with the Grateful Dead logo? Awesome. You want to put a motor on your bicycle? Knock yourself out. You want to ride a recumbent? Well hey, at least you're on a bike (and good luck to you as you start work on growing your beard).

But occasionally, something will get under my skin. I'm not even sure why, but it usually happens when something completely silly demands attention — real, serious attention — from the cycling press. And then gets it.

And when something gets under my skin, well, I tend to pick on it. Just a little bit:

1. **The Tour of America:** A clearly-impossible dream on an even more impossible deadline. It had no more chance of being realized than a bike race to Uranus (pronounced "your anus" in this case). And yet, every single major bike

publication — *VeloNews, Bicycling, CyclingNews*, others — covered this joke with at least mostly-straight faces.

2. **Rock Racing:** I don't mind that someone founded a bike team on the back of his $300+ jeans. What I disliked about Rock Racing was the wrongheadedness and arrogance of Michael Ball, the owner of the team. Spending like there was no tomorrow, hiring and firing capriciously, and in general strutting around like the universe of pro cycling was his own little playground. Outrageously, the cycling universe seemed willing to put up with this.

Stuff like this? Well, it's fair game for poking with a stick. Repeatedly. Which is what I do in this section.

EVEN-LONGER COMPETITOR TO THE TOUR OF AMERICA ANNOUNCED

When the "Tour of America" was announced, I was incredibly upset. Specifically, I was upset that I had not already created a series of posts about such an event, publishing each in the series as an increasingly improbable gag.

But it wasn't a gag. It was in earnest. But it was also completely nuts. Insane. Especially within the timeframe announced (a year from the time of the announcement). Especially with the lack of a route. Or teams. Or anything, really.

They had a website and a form asking for sponsors. And some wild claims. Which seemed like something I should probably do too.

Of all the fake news I've ever written, this may well be the one that comes closest to being actual satire.

Amazing.

Seattle (Fat Cyclist Fake News Service) — PorkoVelo[1] Enterprises, LLC, a heretofore-unheard-of USA cycling race promoter, announced today in a hastily-called press conference that it would be offering a proposal for a United States-based Grand Tour, competing with the just-announced Tour of America. The race, according to PorkoVelo CEO Rick Sunderlage,[2] will be called "Ride Around the US a Lot of Times" (RATUSALOT[3]).

According to Sunderlage, "We've been thinking, lately, that what the world really needs is another Grand Tour. Except one that's not so *easy*. And it should be somewhere where road biking isn't as popular as it is in the rest of the world. And it should happen right after the biggest, most successful top-tier US-based racing team ever disbanded, due to lack of sponsor interest."

---

1 PorkoVelo is actually a pretty cool name for a bike race. I'll have to keep this one in mind.

2 I always like to plop the names of my friends into my press releases. I believe this is the first time I've ever used Rick Sunderlage's name without adding (Not His Real Name) after. A tragic oversight.

3 When I discovered the race name had this acronym, I knew my work was done. This piece was going to write itself.

"I swear," continued Sunderlage, "We were, like, 75 percent finished with our plan when those jerks at Aqu Inc. came out and announced their race, which I guess kind of forced our hand. So we had to rush to get our proposal out the door, which means it's kind of half-baked, unlike the Aqu idea."

"Man," said Sunderlage, a trace of frustration showing on his face, "those guys have their plan totally nailed. You can tell they've thought everything through."

"Anyway," concluded the PorkoVelo CEO, "I think most people will find our idea for an American Grand Tour has everything the Tour of America has, but more of it. And more's better, right?"[4]

THE PLAN

According to RATUSALOT Logistics Director Rob Sunderlage,[5] "The problem with the Tour of America is that it's just too darned short. I mean, only 27 stages? Just 4000 miles? Geez, guys, these are professional cyclists. Don't you think it's time we tested them a little?"

Sunderlage (Rick, not Rob) then said, "So I guess now's as good a time to show off our route for RATUSALOT:

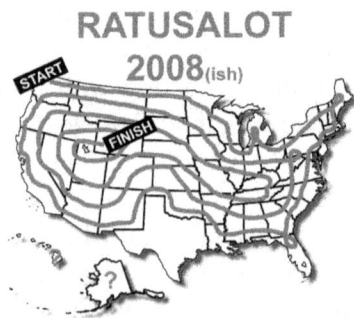

RATUSALOT
2008(ish)

"There are still a few kinks for us to work out," said Sunderlage (Rob, not Rick), but I think you can see that this sucker's a *real* bike race."

According to Race Logistics Director Rachele Urqhart-Sunderlage,[6] "RATUSALOT — unlike the Tour of America, which goes through a mere 22 states[7] — goes through each and every state of the Union, often multiple times."

Then, correcting herself, Urqhart-Sunderlage said, "Well, actually I'm not sure we go through some of those North-Eastern states. Those things are tiny."

---

4   You have to admit, in this way the RATUSALOT is a uniquely American tour.

5   Rick Sunderlage really does have a twin brother named Rob.

6   Rachele is also real. The gag here is of course that this "race promotion organization" is just a family sitting around the kitchen table.

7   Yes, the Tour of America really did propose to go 4000 miles, through twenty two of the states in the U.S.

"Oh," continued Urqhart-Sunderlage, "We also don't go through Hawaii or Alaska, because it'd be a pain to have to charter all those planes. Unless we build some bridges between the mainland and those two states. Which we are looking into."

"And I guess it's obvious that we had to go around Texas,"[8] said Urqhart-Sunderlage. "They wouldn't let us in. They're standing all along the border, saying things like, 'Ain't no spandex-wearing, pedal-pushing, leg-shaving, pansy-boys coming into Texas! This is *oil* country!' So we thought we should just let them be."

Urqhart-Sunderlage pointed out several interesting aspects of the race, including:

- **Distance**: "At this point, we're not exactly sure how many miles the race is. For one thing, it's got a lot of curves, so it's hard to figure out the distances. For another thing, we're having a rough time converting the miles into kilograms. But we guess it's between sixteen and twenty-three thousand miles."

- **Race Timing/Number of Stages**: "The RATUSALOT will have 120 stages, beginning the first day of May and running through the end of August. We understand that this may mean some racers may have to miss other races, but we're sure they'll understand."

- **Stage Breakdown**: "The RATUSALOT will have 25 time trials, five Team Time Trials, and 60 climbing stages. Unlike Aqu Inc., we're not afraid to go into the mountains."[9]

- **Longest Stage**: "We're thinking that with all the miles we've got to cover, we're going to need to have some pretty long stages. That said, we don't think it's wise to have 250-mile stages; that's just too much to ask of a racer, even a pro racer. However, we don't think it's a problem to have a 140-mile stage in the morning, followed by a two-hour break, and then a 160-mile stage in the afternoon. Some of the riders might want to have light systems mounted on their bikes, just to be safe."

- **Prize Purse**: "In order to draw the best cycling teams in the

---

8   I've ridden in Texas numerous times, and have never ever gotten any grief from anyone about it. So I don't know why I singled this state out for ridicule. Maybe because it's one of like three states I can identify on a map?

9   "Also, we haven't really counted how many stages that totals out to or where which stage goes and when, but we're planning to put it into an Excel spreadsheet any day now."

world to the RATUSALOT, we have put together one of the most incredible prize purses in the history of cycling. In addition to $12 million — no, let's make that $12 *billion*[10] — in twenty-dollar bills to be awarded to contestants, we'll be giving every racer a gift bag containing an assortment of candy bars, lip balm, cheeses, coupons, sample packets of sunscreen, a crisp new $20 bill, and all the Coca Cola products they can drink, including Gatorade. Not to mention an event T-shirt and bumper sticker."

- **Sponsors**: "It's not our policy to announce potential sponsors until we've got a signed contract and money in the bank. But we're open to suggestions. If you're a company and you've got untold millions of marketing dollars laying around, please, please, please give me a call. Please."

DATE SET, SOMEWHAT

PorkoVelo CEO Rob — no, Rick — Sunderlage notes that the inaugural RATUSALOT will begin less than one year from now, on May 1, 2008. "That date's not set in stone, however," notes Sunderlage. "There are still a few details we need to nail down. For example, we've still got to figure out whether there are roads in some of the places where we drew the course."

---

10 I mean, why not?

(EDITED) PRESS RELEASE: TOUR OF AMERICA RESCHEDULES FOR 2009

You know how amazed you are when something you thought was impossible, something you thought nobody could ever pull off, actually happens?
This is not one of those times.
As expected, the 2008 Tour of America never happened. Hungering for a taste of the delicious press of yesteryear, they sent out a press release, saying, essentially, "Hey guys, this time we're going to do it. For reals. Honest."
I decided that this press release needed a little help. A little deletion here, a few new words there, and it was ready to go.[11]

Dear Mr. Arokiasamy,

I just got what I assume is the first draft of your new press release; thanks for sending it my way.

I've got to say, Frank, this sucker needed work.[12]

Luckily for you, I — in addition to being an Award Winning Blogger (2008 Weblog Award, "Best Sports Blog in the Whole World" Category) — have spent most of my career as an editor. As a favor to you, I'm sending you back your press release, edited for accuracy, honesty, and pragmatism.

Stuff I added is in redline, stuff I deleted is in strikeout.

Kind Regards,

Fatty

The Fat Cyclist

---

11   Just in case you were wondering: Yes, I did in fact really send this to Frank Arokiasamy. He did not reply.

12   This is literally true. The idea for this piece came to me when I read through the original press release and thought, "This thing needs an editor." The rest was easy.

FOR IMMEDIATE RELEASE

In an Effort to ~~be Included on the UCI Calendar~~ Re-Animate the Corpse of Its Completely Unrealistic Fantasy, Aqu, Inc. Reschedules Inaugural Tour of America ~~Until 2009~~ to 2112[13]

Pressing forward in the face of ridicule, eye-rolling, and general snorts and giggles, with ~~route details and sponsorship agreements~~ unwarranted bravado, Aqu also announces executive team is high on crack.[14]

Lumberton, N.C., March 31, 2008 — Aqu, Inc., would-be organizers of The Tour of America (voted "least-likely to succeed" by its peers), a totally hypothetical multi-stage coast-to-coast professional bicycle road race, today announced rescheduling of the inaugural race until September 2009 or 2112 or when hell freezes over. Whichever comes last.[15]

Since the original announcement of the Tour of America in September 2007, Aqu executives and staff members have ~~met~~ tried to meet with cities along the proposed route, as well as with potential sponsors and race teams. Unfortunately, not a single person has yet returned their calls. They have, however had success reaching, ~~as well as~~ staff members of USA Cycling and the Union Cycliste Internationale (UCA), the sport's governing bodies. Specifically, they have reached the receptionist and night janitor, and are thoroughly looking forward to having lunch with them sometime in the next two years.

"After we announced the Tour of America last fall, we jokingly said we were going to do the race ~~hit the ground running to make the event happen~~ in 2008," said Frank Arokiasamy, Aqu's president and would-be director of what would be called the Tour of America, if such a thing were to ever happen.[16] "Everyone we have spoken with ~~wants to see a 'Tour~~

---

13   The "2112" date is going to be immediately understood by about half a dozen people as a reference to the Canadian rock band, Rush. Hey, not every joke has to appeal to every reader.

14   Or whatever drugs are currently popular right now. I've never really been cool enough to know.

15   Originally, this read, "...whichever comes first." Which was pretty stupid of me, because obviously September 2009 was going to come first, unless hell happened to freeze over even earlier than that. Sometimes, I can be such an *idiot*.

16   True confession time: I have a lot of empathy for Arokiasamy. The fact is, he and I are a lot alike. If I were to create an event, I can imagine making grand announcements and proclamations before ever doing the work. Because that's the fun part.

~~de France-style" race here in the United~~ [17] ~~We want to work with USA Cycling and UCI to establish this event as a compliment~~[18] ~~to the major international races, and at the same time not conflict with established races in the United States. Overall, we want to make sure the Tour of America strengthens the sport of cycling and the race calendar. In addition, potential sponsors and route cities have expressed strong support for a fall 2009 race~~ laughs at us. I suspect this might be because we so far have not been able to get any teams to sign up, or any sponsors to sign up, or any cities to sign up. Other than that, things are going great."

At this point, Arokiasamy began to weep.

Exact dates for the fall ~~2009~~ 2112 — the first year at which this event could realistically happen — edition of the Tour of America has not been finalized, because climate change may have drastically altered the riding season by then, plus we'll all be dead before it happens anyway.[19] Tour of America staff are currently ~~finalizing route details~~ calling chambers of commerce all across America, trying to find out who the right guy is to ask if their bike race can take over their town for a day, hosting an event nobody's ever heard of, sponsorship agreements (current sponsors include *Peggy's Bridal and Floral, All-A-Dollar*, and *Primal Jerseys*) and proposed dates to comply with USA Cycling's race application process. Once the application is submitted, USA Cycling will review it, find fault with it, demand a revised version submitted in triplicate, demand drug tests of every person who lives along the race route, send the proposal to committee, where it will sit for 104 years.[20] At that point, an archaeologist will discover and submit the ~~2009~~ 2112 Tour of America's dates, along with all of the races on the national calendar, to the UCI for approval. UCI (also known as The Priests of the Temples of Syrinx)[21] will then reject it without comment.

The Tour of America currently includes a staff of more than 25 people, including the following:

---

17   Yes, in the real press release this sentence is just sort of abandoned without closing punctuation, with a new one smashed on top of it. It's a thing of beauty, in much the way watching a train wreck in ultra-slo-mo is beautiful.

18   As opposed to "complement."

19   Sorry, but it's true.

20   For those of you who suspect this part is an homage to an early chapter in *The Hitchhiker's Guide to the Galaxy*, you are absolutely right.

21   Rush fans will giggle at this; the rest of you should feel to just keep on reading.

Tour Director and Sponsorship — Frank Arokiasamy
Race Director — Richard Dunn
Team Relations Director — Todd Nurnberger
City Relations Director — A.M. Noel
Events Director — Rachel Enter-Guzman
Volunteer Director — Rick Warren
Marketing Director — Brian Ispen
Merchandising Director — Auburn Collins
Snacks — Elden Nelson
Public Relations — Dick Pound

For more biographical information about the above staff members, please visit the About Us page. Do it soon, however, because we're about to lose our domain name and don't have the budget to get it renewed.

The 2009 Tour of America is also looking for volunteers to help with city and race coordination along the race route. For more information about volunteering, please visit the Volunteer page.[22] Please. We're begging.

BACKGROUND

Originally, we wanted The Tour of America ~~will~~ to be a 21-stage, 2,200 mile (more than 3,500 km) professional bicycle road race. Unfortunately, there's no chance in the world that will happen, so we're thinking maybe we'll settle for a two-stage, 200-mile race.[23] ~~It will be the largest spectator event in the history of U.S. sports, traveling from the Atlantic Ocean to the Pacific Ocean.~~ The event will include close to 200 riders (194.72 riders, to be precise), from 21 of the world's ~~elite cycling~~ most imaginary teams ~~in the world~~ to participate and will boast a prize purse currently pegged at $10 million (in Monopoly money), the largest purse of any international cycling event. And hey, as long as we're just making stuff up, let's also say that everyone who participates gets a free pony.

On the first day of The Tour of America ~~will start~~ the racers will ride around in a parking structure about twenty miles from ~~in~~ New York's Central Park. On the next day, we'll have them fly across the country and

---

22   I like to imagine that the volunteers who signed up are still patiently waiting by their email inboxes, thinking that, someday soon, they're going to be called up to do their part.

23   And if pressed, we might drop to a 1-stage, 25-mile race.

finish in the San Francisco Bay ~~Area. (To see the complete schedule, please visit the Routes page.~~[24]

~~Until this venture by Aqu, all major international cycling races were held outside the U.S. Smaller stage races are currently held throughout the United States and draw respectable spectator crowds and provide significant economic impact to local communities. However, these races are geographically located within single states, while The Tour of America will span approximately 18 states and will travel through hundreds of towns and cities along the way. As such, the~~ The 2009 Tour of America is expected to attract literally ~~millions~~ dozens of spectators along the ~~2,200~~-mile route.

Cities the racers will fly over ~~along the race's route~~ include New York City, Philadelphia, Cincinnati, Indianapolis, St. Louis, Denver, Las Vegas, Sacramento, Napa, Santa Rosa and Palo Alto, to name a few. It would be totally awesome, but it is of course nothing but a pure fantasy.

For information about The Tour of America, please visit www. TheTourofAmerica.com.[25]

ABOUT AQU, INC.

North Carolina-based Aqu, Inc. is the parent company of AquSports. Founded in July 2007 by Frank Arokiasamy, AquSports ~~is~~ dreams of one day being the producer and organizer of the 2009 Tour of America, a multi-stage, coast-to-coast, professional international bicycle road race. For more information about The Tour of America, please visit ~~www.TheTourofAmerica.com~~ your happy place, where all daydreams come true.

> COMMENT BY KANYONKRIS
>
> My cousin owns Carl's Lube Stop and will sponsor me and a few other guys for a Tour of America team. I tuned up my bike and did my first crit this week — I'm ready!

---

24   This page never had anything more than a bunch of "TBDs" for dates, places, and type of stage. It was the Internet's loneliest table.

25   Don't actually go to this site; it's no longer has anything about the race in it. In fact, it now is a Japanese page with a headline that translates (according to Google), "Have never made a sex partners?"

COMMENT BY ETHAN

Wow. I am (pleasantly) speechless that you managed to weave not one but TWO references to Rush into this post. They were my first rock concert (6th grade). Well done Elden.

COMMENT BY LOWRYDR

Wow, if I sign up I even get a special Security T-shirt. I'm so there for this one, I can hardly wait for 2112. Oh wait. I'll be Dust in the Wind by then.

COMMENT BY ADAM

They already have the LEADERS JERSEY'S planned out. This race is as good as already happened.

NEWS FLASH: AQU SPORTS ANNOUNCES TOUR OF AMERICA PLANS FOR 2009 AND BEYOND

I had been waiting. Waiting and watching. I knew nothing was going to happen, but I waited and watched anyway.

And as expected, a year went by after Aqu Sports sent out its press release (see the previous story in this book), saying they were going to wait an extra year to put on their Tour of America.

I imagine that, during this time, Frank Arokiasamy had every intention of making this race happen. At least at first. I kind of suspect that everyone else would just sit around in the office, playing solitaire, except whenever Frank came in. Because there's no way at all they actually thought this race was going to happen. So why try?

Anyway, after about nine months, I figure they got together and each of them told Frank how, in spite of their valiant efforts, the race just wasn't shaping up.

And he told them they were about out of money. And then they all found new jobs, and the race died a quiet death, leaving no trace. Unremarked upon by any of the cycling press which had, a year ago (and the year before that) dutifully reported anything Arokiasamy had sent their way.

Well, if the crack team at Aqu wasn't going to put out their annual press release, I guessed I was going to have to do it for them.

Wilson, NC (Fat Cyclist Fake News Service) — In a packed press conference today, Aqu Sports announced details for its much anticipated and talked-about Tour of America.

"It's been almost exactly a year since

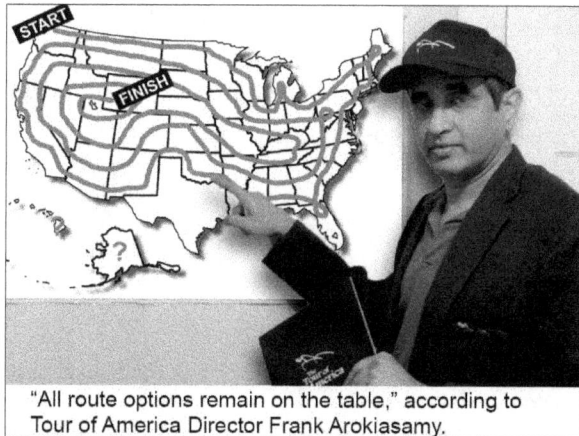

"All route options remain on the table," according to Tour of America Director Frank Arokiasamy.

we sent out a press release asserting the Tour of America would begin in September of 2009," said Tour Director Frank Arokiasamy. "We felt it was high time we start filling in the blanks."[26]

2009 PLANS

According to Race Director Richard Dunn, "2008 went by really fast, and before we knew it — whoa, there was December and we still hadn't signed up any cities or sponsors or teams for the 2009 event."

"We probably should have started making calls before November, but you know, it's really hot in North Carolina during the summer and the air conditioning in our office kind of sucks, and then when autumn comes it's so beautiful and the weather's so nice that you just want to get outside," continued Dunn.

"And by the time we got to November, we figured everyone else would be winding down for the holidays for the rest of the year, so we decided to take some time off and then come back to it in mid-late January."[27]

"But then you get into January and it's just such a dark, ugly time of year; nobody really wants to think about racing then. So we took a trip to Mexico and got some much-needed sun, promising to recharge our emotional batteries before diving in head-first when spring began.

"Long story short, our plan for 2009 changed a little bit. We moved from the unrealistic expectation that we could put a race together in a year to the much more achievable focus on writing a really solid plan for 2010–2012 and calling 2009 a mulligan. And I feel we did an excellent job of that," said Dunn.

"Or at least, we'll *do* an excellent job on it, I swear. I plan to hop on it starting next month, for sure.

"I'll leave the details up to Karen, our Logistics Director, to give you the outline of those plans now."

---

26   Imagine here a Mad-Libs-ish fill-in-the-blanks puzzle, consisting of nothing but blanks.

27   You may be thinking that I am writing this paragraph just a little *too* convincingly. I assure you, however, that I personally am nothing like this.

2010 PLANS

"For 2010," said Karen D. O'Neill, logistics director for the Tour of America, "We plan to...uh...to...well, actually we hope to blame the poor economy for our not doing the race."[28]

"Of course," explained O'Neill, "that's not the way we'll start out. A few months from now we'll announce that we're going to do this race in 2010. Then we'll go dark again for a while. It won't be until sometime in early 2010 that we'll actually make the announcement that either the economy is still too bad to support a race of this magnitude, or that the economy has recovered too recently for us to meet our financial obligations in a timely manner."

"Which, of course," concluded O'Neill, "leads us to 2011."

2011 PLANS

"For 2011, we actually do plan to conduct a Tour of America," said Arokiasamy. "However, it will be in South America. And it will be unsupported. And it will be raced entirely on motorcycles, instead of bicycles. Also we will avoid cities and roads altogether, having the course go up and down the coastline...and under water, when there is no beach...or when the tide is high."[29]

Interrupted Arokiasamy,[30] "We feel that this will give us precisely the kind of experience we need to come back to North America the following year for the *Fifth Annual* Tour of America."

2012 PLANS AND BEYOND

"By 2012," said Arokiasamy, "we will have established ourselves as the premier stage race in America, having either put on a race or had a very good excuse each of the preceding four years."

"And for 2012, we hope to begin planning very exciting plans indeed," effused Arokiasamy. "Namely, we will tell everyone that the race is planned for a certain date in July. Then, when everyone shows up on that date, we will look confused for a minute and then take a

---

28   "We have every confidence in the world that the economy will not be good by 2010. We do have a fallback excuse, however, should this excuse turn out to not be sufficient."

29   I'd watch underwater motorcycle races. You would too. Someone call Red Bull and let's make this happen.

30   Actually, Arokiasamy was already speaking. I'm just checking here to make sure you're paying attention.

quick look at our printed materials and slap our palms to our foreheads and exclaim, 'Oh my! We actually meant to have the race back in *June*! I can't believe we said *July*. Sorry about that!' And then we'll all have a good laugh."

Concluded the owner of the fledgling race, "And then, of course, we'll get busy working on the 2013 race. We're still working out what we'll fail to do that year."

The news conference did not have a Q&A session, with the race promoter citing "important drawing of colorful lines on maps to do."

ROCK RACING Q&A

Here's the thing about Rock Racing. On one hand, you've got a guy who looks like Eric Estrada and acts like Donald Trump, but with less warmth and charm, and also with less business sense.

And he decided he wanted to have a professional bike racing team.

Since he had a lot of money from selling a lot of jeans for more than I'm even comfortable saying (around $300), he got to have a professional bike racing team.

That, I suppose, means he got to do whatever he wanted with that team. Which included firing people just for the hell of it. And being a bully. And having tantrums about not being treated like first-class citizens in the cycling universe.

Astonishingly, Rock Racing fizzled out in just a couple years, and Rock & Republic went bankrupt, getting bought by the Kohl's discount clothing chain.[31]

Which means that my stories about Rock Racing are its longest-lasting legacy.[32]

Much has recently been made of the Rock Racing professional cycling team, what with the wacky, hilariously insane behavior of the owner, Michael Ball, as well as some of the cyclists he has hired for the 2008 season. And while Ball's management style can be truly be called anything but dull, the same thing can also be said of a pickaxe to the groin.

What, then, should a self-respecting cyclist think of Rock Racing? Certainly, you've been asking yourself that question, along with others, such as:

1. Should I root for them, since they've got some of my favorite racers of days gone by?
2. Should I hate them for face-slapping a sport that frankly is all slapped-out at the moment?
3. Should I just grab a bag of popcorn and enjoy the circus?

---

31   You can now purchase a pair of Rock & Republic jeans for $18 when they're on clearance. And at Kohl's, everything is *always* on clearance. And in short, I am mildly ashamed to admit that I now own two pairs of Rock & Republic jeans.

32   As I edit the original stories from my blog for this book, I'm amazed at how often links I made to other sites are now dead. For example, rockandrepublic.com now shows nothing more than a "hello world" page. Which, I confess, made me chortle. Yes, I *chortled.*

These are all excellent questions, none of which I intend to answer.[33]
I will, however, endeavor to answer some of your other pressing questions about this most unlikely of pro racing teams.

Question: *So what's the deal with this Michael Ball guy?*

Answer: Michael Ball is the owner of Rock & Republic, a clothing store not in any way affiliated with Banana Republic. If you find yourself confusing the two, you can easily resolve your befuddlement by remembering that Banana Republic sells clothes in more colors than black and also carries some items that cost less than $300 (I think that converts to about 0.4 Euros right now).[34]

The reason that Rock & Republic is able to sell clothes for the square of their actual value is because Michael Ball brings "attitude" to those clothes. And by "attitude," I mean that he augments his natural unlikeability with aggressive meanness, and the confidence brought on by the self-certainty that he is never, ever, ever wrong.

In fourth grade, you called people like this "bullies."[35]

Well, now he owns a bike team. And he has not yet realized that at some point (possibly already reached), nobody is going to want to do business with him.[36]

For this reason, you should by default hope for the failure of the Rock Racing bike team, and feel a certain amount of glee whenever a racer leaves the team or Ball has a tantrum stemming from his staggering oafishness.

And as a point of honor, you should never wear jeans that cost more than $40,[37] a sum which no longer translates to anything at all in Euros.

Question: *Why isn't Frankie Andreu the director of Rock Racing anymore?*

Answer: This separation stemmed from an honest disagreement between Frankie and Mr. Ball.

On one hand, Frankie thought the directeur sportif[38] of Rock Racing would be in charge of both strategic and tactical operations for the team, from the hiring of the racers to the race-day plans.

---

33   If pressed, I'd say I pretty much went with #2 and #3.

34   This has since sunk to 0.09 Euros.

35   Among other things.

36   In hindsight, I was totally right. This doesn't surprise me even a little bit.

37   You've got to admit there's a certain beautiful irony in the way I now wear Rock & Republic jeans AND hew to my rule of wearing only the cheapest clothing money can by.

38   "Directeur sportif" is probably French for something.

On the other hand, Michael Ball thought main job of the directeur sportif of Rock Racing was to run odd errands, chauffeur the team Escalade, and give Mr. Ball soothing neckrubs when he is feeling stressed out.

The truth is, though, Michael Ball fired Andreu because he discovered that Andreu had used — and then kept secret for many years — EPO as a professional cyclist, and that kind of unethical behavior is simply not to be tolerated on this team.

BWAHAHAHAHAHAAH! Sorry.

Question: I heard that Tyler Hamilton's on the team, too. Is that true?

Answer: Yes. Yes, it is. And you can tell that he's really enjoying himself and happy to be racing for Mr. Ball, by the way he looks completely miserable in every single photo he has appeared in since joining the team.[39]

Question: But I thought Tyler was supposed to be this really nice guy. I can't imagine him wearing the Rock Racing skull and crossbones kit and hanging around someone like Michael Ball.

Answer: Maybe he's become bitter and angry.

Question: Do you think maybe he's become bitter and angry enough that at some point he'll punch Michael Ball in the throat?

Answer: That would be awesome.

Question: I heard Mario Cipollini is also racing for Rock Racing. When was Cipo caught doping?

Answer: Actually, you aren't strictly required to be a known doper to be on the Rock Racing team.[40]

Question: So why is Cipollini on the Rock Racing team, if he is in fact on the racing team?

Answer: If Cipollini is on the Rock Racing team — and we are happy to both confirm and deny that this is the case[41] — it is for one extremely important reason: Cipollini looks like someone who would wear $300 pants.

Question: I understand that Michael Ball told his racers they had to win or be fired.

Answer: Actually, he now claims he said something different, but

---

39 Sadly, I can't show you any of these pictures, because they don't belong to me.

40 At this point, it's pretty well accepted that Cipollini also doped. Nobody cares about this very much, though, because he has great hair or something.

41 Cipollini was incredibly coy about being on the team. Even now, he may still be on the Rock Racing team. If you happen to see him, please ask.

with the same meaning. Where before we thought he had said, "I will fire you if you don't win," he actually said, "Don't ever not come in first if you don't want to be fired."

Question: *OK, that's fine, but really my question was: does Ball know anything at all about bike racing? I mean, even one little thing? Does he even know what a domestique is?*

Answer: No.

Question: *You know, now that I think about it, "Win or Be Fired" would make a great premise for a reality show.*

Answer: You mean, every week have a bunch of semi pro racers do a race and the winner gets to be on a newly-formed pro cycling team?

Question: *Yeah, that's pretty much what I was thinking.*

Answer: You're right. That *would* be a great reality show. Michael Ball has missed his calling.[42]

Question: *So what is "Fast Freddie" Rodriguez doing on the team?*

Answer: Regretting his decision, most likely.

Question: *Do you suppose it's ever occurred to Fast Freddie that putting "Fast" in his name is a little bit weird? I mean, are there any professional cyclists that aren't fast?*

Answer: You miss Fast Freddie's point. He's not putting the "Fast" in "Fast Freddie" because he thinks he's faster than other cyclists. He is merely asserting that of all Freddies in the universe, he is the fast one.

Question: *And how about Oscar Sevilla and Santiago Botera?*

Answer: I'm sorry, I'm losing interest. Could we wrap this up?

Question: *Sure, just one last question. What about the Rock Racing jerseys — Is it OK for me to wear their jersey?*

Answer: Only if you also wear an eye patch and have a parrot perched on your shoulder.

> COMMENT BY WEEAN
> For a fashion chain, aren't their jerseys really ugly? Am I just too old or too European?

> COMMENT BY YEAGERMEISTER
> I've made enough popcorn for everyone.

---

42   "It'll be like *The Apprentice*, but on bicycles! And still with a crazy and unreasonable boss!"

COMMENT BY DNATSOL

I think of Michael Ball as the Marge Schott of cycling.

COMMENT BY REALDEAL

Don't be naive folks, Ball knows exactly what he's doing. It's an act...and a darn good one. What makes for good ratings and a fan-base is drama. Where would Armstrong have been without Ullrich? Where would professional football be without the Raiders?

You hate him...but you love it, don't you?

Mark my words, you're going to see kooks all over your favorite ride-routes rocking his kits too.

AN OPEN LETTER TO ROCK RACING, WHICH IS GRACIOUSLY ALLOWING ME TO BUY ONE OF THEIR NEW TEAM JERSEYS

There are lots and lots of really genuinely good jerseys out there in the world. Starting at around fifty or sixty bucks, you can get a jersey that is comfortable, is lightweight, breathes well, and looks good.

If you're willing to spend close to $100, you can get a fantastic *jersey. Any money you spend beyond that, well...you've kinda hit the point of diminishing returns.*

And when you hit $200...well, you'd better be Assos. And you'd better still plan on having your chops busted a little bit. Especially if you have very, very little to say about why your jersey costs roughly three times as much as others that look essentially just the same.

Minus the pirate imagery, natch.

Dear Rock Racing and Michael Ball,

I'm so excited right now, I can hardly type straight! Why? I'll tell you why. Because I just got the email letting me know the new Rock Racing Jerseys have arrived!

Before I go any further, I want to take a moment for thanking you for your consideration in not spamming me. I know that since Rock Racing does a new jersey every time they have a long training ride, you could easily be sending me notifications like this two or three times per week.[43] By saving up your email blasts so that you only send out an announcement when you have a dozen or so new jerseys to sell, I'm assured that I won't be getting more than two or three of these messages per month.[44]

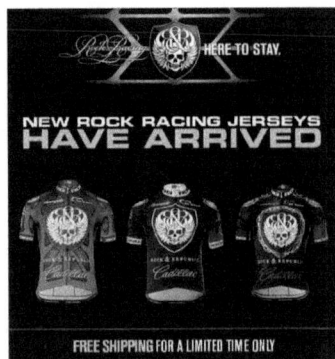

---

43   It's not terribly difficult to imagine an old refrigerator box full of nothing but Rock Racing jerseys in Tyler Hamilton's garage.

44   Imagine the poor harried Rock Racing jersey designer, working under the near-impossible constraints of always needing the jerseys to be primarily black and white

Anyway, I was so excited that you have some new jerseys I can buy from you that I zipped right on over to your website, where I beheld all of your incredibly distinctive and original designs.

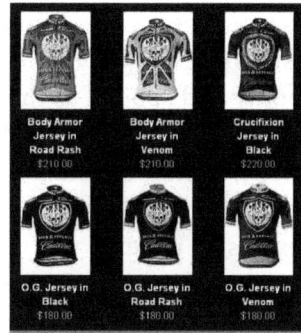

When I looked at these, Rock Racing, I admit that I briefly panicked. Since I only have a budget of $500 for bike jerseys this month, which *two* of these fabulous jerseys should I choose? The black one with the winged skull? Or the black one with the winged skull and red collar and cuffs? Or should I go with the black one with the winged skull, the crown of thorns, and the "Cadillac" logo in blood red?

So many choices! Such very different jerseys!

I have to be honest with you, though, Rock Racing. While I'm really excited about every one of the jerseys you have on your site and intend to buy one of each[45] (and have taken out a third mortgage on my house to facilitate this intention), I find myself looking askance at some of your less expensive jerseys.

For example, while I am unquestionably drawn to the "O.G. Jersey in White," I'm a little bit put off by the $180 price tag.

What about it makes it worth $40 less than the "Crucifixion Jersey in Black?" Is it because the black ink is a lot more expensive? Or maybe it's because Labor Day (U.S.) is coming up really soon and you want to get rid of all your white jerseys before then, so you're selling them at blow-em-out prices?

If that's the case, good call.

If, however, the "O.G. Jersey in White"

O.G. Jersey in White
$180.00

---

and always needing the same logo placement, while simultaneously needing to come up with a new jersey design every single day of the week. If I were the jersey designer, I'd probably start recycling designs. I don't think anyone would notice.

45 Upon further reflection, maybe I'd better get a spare of each, to keep as a collector's item.

is less expensive because it's somehow different — like maybe the skull isn't quite evil enough for your tastes, or riders who wear it don't look as pouty and spoiled as they ought, could you let me know? Because, after all, I have standards and don't want to be seen in a second-rate jersey.[46]

Or, failing all that, would you mind if I just go ahead and pay you $240 for that jersey, so I'll feel like I'm getting a really, not just nearly, exclusive jersey?

Thanks in advance!

Of course, Rock Racing, I like to be an informed consumer. So, even though I would gladly pay top dollar for these jerseys even if they were made of cheesecloth, I like to know my facts. So, as I went to the details page of one of your most expensive jerseys, I was elated to find you did not disappoint.

Frankly, I'm still suffering from information overload, guys, but let me see if I've got this straight:

It's a polyester jersey with *three* pockets in the back. And a zipper in the front.

My head's still reeling from this, but I still want to know a few things. First of all, how can you guys possibly afford to sell such incredibly distinctive jerseys at this deeply discounted price? This is America, guys; nobody's going to fault you for trying to make a profit.[47]

Next, why'd you go with three pockets, when you could have gotten away with two, or even one, like most jersey manufacturers? Your constant innovation shows that you're not just making jerseys to make a quick buck; you're thinking deeply about what cyclists need. And if that means the rest of the cycling apparel industry has to play catch-up for the next several years, well, so be it.

I can see you went with 100% polyester for the jerseys. Unless, as according to your Sizing and Technical Info page, they're actually 75%

---

46 I want to look like I'm wearing a pirate flag, but I don't want to look like I'm wearing some *proletariat* pirate flag.

47 Unless you're an amateur race promoter, in which case if you're making money you're a bad person.

polyester. Either way, I think you went with exactly the right amount of polyester.

And to top it all off: an elastic grip at the bottom? A mandarin collar? Raglan sleeves? You guys are going to blow this industry wide open with that kind of out-of-the-box thinking. $180–$220 for polyester jerseys with zippers in the front *and* pockets in the back is just not enough.

And that actually leads me to a couple of small — oh, ever so small — grievances I have with you, Rock Racing. The first one is this:

FREE SHIPPING FOR A LIMITED TIME ONLY

Do you really mean to tell me that in addition to having pockets *and* zippers in your $210 genuine 100% polyester[48] jerseys that you're going to foot the bill for shipping (ground only), too?[49]

C'mon, guys. Give yourselves some credit. We know you care more about your customers than yourselves, but I feel like I'm stealing food right out of your children's mouths.[50]

Seriously, I demand that you let me pay shipping for my $220 jersey. $84 sounds about right for that, doesn't it? I'll just put the cash in an envelope and mail it to you. I wouldn't feel good about this transaction otherwise.

But then you guys take it one step further. You go and tell me you'll give me a free poster if I spend more than $250 (e.g., if I buy nothing more than the $220 Crucifixion jersey and the matching $45 Crucifixion gloves).[51]

Of course, you stipulate that the posters are only free as long as supplies last. And if I don't miss my guess, those posters are long gone by now, because people are going to climb over the tops of each other getting their $250+ orders in so they can get that free poster.[52]

I, for example, made 18 separate $250+ orders as soon as I became aware of this offer.[53] Free shipping on all of them! 18 free posters! And

---

48   Or, possibly, 75%.
49   How can you possibly afford to do that?
50   Not that I think you have children. I imagine you are too cool to have children.
51   I would have googled "crucifixion gloves," but I admit I was unwilling to confront the variety of results.
52   In a garage somewhere, Michael Ball almost certainly has a large box containing a box that can hold up to 100 posters. That box currently contains 94 posters.
53   Well, so much for my $500/month jersey budget.

I only spent $4,680, for which I got 14 jerseys, two pair of gloves, ten t-shirts, and 4 pair of bib shorts![54]

But now, after the fact, I admit that I feel guilty. I took advantage of your kindness, greedily hogging those posters for myself.

I am such a heel.

Please, Rock Racing guys, let me pay for those eighteen posters. I'll bet that you innovatively printed them on glossy paper, lovingly roll them up, and insert them into a super premium cardboard shipping tube. For this kind of distinctive, elegant product and service, I expect to pay a fair price.

$96 per poster sounds about right to me.

Kind Regards,

Fatty

The Fat Cyclist

> COMMENT BY CARL
> I think I'm going to sell one of my children. I have to have one of those jerseys!!!

> COMMENT BY BOB
> If I can get a jersey with a zipper in the front, three pockets in the rear, and semi-form fitted, isn't it a bargain at any price? I mean, I'll be darned.

> COMMENT BY REGINA
> At those prices you should be able to send in a plaster cast of your torso and get it form fitted to that.

> COMMENT BY GOOSE
> This just underscores how Wal Mart esque the entire Rapha line is compared to the fashion-advanced Mike Ball Rock Racing empire.

---

54 A bargain!

COMMENT BY CLAY

Your condescending nature is unwarranted.

Did you even bother to look at their signature line of T-shirts, which are "100% Cotton" and "Made in the U.S.A."...a steal at $30! And, they come in innovative colors, such as black and "juice" — which is not the same as venom, which is good, because that would probably cost extra.

COMMENT BY SCOTT

I saw a guy in Santa Monica yesterday wearing a full RR kit, actually...on a Sora-equipped Fuji with platform pedals. There's something wrong with you if the clothes you're wearing cost you more than your bike.

7.
Fake News and Outright Lies

IF THERE'S ONE SECTION IN THIS BOOK TO WHICH I'VE BEEN LOOKING
FORWARD, THIS IS IT. THIS IS THE SECTION WHERE I CAN TAKE A BREAK
from all the tedious research I have to do elsewhere. This one's where I
can cut loose a little and not focus on the exacting lingual precision for
which I am so well known. Here, I put aside the nonstop fact-checking
and careful consideration to accuracy I usually put into my writing.

It is where I can basically just lie my butt off and make wild and inaccurate claims, unlike in the rest of the book. Uh huh.

OK, fine. I confess, I don't consider accuracy to be a critical component of anything I write, really. It's not that I actively avoid accuracy; I
just don't find it particularly compelling.

So, having confessed that this book is, more or less, a bunch of
nonsense, what makes this section any different than the rest of the book?

Well, in the rest of the sections I'm writing inaccurate, misleading
stories because I don't know any better. In this one I'm lying on purpose.
Although it's pretty likely that there's plenty in here that I got wrong
just because I didn't know better.

It is my hope that you will not be able to tell which is which.

NEXT YEAR'S TOUR DE FRANCE WINNER STRIPPED OF TITLE

When I originally wrote this story, way back in April of 2007, I titled it, "2007 Tour de France Winner Stripped of Title." And that was a fantastic title, back when it was created.

What I neglected to consider was the possibility that time would continue to pass, which meant that when people saw the headline anytime after the 2007 Tour de France, they would think that this was a post about an astonishing piece of news: that Alberto Contador had had his Tour de France victory stripped from him after the race had ended.

Which is just crazy talk.

Because that wouldn't happen until 2010.

So, I have now appended this headline, making it so it is permanently set in the future. Which means that now, for this year and forever, next year's Tour de France winner may always be stripped of his title.

Oh yeah, one more thing: I should probably have also put blanks where the names for the authorities go; these seem to be changing lately. But I didn't, because you don't know most of their names anyway. Or at least I don't.

PARIS, FRANCE **(Fat Cyclist Fake News Service)** — Three agencies integral to the sport of professional cycling held a joint press conference today, in order to make a number of important announcements regarding next year's Tour de France.[1]

"First and foremost," said Patrice Clerc, President of Amaury Sport Organization (ASO), the promoter of the Tour de France,[2] "I want to congratulate whoever wins the Tour de France. You are truly a great champion, and ASO thanks you for making our business possible. While we do not yet know who will win the Tour, I feel it is vital we acknowledge that person as the pinnacle of strength, conditioning, and personal sacrifice he undoubtedly must be."

---

1   Here's how shaky my understanding is of actual cycling organizations and politics. I did not know the names of any of these people, except Dick Pound. I will never forget the name of Dick Pound.

2   I had to look this up.

"Next," continued Clerc, "I'd like to take this opportunity to accuse the aforementioned winner of using unscrupulous and nefarious methods to obtain this prize, and hereby accuse him — whoever he[3] is — of doping."

AN OPEN AND SHUT CASE

Dick Pound, Chairman of the World Anti-Doping Association (WADA),[4] was on hand to elaborate.

"When was the last time we had a Grand Tour winner who was not eventually accused and — at least in the court of public opinion — convicted of doping?"

Continued Pound, "Our problem, in the past, was one of timing. We keep waiting until after someone has won a grand tour to make our case. By then, the public has gotten behind the rider[5] and we've got a public relations nightmare on our hands."

"Really, it's very simple," said the Chairman of WADA. "Follow my logic, if you please. Every single rider at the Tour de France is a superior athlete. If one person is able to beat all these other people, that person must be doing something the others aren't doing.

"However, everyone knows that every single one of these athletes is doing every legitimate thing he can to be the best racer he can be. And since every racer is doing every allowable thing, but only one person can win, the person who wins must be doing something that is not allowed."[6]

"And what is not allowed?" asked Mr. Pound. "Doping is not allowed, that's what."

Concluded the Chairman of WADA, "I think it's time we stop beating around the bush and be direct about this: If one wins the Tour de France, one is quite simply nothing but a doper, and deserves to be punished for the crimes that one's certainly either currently committing or is about to commit.

Thus, while I admire the future winner of the Tour de France, I

---

3   Or she, if you're reading this far enough into the future.

4   Yes, I know this is no longer true. But I don't care.

5   I was thinking back to Floyd Landis when I wrote this, and how I had fully bought into his innocence. Nowadays, we still get behind riders accused of doping; the difference is we get behind them with pitchforks.

6   I took an "Introduction to Logic" class when I was in college, before I dropped out. So I can assure you that this is completely logical.

have nothing but contempt for the unethical way in which they will go about winning."

NEW FEATURES IN THIS YEAR'S TOUR

Brian Cookson,[7] President of the International Cycling Union (UCI) announced that in conjunction with this preemptive dismissal of the winner of the TdF, several useful and interesting new features will be added to the race.

"In addition to having the team car following the race leader," said Cookson, "we will now have a police car, just in case he tries to make a break for it. We will also have GPS-based location transmitters sewn right into the yellow jersey."

"The award ceremony will have some new drama, as well," said McQuaid. "In addition to the stuffed lion, the flowers, the kisses and the yellow jersey, the holder of the *maillot jaune* will be handed a pair of ceremonial handcuffs by myself and Mr. Pound, and then we will slap him with a yellow glove and challenge him to a duel."

"The final ceremony will be even better," concluded the UCI President. "In addition to the traditional pomp and prizes, we will also have law enforcement personnel, a judge, and prosecuting attorneys on hand to serve notice of arrest, a search warrant, and in fact begin the arraignment proceedings. It will be spectacular."

RACERS REACT

"I suddenly don't feel so well," said Ivan Basso,[8] following the press conference. "Also, I have a pain in my knee and my goiter's acting up. I intend to race still, but frankly don't see my prospects as all that good."

"My back is killing me," commented Alexandre Vinokourov.[9]

"I feel a general sense of malaise," noted Iban Mayo, though nobody asked.

---

7   Of course, this was "Pat McQuaid" in the original version of this story. But since, as a cycling expert, I know Cookson's name without having to look it up, I have updated this story with the new UCI president's name. Because I want this story to be timeless, that's why.

8   In hindsight, it's kind of adorable who I had pegged as the 2007 favorites.

9   Vinokourov was, of course, caught doping in 2007.

FINAL WORD

Concluding the presentation, Christian Prudhomme,[10] Director of the Tour de France, said, "I'd like to make a couple of final points. First, I'm afraid that once we strip the outright winner of the Tour de France of his title, the second place winner will be promoted to the winning spot and is thus a doper as well. And so on and so on, until we've lost interest."

"Second," concluded the race director, "All of this is null and void in the event of a Frenchman winning the Tour."

> COMMENT BY BOTCHEDEXPERIMENT
> Pffft. This is SO ridiculous. It's so PREPOSTEROUS. I've never read such HYPERBOLE!
> I mean, come on, isn't it obvious that Pat, Dick, Patrice, and Christian would never agree on anything!

> COMMENT BY ANGRYROADIE
> I watch it for the crashes. And for the outfits. Vive le lycra!

---

10 Still, as of this writing, in the same job! No revision required! Yay?

TOUR DE FRANCE FINALLY CLEAN!

I'm not going to talk a lot about doping in this book. I'm just not. And I'm not going to talk a lot about it on my blog, either. It's too tiresome, and it's about a part of the sport that is only barely even tangential to why I like cycling.

That said, you should probably read the previous story before reading this one. I say this because I assume that you're otherwise just sort of randomly sampling stories in this book whenever you have to use the bathroom for an extended period of time. The last story kind of hints about the possibility of Alexandre Vinokourov doping in 2007.

I wrote this one immediately after he tested positive.

And of course, I wrote this one years and years before Armstrong finally confessed to doping.

All of these doping watersheds bring up a really interesting question: has there ever been a grand tour that has been raced completely clean?

No, I don't think so either. But what if someone was the very last, final doper — and now everyone else in the Tour de France was clean?

PARIS, FRANCE (Fat Cyclist Fake News Service) — Following the positive homologous blood doping test of Alexandre Vinokourov and subsequent withdrawal of Team Astana from the Tour de France today,[11] Race Director Christian Prudhomme announced that everyone else racing in the Tour de France is clean.

"Well, that about wraps it up," said Prudhomme at a hastily-called press conference. "We finally got the last doper. Everyone else racing the Tour is as clean as a whistle. Possibly even cleaner. You can now watch the rest of the race with full confidence that everyone still in the race — especially all those guys who had like half an hour's advantage on the once-frontrunner Vinokourov — are not doping. *At all.*"[12]

Asked about current race leader Michael Rasmussen and the cloud of suspicion hanging over him, Prudhomme responded, "Well, is he still in the race? Yes, he is. So he must not be doping, or we would have

---

11   If you need a refresher course on these events — and you have the stomach to relive them — you'll find the story at http://bit.ly/fatsby01

12   Why would they?

caught him, just like we have caught all the dopers."[13]

Smiling for the now-completely reassured press, Prudhomme noted, "It's a fantastic time to be a fan of professional cycling, now that we're finally finished cleaning the sport up."

FANS AND RACERS REACT

"I used to worry about whether some of the pros were doping," said Matt Carter,[14] an American cycling fan visiting France to see the Tour firsthand. "But now that the sport has these really reliable drug tests in place, anyone who's foolish enough to cheat will be caught and punished. I'm just glad that Alexandre Vinokourov was the only one left cheating, and that the other general classification guys, each of which were just about forever ahead of Vino, aren't doping."

Said Alberto Contador,[15] a clean racer currently in second place in the Tour de France, "I don't understand why anyone would need to dope anyway. I mean, look at me! I don't dope, as clearly witnessed by my negative test results, and I'm still able to take first and second place, stage after stage after stage!"

"What's crazy," said Nick Abbott,[16] an Australian race fan, "is that Vinokourov somehow thought he could get away with it! Didn't he realize that anyone who dopes is going to get caught by this foolproof dope detector machine (World Anti-Doping Authority) WADA has built?

NO MORE TESTS NEEDED, EVER AGAIN

WADA Chief Dick Pound took today's announcement as an opportunity to say, "I'm very pleased that we've finally arrived at the point where our sport is all cleaned up. Effective immediately, there will be no more tests, since they are no longer necessary. Also, I am disbanding WADA, since it has so thoroughly done its job that it is no longer necessary.

---

13   Of course, Michael Rasmussen was "removed from the Tour" by Rabobank for being in one place when he said he had been in another. And, oh yeah, he had been doping, a fact so obvious that even I could tell.

14   Matt Carter was my manager at Microsoft, as well as my manager at a prior company.

15   I of course wrote this before Contador ever tested positive for anything. I was speculating. And I'm going to be honest: it bums me out that I was right.

16   Another former co-worker and riding buddy at Microsoft. Who also is, in fact, Australian.

"I feel immensely gratified," concluded Pound, "to have played my part in this highly effective anti-doping campaign in the great sport of cycling. With the capture of the final doper in the pro peloton, we've crossed the finish line, and we've won. It's a great day for all of us."[17]

> COMMENT BY MTB W
> How long before Rasmussen is DQ'd? After he wins?

> COMMENT BY EUFEMIANO FUENTES
> Well, at least Armstrong was clean. Right?

---

17 My final thought on this story: it holds up as an artifact of the period. Also, it's pretty funny. But even more than being funny, it is kind of sad.

EXCLUSIVE! DETAILS OF SHIMANO'S ACQUISITION OF PEARL IZUMI

Really, all I have to say about this, by way of introduction, is that Shimano really did buy Pearl Izumi.

No, now that I think about it, I guess I have a little bit more to say, because it's at least remotely possible that not everyone who reads my book is necessarily a huge bike nerd. In which case, you may not even know what Shimano and Pearl Izumi are manufacturers and make stuff.

So:

- ***Shimano** makes parts for your bike. Also, it makes really nice fishing reels, but I am pretty sure that's not relevant to this story.*
- ***Pearl Izumi** makes biking clothes and shoes, among other things (by which I mean clothes for much less dignified sports, like triathaloning).*

OK, now you should be up to speed.

BROOMFIELD, COLORADO (Fat Cyclist Fake News Service) — Shimano American Corporation announced earlier today[18] that it is acquiring Colorado-based Pearl Izumi, Inc.

Many news stories have noted that management of Pearl Izumi would remain independent. No details, however, have been revealed as to product lineup and brand changes at Pearl Izumi.

Until now.[19]

COMPANY NAME

The first change that will be made is to the company name, which will now simply be "Shimanzumi."

"We're very excited by this new company name," said Shimanzumi's Marketing Director, Geoff Shaffer. "It's very fun to say."

---

18   If you'd like to read a really old press release on this acquisition, you'll find it here: http://bit.ly/fatsby02

19   OK, here's where the fake part begins.

"Shimanzumi, Shimanzumi, Shimanzumi!" continued Shaffer, by way of proving his point.[20]

CLOTHING LEVELS

Shimanzumi clothing will be aligned with component Shimano mountain and road group levels. Selected features of the new clothing lines are as follows:

- **Dura-Ace**: The lightest, sexiest cycling clothing available for the road cyclist will be the hallmark of the Dura-Ace line. As precise as it is elegant, it will make Assos look sloppy in comparison.[21] The only reason thread made of actual gold is not used in Dura-Ace jerseys is that it is too heavy. In order to keep your Dura-Ace clothing working properly, Shimanzumi recommends having it maintained by a certified Shimanzumi clothing mechanic every three rides.[22]

- **XTR**: XTR clothing will be much like Dura-Ace, but will come out two years later.

- **Ultegra**: Ultegra cycling clothing will fit as comfortably as Dura-Ace, will weigh only trivially more, will cost less, and will in fact be more durable. However, it will be imperceptibly less sexy-looking, and your riding friends will know that you don't consider yourself as deserving the very best.

- **LX**: The LX clothing line will be nothing more than the XTR clothing line from two years prior, with different silkscreens applied.

- **Tiagra**: The Tiagra clothing line will fit and feel just fine, until your friend persuades you to try on a pair of Dura-Ace shorts, "just to see how they feel." From that point forward, you'll never be happy with your Tiagra shorts again. This is by design.

- **Alivio**: The Alivio clothing line will be made of burlap bags that have been specially treated to combust in sunlight and dissolve in water.

---

20 I highly recommend you join Mr. Shaffer in saying "Shimanzumi" aloud, loud and often. I know I do.

21 Although I'm confident that Assos will always retain the edge in the "Luxury Body" product category.

22 Di2 will be coming out in a couple years, at which point your jersey will put itself on for you, at the touch of a button.

NEW COLOR SCHEMES

All Shimanzumi clothing will be black, grey, and highly-polished silver. No exceptions.

SHIMANZUMI TOTAL INTEGRATION

Shimanzumi clothing is designed to be worn together: shorts, jersey, socks, shoes, and gloves. While it is theoretically possible for cyclists to ride while wearing other brands of clothing mixed in, it is not recommended.

The jerseys have been made two inches shorter, for example, to accommodate the fact that the shorts have been made to go two inches higher. As long as you wear both, you'll have excellent midriff coverage. If, however, you wear Shimanzumi shorts with a Castelli jersey, your warranty is void, for starters. Also, Shimanzumi clothing has been found to cause rashes and chemical burns when mixed with other clothing brands.[23]

You're just better off discarding your existing clothing and going forward with an integrated Shimanzumi setup. It's inevitable anyway, so you may as well embrace it.

NEW MARKETS

The Shimanzumi alliance is uniquely positioned to cross over into additional sport markets. Specifically, look for wicking, lightweight, form-fitting hip waders to come out in 2009.[24] This will be followed by a fishing vest made of high-tech fabrics in 2010, with extra-deep pockets and elastic arm gathers.

YEARLY REVISIONS

Shimanzumi will implement a planned obsolescence strategy into its clothing line,[25] where every three years, an entirely new clothing line with new sizes and exponentially more complex clothing parts are shipped. They will be lighter and fit 15% more precisely, at which point

---

23   It occurs to me that I just metaphorically described the Apple business model.

24   So I guess it was a good thing I mentioned that Shimano makes fishing equipment, after all.

25   Wow, I really *have* described the Apple business model, haven't I?

you can expect to be scorned for wearing your previous-generation Shimanzumi clothing.

ENTHUSIASM AND A PRECAUTION

Says Shaffer, "We're very excited by the new directions and opportunities this melding of two great cycling companies affords us."

"If, however, you get a slight tear in any article of Shimanzumi clothing, discard it at once and buy a replacement. Shimanzumi clothing is not designed to be patched or otherwise repaired. Contact your nearest cycling clothing service center at once for a replacement."

COMMENT BY AL MAVIVA

I'm a little disappointed, Fatty, that you left out the most interesting features of the Shimanzumi line. Your friends who ride their Fondriest or Colnago exclusively with licensed Campagnolo Wear will stop talking to you on the assumption that you are too stupid to actually use words, and if you could use words, they wouldn't be artful or useful in any meaningful respect. Plus if you try to mix and match — say wearing Campy socks with Shimanzumi shorts — the border between the two pieces of clothing will break out in something that looks like shingles, but is much more painful and harder to get rid of, plus spaghetti will shoot out of your body like guinea worms. Um, so to speak. And if any part of either clothing line touches any part of a SRAM Red gruppo at any time, the clothing immediately bursts into flame, killing the user, similar to a Sony laptop if you try to use aftermarket batteries.

Shimanzumi, naturally, is working on improving the design: The Dura-Ace ST line will have electronic climate control along with bib shorts that actually pull themselves down if you want to take a pee while on the bike.

The motto of the new clothing line is supposedly: "Shimanzumi: We're Too Good for You."

LEVI LEIPHEIMER ENDORSES THE ULTIMATE SPORTS HYPNOSIS CD, ANNOUNCES PLEASURE AT BEING CONTADOR'S SUPER-DOMESTIQUE

I like Levi Leipheimer. I like him a lot. I like him so much that I asked him to send me a blurb to use in my book, to help promote and sell it and stuff.

And from time to time, I talk with him. About all kinds of stuff. Including some very serious stuff. But I have never broached one very taboo topic:

The fact that he has, at one point, endorsed a cheesetastic hypnosis CD and had his picture featured in this ad. Honestly, I just don't know how to deal with that.

Except, of course by writing some fake news about it.

MADRID, SPAIN (Fat Cyclist Fake News Service) — In a post-stage team press conference today, U.S. National Road Race Champion Levi Leipheimer announced he is endorsing The Ultimate Cyclist CD.[26]

THE ULTIMATE CYCLIST

Used and endorsed by Levi Leipheimer

Ultimate
SportsPsychology.com

"Since winning the 2007 Tour of California, the Ultimate Cyclist[27] has become an indispensable part of my training arsenal," said Leipheimer.[28]

Added teammate Alberto Contador, apropos of nothing, "phosphorus," at which point Levi Leipheimer stood up, climbed up on the table, and began clucking like a chicken.

---

26   Yes, you can still buy a copy of the CD. No, it no longer has a picture of Levi on it. And I'm not exactly sure where you can find a working CD player anywhere, but you can also just download it. So that's a relief.

27   He neglected to mention which part he likes best: the "trance inducing theta rhythm," the "guided meditation by Dr. Rick Collingwood," or the "powerful cycling specific affirmations and visualizations."

28   Yes, he *actually said that* at some point in his life.

Oddly, when Contador snapped his fingers, Leipheimer returned to his seat and resumed speaking normally.

"This has been an exceptional year for me," said Leipheimer. "I really feel that I have the will, fitness, and determination to win a major tour."

Interrupted Contador, "sodium."

Leipheimer continued, in a stilted voice, "But the greatest thing I could ever do is reject my own selfish desires and to do all I can, regardless of consequences, to help my glorious and exalted teammate Alberto Contador win the Vuelta a España."[29]

Leipheimer then shook his head a few times, pressed his palms to his eyes, and then looked around as if he were lost.

After taking a few moments to evidently collect himself, Leipheimer asked, "Are there any questions?"

One reporter asked why Leipheimer had recently pulled over on the side of the road for several minutes, completely stopping until Contador had caught up with him. Unfortunately, Leipheimer's response was not audible, due to a sudden and quite severe sneezing fit on Contador's part.

Asked why, earlier in the stage that day, he had begun mooing like a cow for ten minutes, Leipheimer had no comment, nor any apparent idea of what the questioner was talking about.

At this moment, Contador's coughing/sneezing fit became so severe, he covered his face with his hands and his entire body seemed to be shaking. The press conference had to be terminated.

Created by cycling coach and Category 1 bike racer Josh Horowitz, and renowned Australian clinical hypnotherapist, Dr. Rick Collingwood, *The Ultimate Cyclist* is the only cycling-specific sports psychology tool on the market.[30]

It is not known whether custom versions of the CD, containing specialized messages and suggestions, can be ordered.

---

29 It took me about twenty minutes to figure out how to get that tilde in that word there, so I hope you enjoyed it.

30 Oh, but I'm sure there will be others soon.

COMMENT BY THE D

I literally had to click on the ad to learn that it was, in fact, "real," at least in the way that the oil from a snake is real.

COMMENT BY KT

That's...scary. They used the arm-crossed staring picture of Levi that always makes me think he's trying to use his psychic powers on me.
Stop it, Levi! You're creepin' me out!

I HAVE NOT YET DECIDED HOW TO SPEND THIS $30,000 I HAVE JUST LAYING AROUND

I remember when I bought my first mountain bike. I went into the bike shop, planning to get whatever bike I wanted and telling the salesperson that I was interesting in buying a really nice bike. He seemed excited about this possibility.

Bragging a little, I told him that I was ready to spend what I considered an exorbitant amount of money. Specifically, I was willing to spend up to...$500.

The light went out of his eyes, and he walked me over to take a look at the only bike he had in the shop that would fit my budget: a Bridgestone MB5.

Things have changed in the past twenty years, and I now have a wonderful little speech I've prepared for whenever someone expresses astonishment at how much I have spent on the bike I am riding. "This is the bike equivalent of a Lexus," I say. "It is as near-perfect a machine as you could ever own. It's strong, light, reliable, and beautiful. It's everything I could ever want, and I use it every chance I can. Further, I love every moment I'm on it."

"And yet," I conclude, "This miracle of a machine costs about a third as much as the cheapest, lowest-quality new car you could find on the market."

That's the thing about cycling. It's delightfully easy to rationalize our exorbitant expenditures. Even so, at some point you hit a point of diminishing returns.

This is the story of a bike that hit — and then just blew right on by — that point. This is all about the Factor 001, which was the proof-of-concept bike for Factor bikes that, amazingly, can now be purchased with (lots and lots) of money.

As a person who is *not* a famous and award-winning cycling celebrity author, you almost certainly spend more than half your waking hours wondering what it must be like to be me.[31]

Well, in order to satisfy your completely justifiable curiosity, today I'm going to give you a little peek into a dilemma in which I am currently embroiled.

---

31 Full disclosure: I also spend about the same amount of time each day, wondering the exact same thing.

You see, as a very famous, beloved, and award-winning author, I make a ton of money. Seriously, it's just ridiculous. I mean, when I got into blogging I knew that it was lucrative, but really, I had *no idea* I'd be making money hand-over-fist like this.

As a result, each month I have given myself a $30,000 allotment for bicycles and bicycle-related equipment.

And that's where the hard part comes in.

For the month of June, I am thinking of focusing on road bikes. I am hence faced with a difficult dilemma: on what should I spend my $30,000? I have narrowed it down to doing one of two things:

OPTION A

I could use my $30,000 to buy a fleet of high-end road bikes, including all of the following:

- Ibis Silk SL,[32] Dura-Ace: $5300
- Seven Cycles V-II, Dura-Ace: $8400
- Cervelo R3, Dura-Ace: $5700
- Trek Madone 6.9 Pro: $9129

This leaves me with $1500 for upgrades. And let's face it, there would be upgrades.[33] That said, I think you might agree with me that this would be a fine road stable, and should mollify me, at least for this month.

OPTION B

However, I can't help but think that instead of buying four absolute beyond-dream bikes, I should perhaps buy this:

Yes, this is the Factor 001: For the serious athlete! And by the way, that "for the serious athlete" and the accompanying

---

32   Ibis no longer sells road bikes, alas, making this otherwise very-dated story even *more* extremely dated.

33   I just wouldn't feel good about my bike purchase if I didn't strip it to the frame and rebuild it with parts that are marginally better, while also being much more expensive.

exclamation point is straight from the company site, which can mean only two things:

1. This bike is for serious athletes.
2. This company is seriously excited about the fact that this bike is for serious athletes.

I can't help but be drawn to the Factor 001. For one thing, since the base model costs $28,000, I wouldn't have to spend all that time — and time is (in my case, *a lot*) of money — purchasing and fitting those other four bikes. Which would be great, because why would I want to get four dream bikes, when I can just buy one really boxy, awkward-looking bike?

Also, the Factor 001 is not just *any* bike. No. It's a virtual cycling lab, containing these very exciting features, which I am taking straight from the press release and then interpreting:

- **Unique ergonometric data collection, logging, and analysis capabilities**: This means the cyclocomputer is included.
- **Biometric, physical force, and environmental data harvested simultaneously**: This means the included cyclocomputer also measures watts. And, evidently, knows which way the wind is blowing and if it's raining.
- **Huge technology transfer potential to other sporting environments**: This means they ran out of ideas for the bullet list, but didn't want it to just have two items.[34]

What they don't list as a feature, but which I fully expect is included considering the price, is that the bike actually uses all this data to *tell you how you're doing*. For example, if I'm not really applying myself, it might say, "I'm sorry, Fatty, but you don't seem to be as serious an athlete as you ought to be."[35] Because, as noted, this bike is for serious athletes. Oops, I mean: serious athletes!

This $28,000 (or in my case, $30,000, because I plan to get the upgraded saddle) bike also has a very exciting feature: all new componentry. This is really good news, because I've been thinking lately that the scores of years and millions of dollars of research Campagnolo,

---

34 For myself, when I run out of ideas before I get to the third item, I like to say, "And much, much more!"

35 As you read this to yourself, be certain to read the bike's voice in the same voice Kitt would use when speaking to David Hasselhoff.

Shimano, and SRAM have spent simply haven't resulted in reliable, honed, time-tested parts. What I need is a bike that uses completely new, albeit strikingly similar to what already exists, and above all, *proprietary* bike parts, designed by a car company.

Oh, also I want the bike to weigh at least a pound more than any road bike that costs a fifth as much and I want it to not be legal to race. Because, as you know, it's silly to expect your training bike to have similar weight and handling characteristics to your race bike.

Above all, though, is the look of this bike. Pure elegance. Nothing says "sexy" to me quite like a lot of rectangles.

And that fork: ooh la la!

DECISION

As you've no doubt guessed, I've made up my mind: I'm getting the Factor 001. The other bikes...well, they can wait 'til next month, I guess.

Unless I decide to use next month's $30,000 to get that matching Arantix[36] and Ascend[37] I've had my eye on.

> COMMENT BY MIKE
>
> I would spend $28,000 on a bike, but only if it was made of hydrogen, and weighed less than 76 grams. That would be cool.

> COMMENT BY RANTWICK
>
> Thanks Fatty. I think I threw up a little bit there. And I love bikes.

> COMMENT BY JIM
>
> You think at that price, they would slap some paint on it!

> COMMENT BY TREKKER
>
> You neglected to mention its most advanced training feature: pedals are included! All those other cheapskate manufacturers make you buy your own. Think of the time you'll save by not having to choose, purchase, and install pedals.

---

36 The Arantix was a bike that looked like a cheesegrater.
37 Same company, same cheesegrater look, also out of business.

8.

Strong Opinions, Trivial Matters

I HAVE A VERY GOOD REASON TO CALL THIS SECTION SOMETHING BESIDES "MISCELLANEOUS POSTS I WANTED TO INCLUDE." WHICH, AS IT TURNS out, is simply, "I don't want to use that title."

But if I were going to be completely honest, which I only sorta-kinda am, this is in fact a miscellaneous chapter. I give advice to Ivan Basso on what I consider to be the weakest, most half-hearted doping mea culpa in history up to that point. I harshly criticize a boy who had the creativity, skill, and tenacity to build a bike out of wood. I plead with the stranger who goes out biking when it's wet and cold outside, thus demolishing my excuse that it's no weather for riding. I muse about my brother-in-law's strange and terrifying mountain biking curse. And I exult in the modern miracle known as convenience stores.

What ties these together? Well, nothing, except that none of these things are important and yet I manage to express strong opinions about each of them.

In other words, they're pretty trivial.

Oh, and also they're some of my favorite stories in the whole book.

EXCUSES IVAN BASSO SHOULD HAVE USED

I've come to the conclusion that I'm at least partially to blame for all the doping scandals in the past five to ten years. Somehow, pretty much every time I decide that I'm going to get behind a pro racer, to really root for him, he winds up being a doper.

It makes me wonder: Is there causation? Does me rooting for cyclists make them start doping?

Suspecting this is the case, I no longer root for anyone.

But I did, briefly, root for Ivan Basso, and, perhaps because I did, he at least "considered" doping, for which he took a two year suspension. Which makes me further wonder: how long of a suspension would Basso have had to serve if he had actually started doping? And even more hypothetically, if he was racing this fast when he was just considering doping, how fast would he have actually gone while on the juice?

I guess we'll never know.

One thing we do know, however, is that Ivan Basso, when confronted, gives what may be the weakest excuse a person could possibly imagine.

On May 8, 2007, Ivan Basso made a major announcement: That he had thought about doping and had maybe even planned on doping for the 2006 Tour de France.

However, it's important to note, he says, that he had never up prior to that date *actually* doped, and that all his victories up to that point (and since) are completely legitimate.

This is, naturally, completely believable. Noble, even. I cannot help but look on in admiration at the conscience of this man, who, ashamed at even the *contemplation* of doing something wrong, has come forth to admit that he has had naughty thoughts cross his mind.[1]

Just for the sake of clarity, let's note that Basso was considering beginning his doping career on the eve of the Tour de France, the most important race of his life.

Which is perhaps a *slightly* more audacious change in regimen for a pro cyclist than trying a new nutrition plan, or a new training plan, or

---

1   Imagine a world where everyone had a press conference anytime they had impure thoughts. No, it's just too horrible to contemplate.

switching to a new bike or riding position, immediately before starting a grand tour.

Like everyone else, I have no problem believing that. Happens all the time.

WE HAVE A NEW WINNER

OK, I confess: I've been being sarcastic.[2]

Basso's excuse isn't just bad, it's *startlingly* bad. I found myself checking the byline to see if I had written it as fake news.

And then I became interested in a question. Is it possible that Ivan Basso has given the lamest of all possible excuses in the history of lame excuses? Will all future excuses be measured against Basso's as a percentage? "You say that you were mugged by masked Dutchmen, who bludgeoned you into submission and then injected EPO into you against your will? Well, that's lame, but only 72% as lame as Basso's excuse."[3]

I mean, was this *really* the best Basso could do? I'm completely addle-brained right now, but even so, I can think of a few excuses that have more credibility than "I was about to dope and had given several bags of blood to Fuentes in order to dope, but I never actually doped, and now that I'm about to be caught, I've had a sudden attack of conscience."

For example, I think Basso would have been better off using any of the following:

- **I doped, but only recreationally.** "Have you ever tried EPO, man? It is a freaking *rush*. You've got all this extra oxygen going to your brain and you're suddenly finding you can remember the quadratic equation, which you haven't thought about since high school. It's a *total freaking rush!* I wasn't doping to be fast, man. I was doping because it's dope."
- **I didn't know it was dope.** "Hey, when you're a pro cyclist, someone's always jabbing you with one needle or another. I didn't know I was being doped; I was just rolling up my sleeve and doing what I was told. It never occurred to me that I was suddenly going 7% faster for any other reason than my

---

2   Or perhaps I was just contemplating being sarcastic. Regardless, the important thing is I've confessed it.

3   I was working on coming up with an excuse that was 90–95% as lame as Basso's, but just can't do it. It's now 2014, but Basso's excuse has stood the test of time.

improved TT position. Also, I didn't get a clue from my suddenly very-pronounced brow line. Nor from my shrunken testicles."[4]

- **I was making a statement.** "Yeah, I was doping, and I'm proud of it. I want to be the best, fastest rider I can be, and if that means taking EPO and percolating pure oxygen through my blood thrice daily, I'm fine with it. In fact, next week, I'm having a second joint placed in my legs, giving me unprecedented leverage in my pedaling power. I'm also having my skull structure modified to be more aerodynamic. Two months from now I will be able to pedal up 30% grades at 48 mph. If the UCI wants to be a bunch of Luddites, that's their problem. The fact is, I will be the fastest man alive, and everyone watching or racing in the Tour de France will know it."[5]

- **I didn't know doping was illegal.**[6] "Whh? Huh? You mean I shouldn't have been taking EPO, human growth hormones, steroids, and suffusing my bones with high-tensile titanium alloy? Whoa. I feel so stupid. I'm really, really sorry. It's just that I've been super busy with my training schedule and haven't really had time to check my email. Seriously, guys, thanks for the heads-up. I'll stop using right away."

- **I only doped occasionally.** "OK, fine, I was doping, but it's not like I didn't have it under control. I'm just a social doper. You know, the occasional testosterone patch on weekends, maybe a vial of EPO on Christmas or special anniversaries. I could totally stop doping any time I want. In fact, I'll quit it right now. There. I hereby declare myself clean. Let's race!"[7]

See, that's five right there. And I'm only quitting because my mind is starting to wander.

---

4   I can't believe I put "shrunken testicles" in this story. This is supposed to be a family-friendly book!

5   If someone actually said this, they would immediately get their own reality TV show. I'm sure of it.

6   This is, of course, an homage to Steve Martin's classic "I Forgot..." bit. Listen to it here: http://bit.ly/fatsby03

7   I didn't think about it at the time, but I'm pretty sure now that I'm editing this that there's a little bit of Steve Martin in this one too. I listened to a lot of Steve Martin as a kid. http://bit.ly/fatsby04

COMMENT BY BOTCHEDEXPERIMENT

"It was only attempted doping." Wait, he actually tried to use that one.

"But I've never even heard of Eufemi-what's his name." Wait, he actually used that one too.

"But I was just storing my blood in case I needed a transfusion." No, Jan's lawyer already used that one on Jan's behalf.

OOOHHHHH, I've got a great one: "I HAVE NEVER TESTED POSITIVE." To really sell this one you have to say it angrily and maybe squeeze a little tear out of the corner of your left eye.

"I have never cheated anyone out of anything." Jan again.

"The blood was for my dog." — Frank Vandenbroucke.

"The EPO, HGH, and steroids were for my mother." — What's his name whose wife got arrested by the French on the last day of the TDF, while transporting a decent sized pharmacy??? Raimondas Rumsas.

Okay, I'm getting disheartened now. I'm not going to post any more.

COMMENT BY MATEO

Jan hasn't admitted to being a vampire yet, so Basso could use that one.

COMMENT BY XCTIGER

I'm not here to talk about the past.

I AM NOT IMPRESSED BY YOUR WOODEN BIKE

You know how you made an awesome cutting board as your final project for woodshop back in high school? And how proud you were of it, and also how excited you were that you now had your mom's Christmas present all handled?

And then the class show-off went and made something like a coffee table? Yeah. That kid was a jerk.

Well, suppose that you had a kid in woodshop who went and built a bicycle, for pity's sake. Then how would you feel?

And furthermore, what if you were an internet-famous cycling blogger and, because everyone knows you like bikes, the entire known universe starts emailing you the story of how this kid built a bike?

Well, I'm not going to take it anymore. I'm going to give this kid — who, by this time, is probably a senior in MIT or something and will soon be making roughly thrice my annual income — a stern critique.

I swear, if one more person emails me a link to the story about that high school kid who built a wooden bike, I am going to *lose my mind*.

For the lucky ones among you who haven't yet received this viral plague, an online woodworking newsletter[8] has an article about Marco, a 16-year-old kid who built a bike, chain and all, out of wood.

Here he and his bike are:

---

8   Yes, you can still read it, right here: http://bit.ly/fatsby05

And here's the detail of the drivetrain:

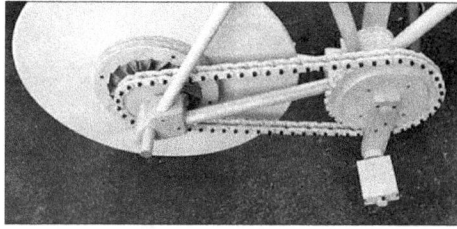

Sure, I can understand why some people would be impressed by a project like this, but I have more exacting standards. So, Mister Wooden Bike Building Genius Person, here are a few questions I have for you.

1. **Where are the derailleurs?** I suppose if you're lazy, single speed was an option, but I think that if I had a bike like that, I'd want to at least set it up as 3 x 8 (though I think we can all agree that a nine speed cassette would be required if you want an A+ in the project). Or maybe, if you're feeling like doing more than just phoning it in, make a nice wooden 14-speed internal-geared hub.

2. **Isn't that bike too heavy?** Looking at that bike, I would estimate it weighs at least 30 pounds. It's going to climb like a pig.[9]

3. **No suspension?** I expect a wooden bike is going to have some measure of vertical compliance built in,[10] but if you want to do ledge drops, you're going to want to build your next wooden bike with wooden suspension. Perhaps you might want to look into some sort of wooden leaf-spring system.[11]

4. **26" wheels?** Dude, all the best wooden plate wheels are being built as 29ers now. Get with the times.

5. **Is your pedal system acceptable?** I suppose some casual riders are okay with a wooden platform system, but next time you might want to carve some Speedplays. I'm thinking a nice natural oak color.

6. **No kickstand?** What's a modern bike without a kickstand?

STUFF I HAVE BUILT BICYCLES OUT OF

I'm sure you are thinking, "Well, Fatty, if you're going to lecture this kid on how he should have made a better wooden bike, you'd better have done something equally impressive."

---

9   And for your information, pigs are terrible climbers.
10 Fact: Pine rides smoother than mahogany.
11 Or something like that. Look, I can't do all your thinking for you, kid.

As it happens, I have.[12]

Here is an abbreviated list of the materials from which I have built bicycles.

- **Money**. I once built a bicycle using nothing but u.s. currency. Curiously, that bike still cost less than half as much as a Pinarello.[13]

- **Pasta**. I was surprised at how easy it was to build a bike using nothing but dry pasta. By wetting the pasta a little bit, it would flex, adhere to itself, and then reharden. Unfortunately, I found the ride quality of the bike problematic. Dry pasta provides a stiff, brittle ride, which is to say, it felt exactly like a GT.

- **Tinker Toys**. This was almost too easy. Took like twenty minutes. And the cool thing was, when I got to a water crossing I took the bike apart and made a bridge out of it.

- **Granite:** This was the most beautiful bike I ever made, but it climbed terribly. The nice thing is, when I decided to abandon it, I just leaned it against the side of the mountain and walked away.[14] I'm pretty sure it's still there.

- **Bubble Wrap:** I built this bike in answer to the question, "What if a bike protected you when you fall?" The bike was also remarkably light. The biggest problem with this bike, in fact, was that if I turned my back for even a minute, riding buddies would start impulsively popping the bubbles, and then I'd have to walk home.

- **Kryptonite:** The only time I ever beat Kenny[15] on a ride, I was riding my Kryptonite bike. You do the math.

- **Duct tape:** Taking the statement "You can fix anything with duct tape" to its logical extreme, I figured I could also *build* anything with duct tape. It turns out you can. As an interesting side effect, I was constantly being pulled over by other

---

12 Sadly, I have no photographs to show you of these magnificent machines. I... misplaced them.

13 When I originally wrote this story, I had "Arantix" here instead of Pinarello. Sadly, however, the Arantix, the original bike that's also a cheese grater, has gone out of business, forcing me to make fun of a more conventional, but still outrageously expensive, bike.

14 The very most pure form of recycling.

15 My fast, bald friend.

less-fortunate cyclists who needed a piece of my bike to fix their bikes. I never stopped using this bike per se; it just got assimilated into a multitude of other bikes.[16]

I'm certain you're grateful for my guidance in this matter, Marco. You're welcome.[17]

> COMMENT BY MBONKERS
> Dude, at least be impressed by the wooden freewheel! Personally, I'd have used pretzels. Good salty snack when you need it, and good traction from the salt studs.

> COMMENT BY BIG MIKE IN OZ
> Is it too much to ask that he put a Powertap or SRM on the thing?

> COMMENT BY STEVEW
> I think the most amazing thing about this is that it started out as an ash tray....

> COMMENT BY MARK
> Where is his helmet? That kid forgot to make a wooden helmet.

---

16   This is probably a beautiful metaphor for life or something, I'm just not yet sure how.

17   Just to be ultra-clear, I'm joking. Like everyone else, I'm impressed by Marco's wooden bike.

ROCKY, THE KARMIC BLACK HOLE

Of all the stories in this book, only one is about someone other than me. That's this story, and it's about my brother-in-law, Rocky.[18]

Rocky and I started riding at about the same time. We both were interested in doing big rides, in going long distances.

These kinds of rides, as it turns out, suit me very well. I'm good at plugging away for hour after hour without bonking, and sweat about a cup per hour.[19]

Rocky, on the other hand, is a technical wizard, able to both climb and descend obstacles I would never consider. But he sweats about a gallon per hour.

Which, as you will learn here, can be a bit of a problem when you're trying to ride for more than ten hours.

When you go on an endurance ride, you've got to choose your partners carefully. You've got to have similar endurance and strength, sure, but that's not really what I mean. You've got to pick people who aren't going to nauseate you.[20]

If, for example, you don't like knock-knock jokes, don't go riding with a guy famous for his knock-knock joke-telling prowess.[21] If you don't like complainers, don't go riding with a guy famous for finding fault with everything.

If you don't like someone paying attention to and remembering every little thing you do,

---

18 Hey, Rocky? Sorry I put this in the book. (But not sorry enough to not put it in the book.)

19 Seriously, I do just fine riding with way less water than most people. I don't sweat a lot, and therefore don't need to drink a lot.

20 Fortunately, nobody *ever* gets sick of me.

21 I'm assuming there is such a kind of person, though this should not be interpreted as an invitation for such a person to introduce her/himself to me.

then eventually writing a story where you're the punch line, maybe don't go riding with...me.

My brother-in-law, Rocky, is one of those guys with whom I can ride all day. He's interesting. He's smart. He's a good rider. He's curiously devoid of annoying habits.

Above all, though, Rocky is a good guy to ride with because he has such remarkably bad luck that you know, with absolute certainty, that something interesting[22] is going to happen when you ride with him. And I'm not just talking about a tendency to have occasional mishaps.

No, indeed.

I am talking about a special gift for bad luck. The Bad Luck Continuum warps and shifts, just so it can find Rocky.

Rocky is, in short, the Karmic Black Hole.

I have examples.

KOKOPELLI: ROUND 1

When Rocky and I first tried riding the Kokopelli Trail — a 142-mile desert trail connecting Moab, Utah up to Mack, Colorado — neither of us had any endurance experience,[23] so I guess we deserved anything that happened to us.

Within the first hour, we missed a critical turn from Sand Flats Road onto the Kokopelli Trail. We didn't figure this out for about another 45 minutes, by which time we figured — wrongly — it would be better to continue on Sand Flats Road until it connected up with the La Sals Mountain Road.

Riding on a flat road in deep sand is harder than a hard climb. We were both cooked by the time we got to the paved road, at which point we still had a long additional climb ahead of us.[24]

And it was summer. I'd guess it was about ninety degrees outside.[25]

Rocky was running out of water fast, because his superpower is to

---

22   And by interesting, I mean "darned near tragic."

23   I'm pretty sure this was the first time either of us had ridden a bike for more than four hours at a stretch. Why didn't someone stop us?

24   My memory of this road is of the sand being ankle-deep and going on for miles. I'd be interested in riding it again now, eighteen years later and with more than a hundred all-day mountain bike rides under my belt. I kind of suspect the road might not be *quite* as bad as I remember it.

25   And we were definitely outside.

sweat faster than he can drink. Still, he didn't complain. That's not his way.

We kept going, and I didn't really pay attention to the fact that Rocky was slowing down. Or that his speech was starting to slur. Or that he no longer was raising his head to look around.

Why not? Because I was too busy having the happiest day of my life. I was discovering I love long rides. I was discovering that the view from Beaver Mesa into Fisher Valley is impossibly beautiful. I was discovering that there was nothing I would rather do in the world than ride my mountain bike in the wilderness.[26]

HEY, WHERE'D ROCKY GO?

To my credit, I gave Rocky half of what water I still had when he ran out. Unfortunately for Rocky, however, I gave him the apple-flavored Cytomax,[27] which was just a flawed concept in sports drinks.[28] So no extra good karma points for me, I guess.

Rocky got progressively worse as we rode toward Fisher Valley. By the time we finally got into the valley, he was no longer fully lucid. He couldn't ride his bike anymore, and could only barely walk it.

His head lolled.[29]

This is, to this day, the benchmark I have for bonked-ness. Yes, Rocky is the gold standard by which all other bonks must be measured. For example, if you were very, very bonked, you might say, "Oh, I was pretty bad off. You could say I was at about a .82 on the Rocky Bonk Scale." I have never ever ever seen someone as cooked as Rocky was.

Just bad luck, really. A one-time thing.

Or was it?

KOKOPELLI, ROUND 2

The next year, we tried the Kokopelli again. This time, we had no trouble finding the turn we had missed the previous year and the first day went swimmingly. Rocky, Bob, and I rode together in the lead group (quite a

---

26 Still true, about eighteen years later. Which is kind of awesome.
27 Seriously, who thought that was a good idea? Because it was *not*.
28 Let's go ahead and call this the kindest understatement I have ever made.
29 Yes, actually *lolled*. I have witnessed lolling. Which does not, I want to make clear, stand for "laugh out loud."

few people joined us this second year, in spite of how the first year went) and made it to camp without any problems. I think all three of us would agree it was about as perfect a day as could be had on a mountain bike.

Of course, we were all starved when we got to camp at Dewey Bridge. My dad was acting as support, and had everything all ready to go, including a massive spread of food my sister Kellene had put together for us and sent along.

I ate my share of the chicken enchiladas — and your share, too — but the salad looked a little . . . I dunno . . . *wilted*. I skipped it.

Rocky had three helpings. Man-sized helpings.

You know what comes next, right? Right. He spent the night barfing 'til there was nothing left to barf.

Then, just to underscore his point, he spent the rest of the night convulsing in dry heaves.

I, on the other hand, slept better than I have ever slept while camping.

To everyone's astonishment, in the morning, Rocky said he would continue on. And he really was something to behold. He was like the little engine that could. He'd ride for five minutes, stop, put a foot down, and heave. Then he'd continue on.[30]

Just after passing the Westwater ranger station, Rocky sat down. He could no longer ride. I've seen people give up on rides before, but this was the first time I didn't think, just a little, "Oh, you could keep going if you wanted to."

Rocky made a call, got a ride, and the rest of us continued on.

Man, that Rocky. He has some bad luck.

KOKOPELLI, ROUND 3

The next year, we tried again. This year, though, it rained.[31] The whole day. Sand Flats Road showed us that there was considerable clay under that sand, and jammed up our bikes. Then we froze riding down the La Sal Road. Beaver Mesa was a soupy swamp. I finally made the no-go call just before we dropped into Fisher Valley, where we could easily have been trapped in muck without the benefit of a support vehicle.

---

30 I'm doing my level best to not make allusions to the *Rocky* movies here, but you can see how difficult that is to avoid, right?

31 For a more complete telling of this story, see "The Day I Hated Brad," in the "Things That (Mostly) Really Happened" chapter of this book.

Too bad about the rain for Rocky, especially, since he seemed the strongest and best-prepared for a long ride that I had ever seen him.

KOKOPELLI ROUND 4

The next year, Rocky declined to do the by-now annual Kokopelli trail ride, saying it was cursed.

We completed it without difficulty and without incident.[32]

LEADVILLE, ROUND 1

I've been riding the Leadville 100 since it was just a little ride. I write about it every year, trying to make a big story out of my race.

The truth is, though, Rocky's Leadville adventures are perhaps more dramatic.[33]

Rocky and I tried the Leadville 100 for the first time the same year. We trained the same and we talked about the ride constantly. We had agreed that we would ride together if we could, but wouldn't make a big deal out of it, because we had different strengths — I climbed fast, he descended fast. If we each held up for each other, we'd be slower than either of us would be alone.

And so, after the first climb, I expected to see Rocky catch me on the first descent.

But he didn't.

And in fact, I didn't see him until we crossed paths on the Columbine climb, more than halfway through the race.

Rocky looked cooked. It was that can't-drink-as-fast-as-I-sweat superpower,[34] coming out in force.

Dug, Brad, and I all finished the race with times pretty close to what we had targeted, which is surprising, since none of us had done the race before. Then we waited at the finish line, expecting each rider we saw on the horizon to turn out to be Rocky.

And we waited.

And we waited some more.

Then Rocky tapped me on the shoulder from behind and said, "Hey, guys."

Evidently, at the final aid station, after he had struggled through

---

32 I'm pretty sure we had a tailwind the whole way, too.
33 And by dramatic, I of course mean, "tragic."
34 Worst superpower, *ever.*

seventy-five miles of the course, Rocky was so wobbly, pale, and dehydrated that the course official yanked him off the course, put him in an ambulance, and sent him off to the hospital, where they loaded him up with two bags of glucose and sent him on his way.

I tell you, Rocky has some bad luck.

LEADVILLE, ROUND 2

That next year, Rocky came back to Leadville with a new Camelbak: the H.A.W.G. It held 200 ounces of water, which, at least for most people, is orders of magnitude overkill for a race that has aid stations no further apart than every ten miles.

But Rocky was playing it safe: this year, he would not be dehydrated.

This was not the only new equipment Rocky brought to the table. He also had a bright yellow riser handlebar.[35]

Dug noticed it immediately. "Where'd you get that Taiwanese piece of crap?" he asked. Dug's gruff, yet curiously unlovable.

Rocky replied, but none of us heard him. We were all looking askance now at this strange-looking handlebar. Now that Dug mentioned it, it did look kinda...I dunno...*cheap*.

Well, it'd be fine, right? Well, maybe it would in fact have been fine if either of the following were true:

- Dug had not singled it out for ridicule.
- Anybody but Rocky were using it.

It almost seems beside the point to say that at mile 85 — yes, with only 15 miles left in the race, after all of the really hard climbs were behind him — Rocky's handlebar snapped in half.

Okay, can we all now agree that this is not just random chance? That Rocky, my super-nice brother-in-law, has somehow angered an evil, ancient spirit?

Rocky, I hate to tell you this, because you're really and truly a great guy, but...you are a Karmic Black Hole.

---

35 Cue ominous music.

COMMENT BY WEILAND

Hmmm, the common variable between the Kokopelli rides and Leadville is you Fatty. It would appear Rocky is able to ride without incident on his own and with others. It is only when the combination of Fatty with Rocky when his rides turn bad. Maybe you are Rocky's Kryptonite? To prove this Rocky needs to ride Kokopelli or Leadville without you being within 300 miles.

COMMENT BY BIKEMIKE

Dude never gives up...freaking awesome.

COMMENT BY KANYONKRIS

"Dug's gruff, yet curiously unlovable."
Did you intend to say lovable?

COMMENT BY FATTY

KanyonKris: No, I did not.

COMMENT BY ROCKY

A few things noteworthy:
1. The Leadville 2 handlebar was silver, not yellow. C'mon man!
2. It has been an interesting fourteen years of riding. Nothing has been easy. Ever.
3. Re-living all of the unfortunate riding events of these years reminds me just how stupid it is that I continue to love mountain biking.
4. This catalog of grim luck events doesn't even scratch the surface. Really.

AN OPEN LETTER TO THE GUY RIDING HIS BIKE IN THE COLD AND WIND AND SNOW AND SLUSH AND RAIN

I love riding, in almost every kind of weather. At least, in every kind of weather that's not ridiculously cold. I'm not a big fan of brutally hot weather, either. And a harsh wind is just stupid.

As for rain, well: I'm fine with riding in it, just so long as I don't get wet. Which I do, so I guess I'm not okay with it after all.

All in all, what I prefer is to ride on calm, clear days with a temperature between 65 and 75 degrees. Otherwise, I'm staying inside, like any sane person would.

And I don't appreciate the folks who go out of their way to show me what a pathetic fair-weather rider I am, either.

This letter, as you may have guessed, is to those inconsiderate riders.

Dear Guy I Saw Riding Last Sunday Afternoon,

I think we can agree that we, as cyclists, need to stick together. We need to have each other's backs, so to speak (although now that I think about it, I don't think it makes very much sense for cyclists to ever be back-to-back). With that in mind, I think you owe me an apology.

You see, it was a very cold day. Alternating between snow and rain and sleet. And it was windy, adding an unbelievable sting to that rain/snow/sleet. The roads were wet, trending to icy.

No doubt about it, it was clearly *not* a day to go riding. And so, using the logic for which I am justly well-known, I did not ride. I didn't even consider it. Instead, I went for a nice *drive* up American Fork Canyon, just to get a sense of when it might be rideable again.[36]

My wife was along for the ride, as we had a couple hours to kill before it would be time to fire up the grill and make burgers, for which I am, again, justly well-known.

From the heated-seat comfort of my car, I commented with authority and machismo, "Well, *this* road's unrideable."

---

36 Sometime in the distant future, I'd warrant.

And then you came around the bend. Riding. You looked up, smiled, and waved.

Oh, the insolence.

It's possible, I suppose, that your smile and wave were perfectly friendly, but I prefer to imagine you as being malevolently smug, because that makes it a little bit easier for me to live with myself.

My wife looked at me, cocked an eyebrow, and observed, "So there's a *real* cyclist."

I had no response at all. Not then, not now. I'm 40 hours into a state of flummox, with no end in sight.

Imagine, if you can, Guy Riding Last Sunday Afternoon, how puny I felt. How very, very ashamed. And, above all, how angry.

Yes, *angry*.

I'm angry because I now have to adjust my self-image, from "steely-gazed, square-jawed, focused, and resolved cyclist" to "fair-weather pansy rider." That's quite an adjustment to make, and not a particularly pleasant one.

Thanks a lot, Guy Riding Last Sunday Afternoon.

And it's not like this was the first time something like this has happened. There are other people who are like you. People who, in spite of the fact that I find the weather too cloudy/wet-road-y/cool/breezy to go ride, are *going out and riding.*[37]

This has to end. Right now.

From this point forward, I would like you, and people like you, to please not go riding until I give the signal[38] that it won't make me feel like less of a man to see you out there. The signal will comprise the following:

- I will post something on my blog saying it's okay to go outside.
- I will emerge from my house, pasty white and fleshy.
- I will ride my bike.

That time has not yet arrived.

Guy Riding Last Sunday Afternoon, let me close with an appeal. In this world, we all have to accommodate others. Or more specifically,

---

37 Imagine me shaking my head in disappointed astonishment as I say this.

38 It will be like the Bat Signal, but with a somewhat different design: preliminarily, it looks like a bike, with a smiling sun behind it.

everyone else has to accommodate me.[39] Please, Guy Riding Last Sunday Afternoon, don't be so selfish. The next time it's cold and ugly outside, think about someone besides yourself for once,[40] and stay inside.

I think we'll both be glad you did. Or at least I will. And that's what really matters.

Kind Regards,

Fatty

The Fat Cyclist

> COMMENT BY WEILAND
> Tell yourself and everybody else it was Jens Voigt.

> COMMENT BY JEFF
> As a fellow "fair-weather pansy rider" I back you 100% Fatty. I hereby pledge not to ride outdoors until it is at least 38 degrees out (or 3.3 degrees Canadian).

> COMMENT BY THE INCREDIBLE WOODY
> I'm a fair-weather pansy rider and darn proud of it!

> COMMENT BY KELLY
> Fatty, I am a new reader and I am with you. Wind, snow, hail, & rain... I'm not a postmaster! I'm a cyclist! Fair-weather and proud. :)

> COMMENT BY PHILTHY IN OZ
> FC, when you next experience a day like you described, I recommend you settle down next to the heater, adjust the dial to HTFU, and then go out for a ride. ;-)

> COMMENT BY BRANDON
> Just ask yourself, what would Andy Hampsten do? Ride. It only looks cold.

---

39   This is pretty much the most honest public assessment of my worldview that I have ever made.
40   Specifically, think about me.

CONVENIENCE

This may well be the single most gushy entry in this book. And I want to be clear here: I am completely, utterly in love with convenience stores.

I imagine your response to this proclamation has got to be one of two things:

1. ***Bafflement**. If you have never been on a bike ride and been so totally hungry, thirsty, and bonked that when you saw a convenience store and realized the endless and amazing possibilities it represents, you will not understand this post. Not at the deeply spiritual level I'm writing it, at least.*

2. ***Agreement**. If you've ever been so hot, tired, cold, thirsty, hungry, or stoned that you thought you would not make it home from your ride, you have thought every single thing that is in this story, and may find yourself silently weeping in profound agreement at what I have to say here.*

There are many, many things I love about road biking. I love how smooth and fast it is. I love how you can start right from your front door. I love how you are going slow enough that you can see what's going on around you, but fast enough that you still get somewhere. I love how elegant a road bike looks. I love the way a road bike feels when you stand up and rock it in a climb. I love how a road bike feels as you lean into a sweeping downhill turn. I love how you can make decisions about your ride as the ride progresses — make it longer, shorter, climbier or flatter — whatever suits you, thanks to the fact that someone has kindly laid pavement all over the place.[41]

And I could go on. See, I wasn't kidding when I said the word "many" twice in the above paragraph.[42]

Of all the truly wonderful things about road biking, however, one thing surpasses them all:

The convenience store.[43]

Truly, the modern convenience store is a marvel of nature, ideally

---

41   I used the word "love" eight times in this paragraph, in case you were wondering.

42   Both of them in the first sentence, JFYI.

43   Please go back and read this paragraph again, this time with the sound of a chorus of angels playing as your mental soundtrack.

adapted for the road cyclist, and in particular for the road cyclist who's been riding for several hours and has a $10 bill in his (or, to be sure, her) jersey pocket. Or, better yet, a credit card — because when you're hungry enough, you never know how much you might want to spend.

Convenience stores are, simply, the very best thing there is about road cycling.

And if you don't agree with me, try riding, as The Hammer and I did about a week ago as we pre-rode the St. George Ironman road course, about seventy miles into a headwind, with another several hours of riding left to go, when you find yourself confronted by a convenience store.

At that moment, I guarantee you will find yourself in grateful, possibly rapturous agreement with me, as you should have been all along.

THE REMARKABLE THING ABOUT CONVENIENCE STORES

Consider this for a moment: You have been on your bike for hours, and you are hungry. And thirsty. For some reason, you cannot get the image of a Fat Boy ice cream sandwich out of your mind.[44] And the thought of a Mountain Dew is lodged in there pretty well, too. And so is a churro. And Twizzlers (or Red Vines — let's not argue over which are better).[45]

You stop at a convenience store, and — really, this is just magical — you can convert a small piece of paper into any and all of these things. It boggles my mind, frankly, that someone would give me *all this food*, for which I would gladly trade my bike, my helmet, my shoes and my glasses...and all they want in exchange is this little piece of paper.

"Look!" I exclaim in delight. "I have turned this silly bit of paper into a delicious *ice cream sandwich*. It's like I'm some kind of genius ice-cream-obsessed alchemist or something!"

Or, if you're all high-techy and stuff, you can swipe a card with magnetic strip in exchange for the same kind of thing. In which case it feels like you are getting something for nothing.[46]

---

44   This is generally true for me regardless of whether I've been riding or just sitting around watching TV.

45   Twizzlers are better.

46   I know, you're not literally getting something for nothing. In fact, you're getting something at a price that is marked up pretty darned high compared to how much you'd pay for it at a grocery store. But considering how much I would pay for a Coke after six hours of riding, convenience store prices still seem really reasonable.

CORNUCOPIA OF GOODNESS

The simple fact that a negligibly light scrap of paper can be converted into a vast amount of food is reason enough to treat convenience stores as a modern miracle. But there's more.

Specifically, the variety is incredible. At one recent convenience store stop — in Veyo, Utah, during the aforementioned death march against a headwind — I purchased and then immediately dispatched a large cup full of soft-serve ice cream. During this episode I demonstrated my ability to stack ice cream *very high indeed*. And then I had a soft pretzel. And a hot dog.[47]

And while I did not have a package of Fig Newtons, nor a plate of nachos, nor a monstrous Snickers bar, nor a Häagen-Dazs bar, I could have. And nearly did. And maybe would have, but people were starting to stare.

Really, the variety of ways I could satisfy my hunger, a hunger understood only by cyclists who have been running on empty for hours, was practically endless, and a delight to contemplate.

I am not ashamed to say that, so great was my gratitude for all these good things, neatly arranged in rows and along the self-serve counter at the wall, I nearly climbed over the counter to hug the clerk.

But he did not look like the kind of person who wanted or needed a hug, so I stuck with profusely thanking him for letting me buy the double-armload of food. "Thank you, sir," I said, my eyes misting over with joy, "for stocking your store so thoroughly and so well. Furthermore, thank you for being willing to part with this food. You can be confident that I will enjoy all of it."

Since this convenience store is the first one in many miles along a very popular cycling route, I'm guessing this was not the first time this clerk has been thanked so effusively.

SOMETHING FOR NOTHING

And now I come to the part where I must shamefacedly admit something. At this particular convenience store on this particular day, I actually had no cash at all, nor a card. I was bumming off The Hammer,

---

47 Which was also soft, but didn't feel like it had to advertise the fact, unlike the other two items I purchased.

who had thoughtfully brought $20 — enough money to let me buy a second serving of soft-serve. Which I did.

But even if The Hammer had chosen to not spot me the money I needed to indulge my most remarkable superpower — the ability to eat vast quantities, all the time — the convenience store would still have been a boon.[48]

True, I wouldn't have been able to feast on ice cream and a churro. And that would have been sad. But convenience stores carry a number of *free* items that can help the cash-strapped cyclist in need of calories.

Take, for instance, water. And sugar, and a number of lemon wedges — all free. What happens when you combine them into your water bottle and shake vigorously? I'll tell you what happens: you've made yourself a lemonade-flavored hobo sports drink.

Need more calories? I have two words for you: mayonnaise packets. They're as plentiful as they are delicious.[49] Did you know, in fact, that ounce for ounce, mayonnaise has more calories than any energy gel in existence?[50] Plus, mayo is free. And it goes great with mustard[51] and is delicious on just about any kind of sandwich.

And there's more. Need sodium? Pickle relish[52] is free. Thirsty? Water's free.

Need to use the bathroom? Yep, free.

Which makes me want to ask: Convenience stores, why are you so *generous and good?*

> COMMENT BY DUG
> It beats the old days when we had to carry doubloons around. Remember those days? We needed bigger and stronger pockets back then.

---

48   But it would have been kind of rotten of her to have not let me have any money, considering how she's my wife and stuff.

49   The mayo is delicious, I mean. The packets themselves are pretty difficult to swallow.

50   I haven't verified this, but it feels like truth, doesn't it?

51   Which is pretty darned effective at stopping cramps in their tracks. For reals.

52   Also very good at stopping cramps. Seriously, try it.

COMMENT BY SPIFF

Wait, those little green pieces of paper can be exchanged for goods and services? Alert the press!

COMMENT BY RYAN IN THE ROCK

It is obvious you don't ride in the south much, because you left off the most important gift of the convenience store: FREE AC. Walking into a nice cool convenient store after 40 miles in the heat and humidity is truly a heavenly gift.

COMMENT BY ADVENTURE MONKEY

It's amazing the things I crave when I make to a convenience on the verge of a bonk. Pickle, Myoplex drink, Red Bull, turkey and cheese sandwich, three Snickers for $2...yes, I will have all of that. No, I don't need a bag.

COMMENT BY JENF

Sometimes there's a convenience store on a wilderness road. Those are really special! Once we made breakfast in a "wilderness convenience store." Donuts, cookies, coffee, score!

COMMENT BY T FOSTER

Am I the only one that also appreciates the fact that I also get to regroup with those that have dropped me?

9.

How To Be Me

WE'RE GETTING PRETTY CLOSE TO THE END OF THE BOOK.[1] SO BY NOW, YOU CLEARLY AND WITHOUT QUESTION BOTH ADMIRE AND ENVY ME, WISHING you had my depth of insight. My well-considered point of view. My beautifully sculpted quads.

I don't blame you for wanting these things. I would envy myself, too, were I not already myself.

But how do you become me? Or at least, more like me? That is a more difficult question, and I don't know if it's possible for me to give you step-by-step instructions. After all, being me has come pretty naturally to me.

That said, these stories will probably help you get going in the right direction, including valuable tips on things in which I feel I have exceptional expertise, including:

- How to give terrible directions
- How to let a nearly intolerable odor build up in your car
- How to be dramatically overcharged for a bike taxi ride
- How to make someone else chase a skunk off the trail you want to ride
- How to justify your recent weight gain

---

1   Although I'd honestly be kind of weirded out if even a single person just read it front-to-back. This isn't really that kind of book.

I think you'll find all of these useful. More importantly, you'll find that once you have mastered these techniques, you will in fact be more like me.

I know you can hardly wait.

MISTER HELPFUL DIRECTIONS PERSON

Imagine the complete assemblage of capability with maps, directions, and location awareness. At one end of the spectrum — the good end — are people who always seem to know which way is north. If they go somewhere once, they know how to get there again. They enjoy maps and understand them. They always know where they are and always know where they're headed.

They are good people to be around when you don't know where you're going.

At the other end of the spectrum are people who are baffled by directions and have anxiety attacks in the presence of maps. While it cannot be said that they are helpful when you're lost, they at least know enough about themselves that they don't try to take charge and get you home.

The most dangerous kind of people, however, are the ones somewhere in the middle of the spectrum. The ones who, if they were going to be honest with themselves, would confess that they aren't really all that good at directions, orienteering, or how far it is to the next intersection. But, and this is key, they are not honest with themselves. Nor are they honest with you.

And so they will do their best to help. They'll give directions, they'll look at maps, they'll make distance estimates. And then, once you're gone, they'll be secretly glad, because they know there's no better than a 50% chance that they gave you good information.

I know this middle-of-the-spectrum type well, because that is exactly what I am. But I'm even more dangerous than most of my sorta-kinda-lousy-with-maps types, because I'm friendly and helpful by nature. So if I see you at a trailhead, on a road, or at an intersection, I'll stop and try to help you.

Allow me to offer this one piece of advice: ignore me. Because you heed me at your peril.

Spring is a good time of year for riding. The winter has been long and I was happy to just be outside, riding my bike. And judging by the number of people on the trail, I was not the only one glad to get outside and on the dirt. A lot of the folks were there for their first time, or at least the first time in a long time.

Luckily for them, I was out there, ready to lend my expert assistance to anyone who needed to know anything at all about the trail system.[2]

Why? Because I love stopping and talking with cyclists and chatting about the trail. I am ... *Mister Helpful Directions Person!*

THE UNFORTUNATE ANTI-SUPERPOWER OF MISTER HELPFUL DIRECTIONS PERSON

As an eager and friendly superhero, I — Mister Helpful Directions Person — actively seek out cyclists and hikers, and even those who hail from Equestria, any of who are stopped on the trail, looking this way and that.

"Aha!" I think to myself. "A cyclist (or hiker, or Citizen of Equestria) in probable need of information! I shall stop and see if I can lend assistance!"[3]

I recognize, however, that there is a burden with being a superhero. I do not want to offend, nor to give out unwanted, unnecessary advice. So first, I stop and chat.

"Isn't it great to get outside and ride after a long winter?" I ask. I am not surprised, of course, to find that most everyone agrees that it is in fact good to get out on one's bike. Very few[4] have replied with a rude comment like, "Actually I hate riding and am out here only because I have done evil and must be punished."

"Isn't this trail network incredible?" is my follow-up question. This, you see, is my clever way of letting the other person that I do, in fact, know this trail system like the back of my hand. How else would I be able to assess its incredibleness?

Some simply agree that it is, in fact, remarkable to have miles and miles of excellent singletrack tucked right into what is otherwise a residential area.

Others, to my delight, pick up on my subtle hint and ask, "So where does this trail lead to?"

And that is all the permission I need to explain:

---

2   It *feels* like I know quite a bit about the trail. I just have trouble expressing this knowledge.

3   As an enthusiastic and supportive superhero, I cannot help but say everything as exclamations!

4   Okay, nobody, ever.

"Well, follow this trail for...I don't know, between half a mile and two miles. Then there will be a really hard climb, or at least it's really hard if you're on a singlespeed and out of shape. Umm, there's a couple of stream crossings you should be aware of before you get to the next intersection, which you will go right through.

"Wait, hold on. I was thinking of a different trail there for a minute. There aren't actually any stream crossings you have to worry about, and you do have to turn at that intersection, except there are a couple forks in the trail before that intersection where I think you follow the main trail.

"And that intersection's actually a fork. I think there's a fiberglass trail marker there, or at least there was two years ago. I think someone stole it last year. It doesn't matter though, because you're just going through that intersection. I mean, you're turning left."

Even as I talk, I realize: I am giving *terrible* directions. The look on my hapless direction recipient's face confirms this, big time. His eyes glass over. He nods, but it's clear he's stopped listening and is now just waiting for me to stop talking so he can go figure out the trail for himself.

As we part, I realize: I am the worst superhero ever.

THE *REAL* MISTER HELPFUL DIRECTIONS PERSON

One of the reasons I give terrible directions is that when I'm riding, or doing anything else for that matter, I don't think about stuff in such a way that lends itself to good directions.

My thought process runs more along the lines of, "Hey, a stream! Look, there's an interesting bug. I wonder what it's called? This trail is fun. My legs hurt. I'm not doing a very good job of turning my cranks in even circles. There's an intersection, I wonder what would happen if I turned left instead of going right? Hey, a stream!"[5]

You see my problem?

Dug, on the other hand, has an actual genuine superpower: He has a GPS and a true-to-scale topographical map of the intermountain West *inside his head.* Once Dug has been on a trail, he can give precise and perfect directions. Furthermore, he somehow knows how trails connect together, what the exact distances are from one point to the next, and recalls landmarks exactly.[6]

---

5   Squirrel!
6   And to scale.

You should hear him give directions to strangers encountered on the trail. "Go two hundred forty yards, during which time you will pass eighteen coniferous trees on the right side, not including saplings. Once you pass a boulder — it looks like a giant potato, has moss growing on the south side, and has a circumference of fifty-four inches at its widest point, you can't miss it — an intersection gives you the options of going to either of the following: Persimmon's Doom on the left, Shimmy-Jimmy Doo-Whop on the right, or continue straight to intersect with Cashmere Nightmare[7] in one-point-three miles."

Yes, we have oddly-named trails around here. But that's not my point. My point is that when people get directions from Dug, they often abandon their previous route, vowing allegiance to Dug and asking if he will be their leader from that point forward.

Unfortunately, Dug is mean-spirited and spiteful, and hence as likely to answer with a chop to the solar plexus and spin-kick to the nose as a "sure, come ride with us."

Which, of course, is why I always carry an extensive first-aid kit, which I waste no time in using.

Unfortunately, I am almost exactly as good at administering first aid as I am at giving directions.

> COMMENT BY JIM
> I too am a Mister Helpful(?) Directions Person. I sent a couple of friends off exploring trails near the Colorado/Utah border. Supplied with one of my custom, highly detailed, hand-drawn maps and accompanying verbal waypoints they were assured that this would become their most favorite ride ever.
> That was Monday.
> I'm pretty sure they made it home, but I've yet to hear the glowing reviews.

---

7   None of these are names of actual trails, which is a darn shame.

MY TRUCK IS STINKY

I love my 2007 Honda Ridgeline. I've had it since I bought it new, back in — you guessed it — 2007, and eight years later I have no intention of ever trading it in. It holds me, three adult passengers, our bikes, and all our stuff, no problem.

Well, there is one problem. A kind of serious problem, actually.

My truck stinks.

I don't think this is a rare problem. Not among cyclists anyway. We tend to put stinky stuff in our vehicles (e.g., our gear and ourselves), and then let the summer sun warm up that gear and bake that smell into the upholstery, dashboard, everything.

This story is about this stench.[8] And, indirectly, I suppose it also answers the question, "Is there anything I won't write about?"

I am not a person who concerns himself with appearances. I'm in my mid-late-forties, balding, portly, have no fashion sense whatsoever, and was never good-looking to begin with.

So I don't worry about how I look, and I don't mind that a lot of people think my Honda Ridgeline is odd-looking, too.[9] This is simply the best vehicle I have ever had.

Unfortunately, however, my truck stinks.

MANY CULPRITS

Naturally, upon detecting that my truck stinks, my inclination is to remove the source of the smell. Sadly, however, it is not that simple. You see, the stench that emanates from my truck is complex. It's a multitude of things, all of which are intensified when the weather's warm. All of them are bike-related.

Helmet, gloves, shoes, shorts, and jerseys: If you are a cyclist, you almost certainly have a bag in which you carry your riding gear. So

---

8   Not about how to get rid of it, because I have no idea how to do that.

9   When I wrote about my Ridgeline for the first time in my blog, I got more than 150 comments, with probably about 15 of them calling my car "ugly." I still maintain that this is the best vehicle a bike lover could ever own, and explain why here: http://bit.ly/fatsby09

here's an interesting experiment: put your head inside that bag and inhale through your nose (no cheating) deeply.

Once you emerge from your coma, go put that same bag, still containing all your riding gear, in the oven and set the temperature to 140 degrees.[10]

Let it bake for half an hour, then go open the oven and breathe deeply. You have just accurately simulated the primary smell component of my truck after it's been sitting in a parking lot all day.

Congratulations!

Tubes: Have you ever smelled a bike tube? You haven't? Go do it, right now. I'll wait.

[Waits for five minutes]

Surprisingly pungent, isn't it?

By itself, that one tube's smell is no big deal. But of course, that smell isn't by itself. It's just a part of the stew of stink in my truck.

Lube: I always keep a bottle of Dumonde chain lube in my truck. And of course by "keep," I mean that there is never a moment in which somewhere in my truck, a bottle of Dumonde is not leaking. And that stuff, in addition to being about as industrial-grade as lube can get, has a *sharp* odor to it. Basically, Dumonde chain lube smells like a flick on the nose feels.

Go ahead and flick yourself on the nose. I'll wait.

The Bike: You wouldn't think a bike would have a smell. Especially a road bike, which is the bike I keep inside the cab; the mountain bikes have to ride in the truck bed.

But bikes do indeed have a smell, if you count the saddle.

Go ahead, go smell your saddle. NO. I WAS JUST KIDDING. DON'T GO SNIFF YOUR SADDLE. THAT'S GROSS.[11]

Passengers: I am sad to report that many of my friends, after riding a bike for 2–14 hours, smell pretty bad. It's a dynamic badness with peaks and plateaus (but alas, no valleys).

While I theoretically could lay out towels and blankets and demand that everyone apply post-ride deodorant, I am not going to.[12]

---

10   No, your significant other won't mind. Why would s/he?

11   But they really do have a smell. How could they not?

12   I could explain that the reason I don't is because I'm not one to inconvenience my friends and act all prissy, but the truth is: I'm just too lazy.

Which means that my passengers leave a little something behind.

Me: I'm just kidding of course. I make no smell at all. Ever.

THE SOLUTIONS

So what does one do when the thing one likes best makes one's vehicle smell like a cross between a locker room and a bike shop?

Well, there are several solutions, each of which I have tried. Sometimes together.

Rolling down the window. This works great, for as long as you have the window rolled down. And the folks in the back seat really really seem to love all that wind, too!

Those tree things you hang from your rear-view mirror: There are a number of problems with these. First of all, they smell nothing like a tree. Go smell a tree right now, then go smell one of those evergreen-shaped air "fresheners."[13] I'll wait.

No, just kidding, I'm going on without you.

The second thing is that these little air fresheners may as well be giant neon billboards flashing the text "VERY STINKY AUTOMOBILE." Which, while undoubtedly an effective auto theft deterrent, is still quite embarrassing.

Incense/potpourri: There are almost too many problems to count with these two. First, it's not easy to keep the incense lit when you've got the air conditioner going. Second, every time you stop, the potpourri spills out of its decorative bowl and gets all over the place. Third, I'd rather have my truck smell like rubber and old sweat than potpourri.

Citrus spray: I've begun using an orange citrus mist spray to de-stenchify my car. I'm very pleased at how effective it is. A quick spray around the cab[14] leaves my truck smelling just like oranges... for about thirty seconds. Then it smells a little bit like sweaty oranges. Eventually, the smell levels off to somewhere between orange-y sweat and a rancid orange creamsicle.

Which is still an improvement. But just barely.

---

13 Honestly, there's nothing even remotely pine-scented about those things. And come to think of it, Pine-Sol doesn't smell like pine trees either. Wow, I just realized there's a massive fake pine scent conspiracy happening right beneath our noses!

14 And a rather more direct and extensive spray at my passengers.

COMMENT BY 29ER

The worst car stench we ever had was from a half consumed gel pack (some gross flavor I couldn't finish). I set it carefully in the door pocket and forgot about it. Luckily it didn't leak and ooze... but it put off an enormous stink after a few weeks. I'll never let that happen again.

COMMENT BY ERINE

I have a friend who lost a foil-wrapped roast beef sandwich in his truck for almost a month.

Of course, this was in the heat of our Carolina summers, he was in the field for a few weeks, and the sandwich had full reign of the locked cab. The smell was unbelievable and defies description. It was a month before my friend could drive his truck without retching. He drove with his head sticking out the window the rest of the summer and into the fall.

After a good cleaning and deodorizing, various treatments and an exorcism by the local priest, the truck still smelled like a**.

Finally, out of desperation, my friend bought a car deodorizer and hung it on the dash. It was cherry scented, but the truth is the cab still smelled- like cherry scented a** rather than plain a**. I can't say it was an improvement.

It's been several years now, but when the moon hangs low over these Carolina shores and the humidity and heat drift up with the coming of summer, the stench returns...

So, good luck with your funky truck!

COMMENT BY RYAN

Embrace the smell, wear it as a badge of honor.

RUBE

I live in a tiny little town in Utah. It's quiet, it's safe, and it suits me fine. Not that everything here is perfect. Utah is home to more multi-level marketing scams than the rest of the U.S. combined.[15] *So I've learned to firmly say, "no thanks" when neighbors I've never met want to drop by to tell me about the opportunity of a lifetime.*

That's fine, for that one kind of scam.

But when a country mouse visits the city, well...he's bound to come away looking a little bit like a fool.

Especially if the country mouse is convinced that he is a kindred spirit with anyone who has ever been on a bike.

I used to travel for work a lot, usually to New York.

Of course a lot of people love living there, including two of my sisters. But I didn't know my way around, didn't like traveling on my own, and felt a little bit exposed.

So I was standing outside my hotel, waiting in a long line for a cab, thinking about how, when I'm at home, I don't ever have to wait for a cab. And I was thinking about how, when I'm at home, I know people. And I was thinking about how, when I'm at home, I'd have a bunch of bikes at hand would have been able to go riding outside that morning, instead of twisting on that cruel mockery of a bicycle: the exerccycle.

And in short, I felt a little bit like a fish out of water. A lonely fish.

And then, behind all the taxis, I saw the answer to all my problems: *a bike taxi.*

I walked over to the guy with the bike taxi.[16] I was thinking about how awesome it is that I was no longer waiting in a line.[17] I was thinking about how it'd be fun to at least talk to another cyclist for a while.

Naturally, he didn't speak any English and my Polish isn't so hot, either.

That's okay, though. I gave him my destination — about eight blocks

---

15   I just made this statistic up.
16   Should I call him the "driver" or the "rider?" Neither seems right.
17   It does not occur to me to wonder why nobody else is migrating from the regular taxi line to the bike taxi line. Because I'm dumb.

away, though I had no idea in which direction, what with my state of being perpetually lost — and he took off.

I was caught between trying to enjoy the ride and feeling very silly.

On one hand, it was nice to be getting around this way instead of in a taxi. On the other hand, it felt wrong for me to be going somewhere on a bike, without being the one pedaling.[18]

I seriously considered asking — via hand gestures, I suppose — whether the guy wanted to trade me places, so I could pedal for a bit. Of course, this has the largish problem that I already mentioned before: the primary reason I was taking a taxi in the first place was that I have no idea how to get anywhere. I wouldn't be a great pilot.

So I rode. And I thought about what a fine story this will make, and how I'd have to make a habit of riding in bike taxis more often, because they're more in line with what I like, and they're environmentally friendly, and how I could hardly wait to tell my sister that I just rode a bike taxi instead of a regular taxi, and then maybe smugly asking why doesn't she start using a bike taxi to get around when she needs to travel in the city?

We arrived at my destination, eight blocks away from where we started.

The driver/rider/pilot said his first English words since picking me up and nodding his understanding of my destination:

"Forty dollars."

I blinked. My mouth went dry.

My ideas of international biking camaraderie and sharing a story about how everyone should ride bike taxis vanished. Instead, I've got a new story in which I was starring: the one where I was the rube.

I had just been on a taxi ride that cost roughly *five dollars per minute.* Which is almost twice as expensive as phone sex.[19]

I realized that this wasn't going to be a story about how cool bikes are, nor how cool bike riders are.

It instead was going to be the story of a small-town fool getting suckered because he thought everyone who rides a bike is cool, and therefore didn't ask about the fare rate before the ride began.

This, as it turned out, would be a story that would leave me so deeply

---

18   And for a third thing, I feel like just a little bit of a dork for riding in something not very different from a baby trailer.

19   Or so I hear.

embarrassed about my naiveté that I would not tell this story to anyone for more than two years.

I got him back, though. I did not leave a tip.

> COMMENT BY LEROY
> At least now I know how to make money on my commute. All I need is a Trail-A-Bike and a short layover in Times Square. Twenty dollars sounds fair if the fare helps to pedal the taxi.

> COMMENT BY MIKEONHISBIKE
> $40 for 8 blocks? Ouch, I must be in the wrong business. Either that or he could spot a fat cyclist coming from miles away and faked a polish accent.

> COMMENT BY TOM
> Same thing in Chicago. Around Wrigley there are tons of these guys but they want like $30–40 for a few blocks. So instead they ride around empty all the time in packs of three to five taxis.

I FEARLESSLY VANQUISH THE TERROR OF THE TRAIL

I love seeing wildlife on the trail. I've seen moose. I've seen rattlesnakes. I've seen owls. I've seen elk, wild turkeys, and deer.[20] I've seen a badger. I've seen lizards, squirrels and chipmunks galore.

And I've seen skunks.

Of all of these, only two have seriously hampered my ride. First, the moose just stood in the trail, with a "Well? Your move," kind of look. Eventually, however, it lost interest and wandered off.

The skunk...well, the skunk was more frightening.

It was early spring, and Dug, Karl, and I were out riding some of the local trail we usually ignore: trail that's good, but since it's lower, we don't use much once the higher trail is available.

I led out for the first climb, because I'm the strongest and most handsome rider of the three of us and I have an undisputed claim to the alpha male role. It wasn't even a question, really. I just took my position at the front and began the climb, the other two falling obediently into line.

This means, of course, that I was the first to see the skunk standing in the trail, facing us, tail raised, eyes defiant.

Challenging my authority.

Taking control of the situation, I calmly locked both my front and back brakes, stopping a mere 20 feet away from the skunk. I was close enough that it knew I had no fear of it, and would not be deterred.

Never one to back down, I said to the others, "Let's turn around. There are other trails."

Dug, however, wanted to press forward. I allowed him to, delegating to him the lead position.[21]

Dug shooed away the skunk by tossing small branches in its vicinity. Immediately, I could see the cleverness of my plan of delegating the "shoo-ing" task to Dug, for the skunk walked off the trail.

---

20 I've seen a deer t-bone a riding buddy of mine. Read about that here: http://bit.ly/fatsby10

21 Note that I did this brusquely.

And then it re-appeared back on the trail, approximately six feet further up ahead. And commenced to wander idly up that trail, at a pace which can accurately and eloquently described as "slow."[22]

After quickly assessing, evaluating, stack-ranking, and otherwise considering all possible options, I re-proposed my bold course of action: "Let's turn around. This trail belongs to the skunk now."

By this, I of course meant that I chose to let the skunk use the trail of which I was in command.

Dug, however, did not want to leave. As wise as Solomon, I therefore told him, "Well then, getting the skunk off the trail is *your* problem."

Dug walked after the skunk, tossing small rocks and branches — hopefully enough to startle without actually seeming to threaten the skunk — to the side of the animal.

Slowly, the skunk disappeared around a bend. In slow-motion pursuit, Dug...um...pursued.

For minutes, I took command of the situation by remaining where I was. Karl also stayed in position, ready to do as he was told.

Then Dug reappeared.

I do not consider it a repudiation of my bravery to say that I was tentative in breathing when Dug first came back.

"The skunk went off the trail, finally," said Dug, when I asked him to report. "I think it's okay to go on ahead."

We rode on. I rode in third position, since a leader must sometimes lead by pushing, not pulling, his troops along.

Also, I kept my fingers on my brakes and my eyes peeled, ready to execute a quick 180 should I smell even the most trivially skunk-like odor.

After all, while I am a great and inspiring leader, I am no fool.

COMMENT BY DUG
Beware the Jabberwocky, my son. And skunks.

COMMENT BY ITMUSTBEKEN
Your calm, authoritative, and wise handling of the situation was surely a comfort to all involved.

---

22   It could also be described as "unconcerned," or possibly even "leisurely."

COMMENT BY MIKE ROADIE

" Brave, brave Sir Robin!!!!

I REALLY DON'T SEE A PROBLEM WITH MY CURRENT WEIGHT

Let's end with where I began.

I created FatCyclist.com because I needed to lose a few pounds. More to the point, I needed to lose about thirty pounds. Okay, forty.

And I did it.

Then I gained it back.

Then I lost it again.

Then, while I wasn't watching, it crept back up on me.

And the cycle begins again.

This...well, evidently it's the story of my life.

It's September as I write this, but yesterday I weighed myself for the first time since about mid-April. I fully intend to disclose my current weight and how I feel about knowing, for the first time in five months, this aforementioned number. But first I'll force you to read a whole bunch of explanatory text, with the hope and intention that you will lose interest in my weight before you find out what it is.

I think, with that first paragraph, I'm off to a good start.[23]

MY INITIAL REASON FOR WHY I HAVE NOT RECENTLY WEIGHED MYSELF

Whenever I've had a big, important race coming up, I've stopped weighing myself between two and three weeks before the race. Why? Because I figure that once I get that close to the race, any weight gain[24] is not going to be significant enough to affect the outcome of my race.

Therefore, anything I know about weight I gain right before a race[25] is only going to mess with my head.

---

23 Rambling is what I do best.
24 Or, hypothetically, weight loss. Oh, who am I kidding?
25 Let's face it: I'm not going to lose weight as I taper down my exercise and carbo-load up the calories.

And so, in mid-April, a couple weeks before I raced the 2010 Saint George Utah Ironman,[26] I put away the scale.

And then I never brought it back out. Because, you know, there's always another race coming up.

Like...um...justasec here...hm. Okay, fine, I guess there might've been a couple months in there where I didn't have a race that was exactly *impending*.

Which is why I've got a very valid, extra-scientifically second reason for why I haven't weighed myself recently.

QUANTUM MECHANICS!

You may have heard of "Schrödinger's Cat," a theoretical experiment wherein the living/dead status of a cat that may or may not have been poisoned is in a state of flux — i.e., the cat is simultaneously alive *and* dead — until that cat is observed.

It's a fun thought exercise, and I recommend the next time you have a child come home with a science fair project assignment that you have this child perform this experiment for his or her classmates.[27]

My relationship with the scale is much like Schrödinger's cat experiment, except instead of a cat, it is my weight that is not observed.[28] And also, I am not kept in a sealed box, and there are no cyanide tablets or Geiger counters involved.

Really, the point I'm trying to get at is that as long as I do not measure my weight, no weight has technically been gained.

Schrödinger's cat. My weight. You get the picture.

Right?

WHY I HAVE FINALLY WEIGHED MYSELF

The problem with the quantum mechanics aspect of "Fatty's Weight" is that, at a certain point, other indicators start to make it evident that while I have stopped training like I'm going to be doing a big endurance

---

26   Hey, I wrote a three-part story about this race. You can find part 1 here: http://bit.ly/fatsby11

27   NO, NOT REALLY.

28   Except you and I both know that it's totally observable, just by looking at me. But let's set that aside for the time being.

race soon, I haven't stopped *eating* like I'm going to be doing a big endurance race soon.

Or in other words, once you start carbo-loading, you quickly develop a fondness for it.

This has led to — for about the thousandth time in my life — the manifestation of my least favorite (because it's true) weight-gain axiom, which is deep enough that it belongs on its own line, centered, in bold and italics.

You will know before it shows.

In this case, I could tell my body is getting ready to hibernate because my pants are tighter. All of them. Which kind of forced me to rule out the "mysterious shrinking pants" theory I otherwise like to cling to so tightly.

MY WEIGHT DOES NOT MATTER

So, anyway, for those of you who pushed on through to this point. My weight. It's 12.07 stone. Which is 169 pounds.

Which is about twelve pounds more than I like to weigh.

Or at least, it appeared to be 169 pounds. You see, there were some ameliorating circumstances that make that 169 pounds really quite a bit less than 169 pounds. Specifically:

- **I weighed myself in the afternoon.** Ordinarily I weigh myself first thing in the morning, right after I pee. I consider that my *true* weight. Everyone knows that you're heaviest during the afternoon. Because you've had both breakfast and lunch. And probably a few snacks. And around 64oz of Diet Coke. So I expect that this 169 probably counts for eight pounds or so.
- **I have recently raced.** Everyone knows that you gain weight after a big endurance race. This is due to the "post-race-3-day-binge" factor, as well as serious inflammation (which is a form of water retention, I suspect) factors. I figure this is worth two pounds. And a half.[29]
- **I was fully dressed.** Actually I can't remember whether I was fully dressed when I weighed myself. Let's just assume that I

---

29   For what it's worth, I actually have talked to a couple of professional cyclists and asked about this post-race inflammation. They both confirmed that it is real.

was, though. And let's further assume that I was wearing very, very heavy shoes. So, maybe seven pounds.

- **It's been a while since I've shaved my legs.** Oooh, and my head too. And my eyebrow hair needs trimming. Between all the excess middle-age-man body hair I need to prune, that's probably two or three ounces of weight I can lose instantly with the help of a razor.[30]

So, when it comes right down to it, when I weighed myself, my reported weight was probably around 17.65 pounds too harsh of a judge.

No need to start dieting. All's well.

> COMMENT BY NEIL
> I use to obsess over my weight like a high school cheerleader but discovered it was easier to buy carbon-fiber parts. God bless technology.

> COMMENT BY STUCKINMYPEDALS
> I never thought of trimming my eyebrows before stepping onto the scale. Yet another good tip, Fatty.

---

30 I would like to apologize for putting that image in your head.

Backword

DAN WUORI

I'm not the kind of guy to say I told you so, but...well, who am I kidding? I'm *exactly* that kind of guy. Still, I'm not entirely heartless, so I'll give you this one last chance:

If you've enjoyed The Great Fatsby *it's probably a good idea for you to just stop reading now. If you choose to continue, don't say I didn't warn you. Because I'm about to go all* Dateline NBC *on the scam artist you know as "Fatty."*

I should have known better from the beginning. Once I finally consented to write the Foreword to this book, I suggested it might be helpful to discuss the idea by phone. But what followed was a litany of excuses as to why a call just wouldn't be possible.

"Can't talk right now," said one text message. "I'm helping a friend reinstall Windows 7."

Elden has often written of his background in information technology. So I thought nothing of it and tried again the next day. "Your call is important to us. Please continue to hold...and thank you for flying Delta," came this most-unexpected response.

It was around this time that I began to question Elden's distinctive email address: Fatty@fatcyclist.in. Why was a guy in Utah emailing from an Indian-registered domain? And how does he know so much about software? After a flight across the globe, I discovered the truth at last.

First the good news: There *is* an Elden Nelson and he *did* create the Fat Cyclist blog in 2005.

But ten years is a long time to keep churning out content. And when he ran out of cycling jokes in early 2006 (as we all do sooner or later), Elden outsourced Fat Cyclist and all of its content development to a team of phone bank workers in Bangalore, each curiously identifying themselves as "Todd."

The real Elden Nelson sold off his bikes in 2007 and now teachers Zumba classes at a local YMCA. He tells me he may get back on the bike someday. "It's something you never forget," he chuckled, seemingly relieved to know his secret was finally out. "It's just like, well, you know, riding a bike."

So there you have it. In the end *The Great Fatsby* owes a greater debt to its namesake than you might have imagined. To wit: both are classic works of fiction.

As for Elden Nelson, you can call him "Fatty" all you want. But from now on I'm just calling him "Todd."

Never trust what you read in a cycling book.

PS: I told you so.

Acknowledgements

THANKS FIRST AND FOREMOST TO LISA (AKA THE HAMMER) FOR HANDLING
PRETTY MUCH EVERYTHING WHILE I DISAPPEARED INTO MY MAC CAVE
and worked on this book. You were supportive, loving, and made sure
I still got on the bike. I love you, Beautiful.

Thanks to Brice, who took a long list of URLs and turned it into
formatted, styled Word documents, ready for me to edit and rewrite.
You saved me dozens of hours of work, without ever complaining.
You're an awesome son.

Thanks to Nigel, Brice, Katie, Carrie, Zac, Erin, Blake, Melisa (my
kids and stepkids), Gene, Janel, Carolynn, Dean, Dee, Jackie, Karen
(my parents, step-parents, and parents-in-law), Kellene, Lori, Jodi, and
Christy (my sisters). It's just a little bit crazy to have so much near-
relation family so close. I appreciate all your support.

Thanks to Kim Dow for taking this book on. Kim took my rough
book idea, both the inside and out, and managed to make it look professional and playful. Thanks also to Greg Fisher for editing, along with
talking me down from the occasional ledge.

Huge thanks to Dan Wuori, who writes an incredibly funny (and often
thoughtful) back page column for Velo magazine. I was astonished that
he'd say "yes" to writing a Foreword, Middleword, and Backword for
my book. And then he did a brilliant job with them in very short order.

Thanks to The Core Team: Dug, Kenny, Ricky, Brad, Bob, and Cori. You guys are still the audience I have in mind when I write, and you're the best guys in the world with whom to ride.

Thanks to Racer for being a great bike-builder, mechanic, and friend. I don't think I could list all the bikes I've owned during the twenty or so years he's been working on my bikes, but I bet he could.